Dr. David Goodman

Personality Development and Social Behavior in the Mentally Retarded

Lexington Books
in Psychology
under the general editorship of
Paul H. Mussen
and
Mark R. Rosenzweig
University of California
Berkeley

Personality Development and Social Behavior in the Mentally Retarded

Manny Sternlicht
Yeshiva University and
Willowbrook State School
Martin R. Deutsch
Willowbrook State School

Lexington Books
D.C.Heath and Company
Lexington, Massachusetts
Toronto   London

To our parents, wives, and families.

Table of Contents

Preface   ix

Chapter 1   Personality Development: Introduction   1

Chapter 2   Personality Dynamics: Meaning of
       Mental Retardation   9

Chapter 3   Environmental Influences on Personality   35
     The Role of the Family   36
     Deprivation and Isolation   41
     Institutionalization   46

Chapter 4   Self-Concept and Personality Traits   57
     The Dynamic Structure of the Personality of
       the Retardate   57
     The Nature of the Self-Concept of
       the Retardate   59
     The Retardate's Ideal-Self   61
     Hostility   62
     Rigidity   64
     Two Personality Studies   70

Chapter 5   Deviant Behavior   75
     The Relationship Between Mental Retardation
       and Criminal and Delinquent Behavior   75
     The Relationship Between Mental Retardation
       and Emotional Disturbance   84

Chapter 6   Social Behavior and Social Problems   101
     The Nature of Retardate Adjustment   101
     Social Reinforcement Variables and Behavior   103
     Follow-up Studies of Retardate Adjustment   105
     Experiments in Social Living Among Retardates   113

Chapter 7   Behavioral Adjustments in the Classroom   123
     The Relationship Between Class Composition
       and Behavioral Adjustment   126
     The Effect of Teacher Attitudes and Approaches
       Upon the Retardate's Classroom Behavior   133

Chapter 8   **The Adult Retardate**   143
             The Vocational and Occupational Adjustment
               of the Retardate   143
             The Leisure-Time Pursuits of the Retardate   162

             Index   175

             About the Authors   181

Preface

Since the present volume is necessarily a pioneering undertaking in the field of mental retardation—the first large-scale work to treat exclusively the personality of the mental retardate—we have recognized our incumbent responsibility to break ground in a fashion that does justice to so vital and challenging a subject. Accordingly, let us at the outset underscore what has been brought home to us as a very real and palpable fact in the course of our investigation, namely that the study of the retardate's personality is indeed only in its infancy. Such a fact is at once disquieting and reassuring: disquieting because it serves as a sober reminder of how little is known; reassuring because it holds out an open invitation to come to know so much more. The present work has tried to bridge the gap and to ease the transition between what is known and what is yet to be known. Intended as a comprehensive, wide-ranging experimental and clinical investigation of the personality of the mental retardate in all its phases, the volume seeks to bring into focus the manifold data and observations of the experimental psychologist, the clinical psychologist, the psychiatrist, the educator, and the social scientist, as well as the vocational counselor, the social worker, the occupational therapist, the recreational therapist, the nurse, and the institutional administrator.

In assembling the various findings in the field, the present work has undertaken at the same time to organize these findings according to certain general principles about the retardate's personality which the present authors have had the opportunity to develop during more than a decade of intensive psychological evaluation, treatment, and research among the largest institutional cross-section of mentally retarded individuals in the world. The volume thus represents not only the culmination of years of systematic study of the retardate in the laboratory and the clinic, but a distillation of repeated daily observations of the retardate in his natural environment as well: talking with his friends over a cup of coffee in the cafeteria; playing cards in the dormitory recreation room; being taught how to read and to write in the classroom, how to paint and to do leather work in occupational therapy, and how to swim and to play baseball in recreation; working as a messenger, orderly, and clerk in the institution's offices and buildings; attending a party or a dance with his girl friend; and reacting with his full repertoire of emotions to the myriad situations and experiences which he encounters in the course of his daily routine. As a result of the close and comprehensive contact with the retardate which has been our fortunate circumstance, we find ourselves in the advantageous position of being able to make the necessary distinctions between what is apocryphal and what is authentic as knowledge concerning the retardate's personality. In a field in which so much has been said and written, it is important to place in proper perspective the single anecdote, the isolated experimental finding, and the lone educated guess.

In so doing, we have found it necessary to be somewhat selective in our inclusion of only those materials which we have considered to be particularly illuminative of the personality of the mental retardate. We have repeatedly tried to pinpoint and to highlight the essence of the retardate's personality, rather than merely to survey the existing body of knowledge in the field. The work is thus intended not simply as a review of the subject, but as an overview as well, and as a directional point of departure for what is an as yet unwritten body of knowledge on the personality of the mental retardate.

The book has been conceived as two separate sections: first, a "theoretical" section treating questions of personality development, personality dynamics, environmental influences, the self-concept, personality traits, and deviant behavior; and secondly, an "applied" section dealing with problems of classroom adjustment, social behavior, vocational adjustment, and leisure time pursuits. Accordingly, the volume is directed toward both the academic student of the subject and the professional worker in the field. To the extent that it defines essential terms, identifies basic concepts, and implements both experimental and clinical research findings in the formulation of a theory of personality, the book is offered as a basic text in the psychological study of mental retardation. To the extent that it explores particular areas and phases of the personality functioning of the retardate in the course of his everyday life and behavior, the book is offered as a ready source of reference for the professional worker whose daily contact with the mental retardate inevitably raises certain questions about the personality of the individual who is under his care or treatment. For both the student and the professional worker, a wealth of source material is provided in the form of an extensive up-to-date bibliography of articles, monographs, and books presented at the end of each chapter. At the same time, the elimination of footnotes throughout the work makes possible a smooth and unencumbered reading of the text. The book's potential readership includes all those who have ever reflected, wondered, or found themselves concerned in one way or another about the personality of the mental retardate and who therefore want to come to know, to understand, and to appreciate this personality in a more systematic and sustained way.

The keynote theme of our approach to the subject consists in the understanding and appreciation of the mental retardate not as an odd or idiosyncratic entity, but rather as a human being with certain deficiencies and limitations which create special problems of emotional and social adjustment. The present work has thus sought to place in perspective the limitations of the retardate, to see them in relation to the intellectually normal world about him, and to offer certain principles which recognize the need for sustaining the retardate's personality through a synergic balance between individual capacity and environmental demands. Above all, it remains our hope and aim that what we have set forth in these pages will help to raise the limit of knowledge on the subject above the existing threshold, so that through our enlarged understanding and appreciation of his personality, the retardate himself might be aided in his own attempt to establish a healthy and happy niche in life and to find his own special place in the sun.

In consideration of the foregoing, the authors should like to express their indebtedness to those who helped make this work possible. To Mrs. Madeline Sternlicht, for her unselfish devotion of time and energy in the ideation and completion of this work. To Mrs. Gragina G. Deutsch, whose untiring efforts in the conception and execution of the present work have been indispensable. Her participation has been a constant source of inspiration during the writing of this book. To the Director of Willowbrook State School, Dr. Jack Hammond, whose progressive and enlightened approach to the care and treatment of our mentally retarded patients has made our work with them all the more meaningful and productive. To our colleagues in the Department of Psychology at Willowbrook State School, whose conversations with us over the years have sparked many of the ideas that have been incorporated into the present work. To Mrs. Lucille A. Hoerle, Mrs. Jo-Ann McAtee, and Mrs. Edwin Schild, for their painstaking and flawlessly careful preparation of the manuscript. And to the wonderfully engaging and lovable human beings who have been the subject of our study—the mentally retarded—in whose service we have devoted our life's work. Without them, indeed, this book could not have been written.

1

Personality Development: Introduction

It is somewhat disconcerting to have to begin by saying that our knowledge of the development of the personality of the retarded child consists of little more than educated guesses. There are several reasons for this. The psychological construct of "self-concept," which is so operative in personality theory and which, because of its importance, will be more fully treated in a separate chapter (see chap. 4), is not wholly reliable for retarded children, especially those under five years of age. Because of the limited verbal ability of retarded children, as well as their tendency to alter their perceptions of themselves because of those diverse interpersonal forces which are in constant daily operation, the assessment of self-concept is, at the very best, a tenuous measure. Further, measurement techniques designed for adults are not necessarily appropriate, when revised downward, for children; Piers and Harris (1964) bemoan the lack of self-concept measurement procedures for young children. Because adapted procedures are often of limited use for young children, due to their dependence upon the ability of the youngster to explore his feelings in depth and to verbalize these feelings, Brown (1966) reported on a technique to assess dimensions of self-concept held by four-year-old children as well as the results of a pilot study in which it was employed. Children, seeing themselves through pictures, were assigned different roles and asked to view themselves over an extended period, the latter procedure undertaken because of their limited attention span. Such nonverbal techniques may eventually yield useful data.

All of the preceding data on limited population samplings, owing to the difficulties inherent in the assessment of self-concept in young normal children, should make us stop to pause and to reflect. If there are so many problems involved with normal children, how much more so must be the case with the retarded child. Just as he is the stepchild of psychological treatment (Sternlicht and Wanderer, 1963), so, too, is he relatively deserted in personality development studies.

Although some overlapping does occur, most of the studies concerned with the personality of the retardate fall into four major groups:

1. Evaluation of the effectiveness of assessment techniques in evaluating personality (and suggested innovations);
2. Observation of the behavior of the mentally retarded in given areas;
3. Cataloging of characteristic personality traits of retardates (usually performed in comparison with a "normal" group); and

1

4. Investigations into possible causes for the manifest behavior of retardates, and proposed solutions to some of those personality disorders observed.

Although it is true that considerable research on personality dynamics has been done with the retardate at different levels of his development, it has had little bearing on the actual stages of development that were taking place. Perhaps the complete absence of intensive, longitudinal psychological studies of the mentally retarded is a reflection of the "inability of the behavioral scientist to identify himself with the problems of that large group of individuals from whom he differs so markedly intellectually and culturally," as Sarason and Gladwin (1958) stated. But it also is doubtless due to the physical impossibility of studying a large sampling of retarded children from early childhood on, and then comparing data and checking for environmental or genetic variables. Large-scale study is usually possible only once the child has been institutionalized, and then we have few clues as to the differing backgrounds which may have contributed to the personality as it has emerged. Gallagher (1959) has attributed the comparative dearth of studies dealing with the personalities of the mentally retarded to "lack of adequate instruments . . . and the variability of behavior in the retarded." And those few studies that do exist deal almost exclusively with "variables (that) can be manipulated in either natural or laboratory settings" (Guskin, 1963).

Also, there is a tendency to study the retarded in terms of their isolated disabilities as separate phenomena rather than within the subject's life situation (Michal-Smith and Kastein, 1962). Perhaps the focus should rather be upon those aspects of the life experiences of a retardate which may be expected to enhance or to detract from effective adjustment and personality development. That is, emphasis should be placed on the given mentally retarded individual reacting to specific situations. We may have to study those behavioral and situational variables which may be critically related to the retardate's general functioning. But, as Gardner (1965) has so eloquently stated, "the determination of the amounts and the kinds of differentiation of the (retarded) child's external world that are either salutary and necessary, or their opposites that are developmentally unhealthy and unnecessary, requires further research by our social scientists."

When an attempt to trace a pattern of development is undertaken, it is usually based upon generalized observations. Cobb (1961), for example, traced the self-concept of the retarded child through five stages of development: primitive differentiation and integration; naming, identifying, and generalizing; accretion and evaluation of attributes and possessions; aspiration level and expectancy of success and failure; and adolescent revision of self. Cobb also emphasized the slowness of cognitive development (especially in relation to physical maturation) which differentiates retarded from normal children, making for greater undifferentiation, for unrealistic expectancies, and for a confused self-image. Retardation is thus viewed as a slower version of normal personality development which results in special problems as well. Intelligence, however, is but one facet of the total personality, and it requires a proportionate and appropriate balancing among the total assets and liabilities of the retardate. This is especially important when one considers that our society offers the retardate fewer environmental supports than it does the normal child. In addition, the general economic situation and the availability of professional assistance must be considered. Miller (1944), too, noted the slow-motion quality of growth and development of the retarded, but stated that the quality of their feelings and emotions did not differ from the normal person's. Whether or not there is anything unique about the development of personality in the mentally retarded is a fundamental consideration for this topic, as well as the focus of this chapter. If the retardate presents a "slower" version of normal childhood development, then we need only dwell on the body of information dealing with normal children, and anticipate slight deviations. If, on the other hand, he presents a totally different developmental pattern—his diminished intellectual functioning creating a concomitant ego disturbance and other dysfunctioning—the implications are tremendous. The existing studies present conflicting views.

Bender (1959) viewed autistic thinking and actions observed in the retarded as a primitive form of behavior—an aspect of normal development which has persisted and has become exaggerated. It also may indicate a defense against disorganization and anxiety in children with defects. In a related vein, McKinney (1962) interpreted those aspects of autism which pertain to bodily stimulation and lack of recognition of social surroundings in terms of a primitive need for self-awareness. Rather than hazard a guess as to differences or similarities of development, Duhl (1958) concentrated upon methodology. He believed that child development studies of normal children could set a pattern of investigation for students of retardation (and indeed, may be prerequisite for any understanding of the retardate), and he cited the determining forces of development as the child himself, his family, and the community, all interacting simultaneously.

Just how important the family is in determining the personality development of the retarded child is underscored in a study by Goldfarb (1947), which showed that a depriving experience (e.g., institutionalization) in infancy exerts an enduring negative psychological effect on children, even if these children are removed from an institution and placed in foster homes at the end of a three-year period. The majority of these deprived children were found to present a continuing history of maladjustment, although individual differences were noted within the group. Goldfarb concluded that "cold, isolated depriving experience during the first months of life impedes the normal development of such mature qualities as personal security and independence, a deep personal reciprocating interest in others, appropriate inhibitions and a reflective, organizing approach to problems."

Gorlow, Butler, and Guthrie (1963) found that retardates who were separated from their parents at an early age manifested more negative self-attitudes, and that their self-acceptance was associated with certain dimensions of social needs and certain modes of response to hostility. Peck and Stephens (1960) found a direct relationship between parental attitudes and behavior toward their adolescent retarded children and their children's attitude and behavior (e.g., where parents were willing to answer the child's questions, there was an exploring attitude in the child). Nevertheless, there was a lack of emotional security in most retardates' homes, and peer relationships were extremely poor. Also, the homes of these retardates were organized about interests different from those of the retardates.

Such studies, although quite inconclusive and merely suggestive, offer tantalizing fields of exploration. If much of the maladjusting behavior attributed to retardates can be traced to infancy and early child-rearing patterns, and if the parents themselves usually react in almost a predictable rejecting pattern, then the behavior of the retardate may be more a function of his early environmental upbringing than of any inherent behavior syndrome associated with the nature of his retardation.

Biller and Borstelmann (1965), although noting sex role development to be related to IQ, also postulated that the slower sex role development of the institutionalized retardate may be due to the lesser availability of role models and the greater probable rejection by the same-sexed parent. Pearson (1942) felt that, because of lack of love and acceptance, rather than directly because of his intellectual handicap, the retarded child begins to live a life more and more different from that of the normal child. Specifically, he stated that "this lack of love interferes with the development of his ego to any close approximation of what it is really capable of," and as a consequence of this, the retarded child never has the same type of security in his parents' love as the nonretarded child does.

Jordan and deCharms (1959) likewise have observed different behavior in the parents of retardates. These authors noted that parents of retarded children did not stress independence training in early childhood, which lack impeded the child's achievement motive and increased his fear of failure. Their experiment was based on an education program whereby special training in special classes produced personality changes, especially in terms of less fear and less anticipation of failure.

Tending to corroborate these findings, Blatt (1958), who indicated that retarded children in both special and regular classes appear to have a greater degree of personality maladjustment than do normal children, nevertheless found that the retarded children in special classes tended to be more socially mature and emotionally secure and stable than those in regular classes. Meyerowitz (1962), however, felt that the special classes themselves may have an adverse effect on the retardate's self-perception, in that he is singled out as being inferior to the rest of the school children.

The implied point to be made here is that the exposure of retarded children to atypical child-rearing practices may produce the differences observed in their personality development.

Without entering into the reasons "why," Snyder (1966) noted that, in the mildly retarded, a close correlation exists between good academic achievement and personality integration. Conversely, the adequately adjusting (with favorable self-concepts) attain more academically. No attempt was made to explain why there was greater manifest anxiety among the poorer achievers who showed learning inhibitions. This study does indicate, however, that even a subgroup of retardates (the "mildly" retarded) cannot be considered as homogeneous, and that we need to search for those factors causing the personality variables which, in turn, were found to play a major role in the extent to which the retarded adolescent maximizes his intellectual potential. Synder's findings also showed that the midly retarded adolescent, in general, shows a poorer level of personality adjustment than does the normal subject. Thus, he infers a "different" personality development.

Higgins (1955), too, regards retardation as creating different developmental patterns. In a normal child, he declares, development is a smooth process whereby the child progresses, when able to do so, but in the defective child, the development is impeded by the lack of incentive to make the next move forward in both the physical and social world. Inadequate intellectual abilities are thus cited as causing anxiety in the child, because he has failed to master the world about him. A clinging, fearful child desperately seeking love and approval is the consequence. Thus, although environmental factors are not disregarded, the focus here is on the "initial handicap" as producing major disability. Damage in one system is viewed as being reflected in another.

In contrast, Bobroff (1960), who studied normal and educable mentally retarded children at several age levels in the areas of ego maturation and socialization, found no differences in the sequence of developmental stages. Although both groups progressed through the same sequence of stages, a significantly large number of educably retarded subjects were classified into lower stages of ego development than normals of similar mental age (based on T.A.T. protocols).

Zigler (1966) has referred to those conceptualizations by theoreticians of the familial retardate as different, as the "difference orientation." Thus, regardless of etiology, all retardates are seen as inherently different. Although he is not referring to the developmental analyses, his summation can be applied here, too, where we have shown that certain researchers have assumed that the different personality development of the retarded individual results from his cognitive structure or intellectual level. Although Zigler has not labelled the converse view the "similarity orientation," for simplicity's sake, we might do so to categorize the position taken by those investigators who dwell on the similarity with normal personality development, and emphasize the influence of environmental history on personality development. Thus, while aware of the intellectual limitations of mental retardation, these authors see a parallel development with the normal child, accounting for the differences in terms of their different emotional experiences.

In sum, whereas both orientations view retardation as a slower process of cognitive development, making the mentally retarded "different," the "difference" orientation sees the emerging personality as resulting from the "handicap," while the "similarity" orientation sees it as resulting from reactions to that handicap.

The question with which we are then confronted is how we can assess those emotional variables that may be influential in the behavioral (personality) functioning of the mentally retarded. Perhaps it might be more appropriate to ask how this can be accomplished at all, in light of the rather restrictive repertoire of evaluative techniques that are available.

Those evaluation and assessment devices that are available might be dichotomized as either objective or subjective. Because of the retardate's intellectual limitations, so especially apparent in the areas of verbal fluency and verbal facility, the employment of wholly objective psychological assessment techniques, such as inventories and questionnaires, is largely ruled out. Objective rating scales, however, such as the Vineland Social Maturity Scale, can be and are being utilized.

The heaviest emphasis in the evaluation of the emotional dimensions in the mentally retarded is upon more or less subjective techniques. Primary among these subjective assessment devices are the projective techniques and observations. In a survey dealing with the psychological testing practices in state facilities for the retarded, Silverstein (undated) found that "more projective testing" was being performed, and the anticipation was that even more would be done in "the next five years." "The greatest needs in testing for the mentally retarded" were viewed to be improvements in "Personality testing" and in "Testing for differential diagnosis." The projective techniques which are currently being utilized with the greatest frequency include the Rorschach, the Figure Drawing Test and other graphic techniques, the Bender-Gestalt, the T.A.T., and the Blacky Pictures. Hopefully, such projective techniques will reveal the retardate's personality dynamics and emotional conflicts via an intensive analysis of the patient's approach to the "test" materials and a thorough exploration of the content of his perceptions, cognitions, and verbalizations. Sometimes this can be done, at least on a gross basis; at other times, however, the projectives are too insensitive to perform the task. In addition, many of the psychologists, in their interpretations of the derived data, tend to highlight the negative aspects of the individual's social and personal functioning, at the expense of the retardate's personality strengths and assets.

Observational techniques are perhaps the most fruitful assessment procedures, especially naturalistic observations made directly within the retardate's functioning milieu. From these kinds of observations, including filmed observations, as well as from observations made within the context of a formal testing-assessment or therapeutic session, hypotheses can be formulated concerning the retardate's level of self-esteem, his modes of relating to others, his degree of personal and social adequacy and effectiveness, his critical and evaluative capacities, his perceptual adequacies, and so forth.

Although on a very general level this procedure is good, on a specific plane its inadequacy is demonstrated in the many unanswered questions that remain. For example, to which behavioral and personality variables are we to pay special attention, and in which ways do they contribute to adequate or inadequate social functioning? Then too, what aspects of maladaptive social functioning are amenable to therapeutic and/or educational amelioration? Should we concentrate on the retardate's weaknesses, on his strengths, or on both? What environmental modifications and structural changes are called for? What reliability and what validity can we ascribe to our observational and projective judgments?

Clearly, we desperately need greater conceptual-theoretical clarity in this area, as well as greater applied research efforts.

References

Bender, L. Autism in children with mental deficiency. *American Journal of Mental Deficiency*, 1959, 64, 81-86.

Biller, H.B., and Borstelmann, L.J. Intellectual level and sex role development in mentally retarded children. *American Journal of Mental Deficiency*, 1965, 70, 443-447.

Blatt, B. The physical, personality, and academic status of children who are mentally retarded attending special classes as compared with children who are mentally retarded attending regular classes. *American Journal of Mental Deficiency*, 1958, 62, 810-818.

Bobroff, A. The stages of maturation in socialized thinking in the ego development of two groups of children. *Child Development*, 1960, 31, 321-328.

Brown, B.R. The assessment of self concept among four-year-old Negro and white children: A comparative study using the Brown-IDS Self Concept Referents Test. Paper presented at the annual meeting of the Eastern Psychological Association, New York City, April, 1966.

Cobb, H.V. Self-concept of the mentally retarded. *Rehabilitation Record*, 1961, 2 (3), 21-25.

Duhl, L.J. The normal development of the mentally retarded child. *American Journal of Mental Deficiency*, 1958, 62, 585-591.

Gallagher, J.J. A comparison of brain-injured and non-brain-injured mentally retarded children, on several psychological variables. *Monographs of the Society for Research in Child Development*, 1959, 22, No. 2.

Gardner, G.E. The next decade: Expectations from the social sciences and education. *Journal of the American Medical Association*, 1965, 191, 223-225.

Goldfarb, W. Variations in adolescent adjustment of institutionally reared children. *American Journal of Orthopsychiatry*, 1947, 17, 449-457.

Gorlow, L; Butler, A.; and Guthrie, G.M. Correlates of self-attitudes of retardates. *American Journal of Mental Deficiency*, 1963, 67, 549-555.

Guskin, S. Social psychologies of mental deficiency. In N.R. Ellis (ed.) *Handbook of mental deficiency*. New York: McGraw-Hill, 1963, pp. 325-352.

Higgins, R. The psychological aspects of backwardness. *Mental Health*, 1955, 15, 8-15.

Jordan, T.E., and de Charms, R. The achievement motive in normal and mentally retarded children. *American Journal of Mental Deficiency*, 1959, 64, 457-466.

McKinney, J.P. A multidimensional study of the behavior of severely retarded boys. *Child Development*, 1962, 33, 923-938.

Meyerowitz, J.H. Self-derogations in young retardates and special class placement. *Child Development*, 1962, 33, 443-451.

Michal-Smith, H., and Kastein, S. *The special child: Diagnosis, treatment, habilitation*. Seattle: New School for the Special Child, 1962.

Miller, H.G. The transformation of the self in children. *American Journal of Mental Deficiency*, 1944, 48, 374-378.

Pearson, G. The psychopathology of mental defect. *Nervous Child*, 1942, 2, 9-20.

Peck, J.R., and Stephens, W.B. A study of the relationship between the attitudes and behavior of parents and that of their mentally defective child. *American Journal of Mental Deficiency*, 1960, 64, 839-844.

Piers, E., and Harris, D.B. Age and other correlates of self concept in children. *Journal of Educational Psychology*, 1964, 55, 91-95.

Sarason, S.B., and Gladwin, T. Psychological and cultural problems in mental subnormality: A review of research. *Genetic Psychology Monographs*, 1958, 57, 3-290.

Snyder, R.T. Personality adjustment, self attitudes, and anxiety differences in retarded adolescents. *American Journal of Mental Deficiency*, 1966, 71, 33-41.

Sternlicht, M., and Wanderer, Z.W. Group psychotherapy with mental defectives. Paper presented at the annual convention of the American Group Psychotherapy Association, Washington, D.C., Jan., 1963, and reviewed in *Journal of the American Medical Association*, 1963, 183 (5), 45.

Zigler, E. Research on personality structure in the retardate. In N.R. Ellis (ed.), *International review of research in mental retardation, v. 1*. New York: Academic Press, 1966, pp. 77-108.

2 Personality Dynamics: Meaning of Mental Retardation

Since the role of the maturation processes in the development of the personality of the mental retardate has been inadequately investigated, our principal source of knowledge in this area is to be found in studies of behavioral manifestations assumed to be "typical" of the retarded. Yet, the very classification "mental retardation" must be examined carefully. In fact, a good number of studies are designed not only to differentiate retardates from normals, but also to differentiate retardates from one another.

As a starting point, our definition of mental retardation is that contained in the current American Association on Mental Deficiency's Manual on Terminology and Classification: "Mental retardation refers to sub-average general intellectual functioning which originates during the developmental period and is associated with impairment in adaptive behavior" (Heber, 1961). While this definition is intended to encompass all levels and degrees of intellectual deficiencies, the term "mental retardation" is clearly rooted in the specific cultural value systems of any given societal group. Thus, depending upon societal values and demands, a given individual may be deemed to be retarded in one society, but may not be so considered in another.

There are a multitude of widely held beliefs regarding common personality dynamics or behavioral characteristics in the retarded, but few of these notions have received research verification, and variable clinical portraits are more the rule than the exception. In tracing patterns of personality dynamics in the retarded, the emphasis should be placed upon specific types of situations which produce specific types of behavioral manifestations. Within such a framework, several patterns may emerge which may demonstrate a similar causal relationship, perhaps in terms of experiential referents.

Zigler (1967) feels that considerable order could be brought to the area if all retardates were not viewed as a homogeneous group arbitrarily defined by some IQ score, but rather were viewed as a group to be differentiated, distinctions being made between physiologically defective retardates of known etiology and cultural-familial retardates. He also maintains that the reported differences in behavior between this latter group of retardates and nonretardates of the same mental age (MA) essentially were due to differential motivational systems, rather than to the existence of mental retardation per se. Notwithstanding, and including, these two categories, nearly 75 to 85 percent of the causes of mental retardation are as yet of unknown etiology. That is, in these cases the primary etiology of the retardation, at this point, is ascribed to psychological, social, and/or cultural variables. Many workers in the field, however, feel that many mildly retarded individuals are best viewed as "culturally deprived," in that they grow up in relatively unstimulating and undemanding early environments. As an example of some of the difficulties in this area, Bakwin (1950) classified two types of retardation, one fitting into the lower area of the "normal" range, with the other being distinctly "abnormal." He then listed twelve reasons that children may be falsely diagnosed as retarded, including improper testing. Benton (1956) speaks of diagnostic errors and "pseudofeeblemindedness," and says that a specific etiology based on neuropathological findings alone is distinctly inadequate—a broader formulation being called for. Sternlicht (1964) postulated a threefold etiological model, as follows:

1. The mental retardation syndrome, as it manifests itself in a patient, is the result of two causes, a primary and a secondary cause.
2. The primary one is the cause of the low intelligence. The secondary one is the emotional response to the former, resulting in an impairment in adaptive behavior.
3. The primary cause may be the result of (a) neurological deficit (b) severe cultural deprivation (c) emotional maladjustment. Primary neurological deficit included all of which we call 'organicity' (p. 620).

Werner (1945 a, b) has noted, through the use of the Rorschach, essential differences in the makeup of various retarded children. His findings indicate that brain-damaged children are impaired in general functions such as perceptual integration and conceptual thinking, impairments which are not to be found in the familial retardate. Two different groups of mental retardates were matched for chronological age (CA) and MA. Responses to tiny, speck-like details were almost absent with the brain-injured children. These subjects perceived a part as a whole (oligophrenic response) about four times as frequently as did familials. They gave significantly greater responses based on white rather than colored or black spaces. As contrasted with the non-brain-injured children, they tended to perceive the background without seeing the objects themselves. Further, brain-injured children, although they saw significantly more human than animal figures, viewed both as much more static. They reacted more strongly (than non-brain-injured retardates) to color, which fits into the critical picture of excessive distractibility to external stimulation. Finally, the organically damaged retardates gave a good many farfetched, bizarre interpretations, a type of "original" response practically absent among the familial retardates. In summary, the characteristics of the brain-injured retardates that were observed were the following: (1) lack of integration of elements into a more comprehensive configuration; (2) lack of sensory control; (3) lack of affective motor control (i.e., hyperactivity); (4) lack of associational control; (5) meticulous behavior; and (6) pathological rigidity.

Tolman and Johnson (1958), in a study of thirteen pairs of organic and familial mentally retarded children, found differences in their need patterns. The organic children were less willing to compete, and they were relatively more accepting of their parents' rejection. The familial group, in contrast, feared rejection and showed a willingness to compete (against a standard of excellence) because of their need for achievement.

Siipola and Hayden (1965), who predicted that prolonged retention of a primitive type of cognition (i.e., eidetic imagery) would be more commonplace among the familial retarded, found, to their surprise, that almost all of those retardates who displayed eidetic imagery belonged to the brain-injured group. If these preliminary results were confirmed, they believed, there may be interesting implications for a neurological theory of (eidetic) imagery, for future research, and for diagnosis of brain injury in children.

Equally eager to show that mental retardation is not a fixed entity but is, rather, a heterogenous grouping to be differentiated according to etiology, Michal-Smith and Kastein (1962) suggested that the subcategory of "brain damaged" is not a homogeneous one, since "cerebral defect itself is not a unified concept, but a multiple one. . . ." Individual differences, whether based on physical inadequacies or differences caused by environmental stresses, produce different types of subjects. A proper diagnosis, therefore, should involve, according to these two authors, an analysis of personality structure, of level of aspiration, of interpersonal relationships, of motivation, of social integration, and of maturity of behavior. The authors thus question the very usefulness of clinical findings on the brain-injured, such as those previously cited and also those specified by Strauss and Lehtinen (1948), which classified the brain-injured as hyperactive, distractible, awkward children, poorly integrated in their motor performance, faulty in their perception, and poorly organized and unpredictable in their behavior. This generalized pattern was criticized because it fails to account for individual differences. "There is no brain injured child," say the authors, "but only a variety of children with brain dysfunction whose problems are quite varied . . . " Yet, the authors then proceeded to describe the personality dynamics of the brain-injured, including the inability to grasp abstract concepts, the intense anxiety that results from unfamiliar or threatening situations, and the paradox of the inability to bear tension resulting from warm relationships coupled with the intense need for them, emphasizing that special problems will be met with each child. While these authors, too, applied generalized behavior patterns, the differences in approach consisted of their denial of *one* basic underlying cause for this condition. There are observable personality dynamics, but they are to be used with caution in diagnosis and treatment, these authors seem to be saying. Michal-Smith and Kastein (1962) noted that there should be no distinction made between brain injury in children and brain injury in adults. In children, the brain has not fully developed, whereas in adults the brain has acquired maturation in learning before the injury took place. Thus, adult defects may be compensated for by the preserved capacities. The brain-injured child thus probably feels greater stress because of environmental demands. Certain types of hyperactivity similarly may indicate the presence of an organic or intellectual defect. Symptoms which include continuous involuntary movements, shaking, banging, and perseverative movements require further evaluation to determine the etiology of these disturbances in the motor area.

Leaving the subgrouping of organic retardation, we are now faced with another major category of retardation which has been studied separately—mongolism, a condition that is always present at birth. The etiology or cause of mongolism is still uncertain, and many theoretical explanations have been offered. Most theorists view this condition as being exogenous in etiology, however, and Murphy (1956) conducted an experiment which tended to demonstrate that mongolism is of exogenous origin. This finding supports Benda's (1949) theory that mongolism is the result of an improperly developed or damaged pituitary gland during the fetal period which causes severe retardation of intellectual development and is not the result of arrested development at a certain mental age, as is the case with many brain-injured individuals. McNeill (1955) traces the developmental patterns of mongoloid children, which he finds to be different from that of normals. There also is a different developmental pattern for institutionalized mongoloids as against those reared at home.

Silverstein (1964), empirically testing the stereotype of the mongoloid as a well-adjusting, cheerful, extraverted individual, employed Peterson's Behavior Rating Scales, and found that the mongoloids scored significantly higher (than a matched group of other kinds of retardates) on general adjustment, thus providing partial support for the mongoloid stereotype. However, there were no significant differences on the introversion-extraversion scores. In addition, a study by Domino, Goldschmid, and Kaplan (1964) did confirm the mongoloid stereotype. Technicians rated a group of twenty-one mongoloid and thirty-five non-mongoloid institutionalized retarded girls on the Sonoma Check List, and they also obtained a "degree of familiarity" score for each subject. A unified and internally consistent pattern of mongoloid personality was found, which was not due to rater bias. The results showed that mongoloids are affectionate, happy, cheerful, good-tempered, and friendly.

Wunsch (1957), in an evaluation of seventy-seven mongoloid children over a three-year period in a state clinic, likewise found 66.2 percent to exhibit the docile-affective type of temperament usually attributed to mongoloids, with only 14.3 percent of the group, and these were mostly boys, manifesting hostile-aggressive behavior. The behavior of the remaining 19.5 percent could not readily be classified or was not noted. In this connection, many mothers have been known to remark that their mongoloid child was "the best baby we ever had. It never made any trouble." (Sternlicht, 1966)

In direct contrast are Blacketer-Simmonds' (1953) findings that mongoloids show no "special desirable personality traits." In this study, an investigation of the temperamental factors of mongoloids was carried out by employing 140 mongoloids with Binet IQ's of less than 46, and 100 controls, matched in terms of intellect and physical aspects with the former group. Contrary to the personality characteristics presented by previous writers, the findings indicated that mongoloids do not generally conform to certain characteristic temperamental types, and that they seem to display the same undesirable habits and tendencies as do nonmongoloids (e.g., they are less docile and more mischievous than nonmongoloids).

Tizard and Grad (1961) also found that mongoloids did not differ significantly in temperament from other retardates, yet they were more commonly kept at home. The authors relate this to the fact that mongoloids include in their number fewer individuals functioning at the idiot level as well as fewer individuals with severe health or management problems. It can thus be seen that in this subgrouping, too, generalizations must be taken with caution.

The following two cases will serve to illustrate the diversity of behavioral functioning that is apt to occur between mongoloids and even within a single mongoloid individual.

Case One

Max is an eight-year-old mongoloid boy, who was born in New York City. His mongoloid condition was immediately noted at birth, though the parents were unable to accept such a diagnosis, hoping that some change would in time take place. The parents attempted to care for Max at home during the child's first seven months, at the end of which time he was placed in a Home, owing to the fact that he was showing very few signs of adequate development, at the same time as his mongoloid features were becoming more pronounced. During his one-month period of stay in the Infants Home, the developmental abilities which the patient displayed consisted in rather elementary behaviors, such as responding to his parents and being able to roll over in his crib. It was reported that Max presented no feeding problems at that time, was in good physical condition, adjusted well to the environmental change from home to institution, and in general appeared to have benefited from the care he was receiving at the Home. At the age of two, however, the patient was confined to a general hospital for eight days with an upper respiratory infection, subsequent to which he would suffer from frequent colds and a constantly running nose. Following his stay in the Infants Home, the patient was placed at Willowbrook since the parents recognized that they would be unable to care for their son at home.

At the time of his admission to Willowbrook, at the age of two, Max was described as a friendly boy, somewhat active, with no bad habits. He was nonambulatory, though he could sit well; nonverbal, though he made sounds; and noncomprehending, though he displayed a fondness for affection and an interest in his environment. The patient's IQ at the time of admission was 45 as measured by the Kuhlmann Test of Mental Development, placing him in the moderately mentally retarded range of intelligence. He had a good appetite, being fed by spoon and drinking from a bottle. Similarly, he slept well. In general, Max gave the impression of being a happy child. One month after his admission, it was observed in the physicians progress notes: "This child is very friendly, smiles and is a very happy boy. . . . He is very affectionate and interested in his environment. He is not self-abusive. He understands a little." One year later, the patient's general understanding of his environment improved. Some incipient verbal behavior was noted as the patient attempted to say some words. Crawling activity was observed as well. Two months later, he was walking with assistance and relating well to the other children. On several occasions during the next two years, the patient developed an upper respiratory infection and in each case was in critical condition for a short period. By the age of five, the patient had made developmental progress in the areas of self-help and motility, being able to feed himself and to walk without support. He was partially toilet-trained as well. He could not dress himself however. At this time, it was reported that Max enjoyed playing with the other children and that he would engage in such socially oriented play activity as reciprocal ball throwing with attendants. During this entire period, the patient was repeatedly described as nonabusive either to himself or to others. By the age of six, Max was comprehending a good deal and obeying simple commands. He was reported to be pronouncing some single words though his speech was unclear. At seven, the patient was able to dress himself with some help. He displayed, too, a desire to be helpful to others. The patient was able to talk in sentences though unclearly. In addition, he would answer questions, presumably of a "yes-no" variety. He remained, however, only partially toilet-trained, though continuing attempts were being made in this area. At that time, the patient was participating in recreation therapy and mixed trainable school classes. In school, his progress and interest were consistently good, though his conduct was variable, with the patient displaying a tendency at times to boss the other children and to try to correct them. Currently, at the age of eight, Max has progressed in school from nonverbal to verbal abilities, and he has demonstrated an ability to retain skills and vocabulary.

Case Two

Dominick is a fourteen-year-old adolescent mongoloid male, who was born in New York City. His father has a history of drug addiction. Dominick's condition of mongolism was diagnosed at birth. He was bottle fed and retained his food badly for the first six months of his life. The patient began to stand at two years, to walk at three years, and to talk at two years. Toilet-training was completed at the age of five years, with occasional omissions. Dominick could feed himself at the age of five. He was described as an extremely stubborn child, always wanting his own way. At times, he would display marked temper tantrums, sometimes hitting and attacking other children. Otherwise his disposition was described as affectionate. His play activities included watching television, coloring, listening to music, and playing with building blocks, puzzles, and clay. At seven years of age, Dominick attended a class for children with retarded mental development (CRMD) at public elementary school. The patient's eyesight was described as extremely poor. He was hospitalized for pneumonia at a general hospital at the age of eight. Admission to Willowbrook was requested at the age of twelve, because the patient was becoming increasingly wild and difficult for the mother to handle. Dominick would typically run across the street without looking in either direction, climb up the fire escape, and play with matches. The mother felt at that time that her son "always wanted to get out on his own."

Upon his admission to Willowbrook, Dominick presented himself as a moderately cooperative boy with normal poise and expressive movements. He appeared sad and showed anger and irritability as well. His speech was irrelevant and incoherent. He was disoriented to time, place, and person. The patient spoke in sentences and followed simple commands. In the ensuing days, he began to display a hyperactive, abusive, and assaultive pattern of behavior. He would, for example, throw chairs around the ward and fight with others. As a result, Dominick had to be closely watched. The patient was placed on Thorazine several days after his admission. Notwithstanding this, he was described as friendly and content. He had a good appetite, fed himself, and slept well. Dominick appeared interested in his surroundings. Two months later, his hyperactive and assaultive behavior appeared to increase. He then became quieter, though he still fought with other patients to some extent. Two months after this, he was reportedly adjusting well, preferring to sit by himself. He would still have temper tantrums when he could not have his own way. He did not show much interest in his surroundings and was described as indifferent. He was occasionally assaultive. A month later, he was characterized as cranky, not playful, and sometimes aggressive. The patient's behavior of the previous several months—quiet, indifferent, occasionally assaultive, and apparently content—continued presumably for another year. Then, the patient developed and was treated for infectious hepatitis. Following this, the patient was granted weekend privileges on the basis of his improved behavior. A month later, he developed cataracts on both eyes and underwent operations, being placed on community status for this purpose. No further reports of the patient's psychological development were made until a year later, when he was described as stubborn, teasing, abusive, and assaultive. In the most recent progress report, Dominick continued to be characterized in similar terms: "This fourteen-year-old patient is rather cranky; likes to be alone; doesn't like to be bothered; is abusive to others, pushing them; also self-abusive." The patient reportedly attended occupational therapy and physiotherapy, though no mention is made of educational training. Dominick is functioning at the moderately mentally retarded level of intelligence, with a 1960 Stanford-Binet IQ of 43.

To complete the picture of the diversity found even among a supposedly homogeneous group of retardates, Chipman (1940) has demonstrated that variations in mental output and in general competence exist even among the group labeled "idiot." The report deals with the undirected activity, under controlled conditions, of a group of fifty-four adult idiots (profoundly retarded) (CAs 18 to 45; MAs 0-6 to 3-6). Chipman discovered behavioral differences among the subjects, even in the linguistic area, traditionally thought to represent the most serious limitation in idiot functioning. The author therefore concluded that their behavior gave evidence that "idiots" cannot be considered as a homogeneous group (from a psychological point of view).

Sarason and Gladwin (1958) similarly concluded, based upon Itard's work, that even in severely retarded individuals, the quantity and quality of interpersonal relationships is an important variable in determining the level of complexity and efficiency of psychological functioning. Thus, even in the severely retarded child, the measurement of intellectual performance and of potential cannot be meaningfully done without consideration of environmental opportunity and stimulation. In this regard, the authors stressed the importance of parent-child relationships, an area hardly touched upon because most professional workers assume that the severely retarded individual "has no personality or intellectual potential to speak of," which does not hold true in all cases. Dokecki (1964) declared that the notion that grossly mentally retarded individuals have very little or no behavior potential "cannot be held in the face of the experimental literature." His review of the literature suggested that there is sufficient evidence available to demonstrate that the severely retarded have behavior potential, and that their behavior is capable of modification, via the employment of appropriate treatment techniques.

An example of a severely retarded boy is the case of Thomas, a fourteen-year-old. His early developmental history is rather scanty, and no anamnesis is available. However, Thomas first walked at the age of nineteen months and first talked between the ages of three and six. The patient's retardation was first noted when he was two years old. There is no history of accident or injury to the patient, defect of the special senses, bodily deformity or anomaly, or epilepsy, and he is in good physical condition. At the age of seven, his speech was limited to a few names of people and several phrases. He was able to dress himself but could not button his clothing or tie his shoe laces. The patient had sphincter control. Thomas reportedly was a restless child who would hit and spit at people repeatedly. He was described as a dependent individual, unable to attend school, whose behavior consisted largely in aimless wandering, fingering of objects, and the aforementioned hitting and spitting. The patient could not safely be left alone at any time and needed constant supervision. He was considered liable to self-injury though not to injury of others. His Stanford-Binet IQ obtained at the age of seven was 30. For these reasons, admission to Willowbrook was requested.

The patient adjusted slowly to ward routine after admission to Willowbrook. He ate and slept well, was toilet trained, and could dress and undress himself with supervision. Thomas spoke in simple sentences and followed simple directions. In about two weeks, he began mingling slightly with other patients and was considered friendly and content. The patient would repeat everything that was said to him. Six months later, it was reported that he seemed to understand a little. No sex activity was noted. His condition remained unchanged for the next four months, and then he was characterized as "indifferent and manneristic, occasionally rocking forward and backward." In addition, it was noted that the patient had a habit of crying during the entire time that he would eat without any apparent external provocation. He had no known pain and the cause of the crying could not be determined. At the age of eight, he appeared cranky and manneristic. He was hyperactive and occasionally developed temper tantrums. Thomas showed an interest in his environment and cooperated on the ward. The crying tantrums became aggravated two weeks just prior to a home leave. Otherwise his behavior and his functioning remained the same. After returning from home leave in August, Thomas continued to have crying and screaming tantrums. He was cooperative in ward routine except at meal time when he would usually have his screaming tantrums. This pattern continued through Thomas' tenth year of life. Thomas participated in occupational therapy, physiotherapy, and school classes. For the academic year, the patient was showing little progress and no interest in school trainable class. His interpersonal relationships in class were poor. He experienced difficulty in communicating and would scream daily in the classroom. By April of that year, our patient had been dropped from school because he was not responding. For a period of time his progress in occupational therapy was somewhat better as suggested by the following report: "Hyperactive! Has made great progress (i.e., staying in seat—works on class projects). Because he is 'busy' he demands a *lot* of attention but understands better than one would believe but needs a 'firm' hand and *lots* of individual attention." He eventually reverted to his old self, however, and he was temporarily discontinued in the O.T. program. At the age of eleven, in addition to his hyperactivity and his tantrums, an assaultiveness against other patients was noted. The assaultiveness continued and one year later was combined with a disturbed lack of general control as well. It was reported at that time: "This 12-year-old patient is cranky most of the time; assaultive to other patients, abusing, pushing and knocking them down; also throws chairs around and pushes benches over. He is easily disturbed." At that time, too, masturbation was mentioned for the first time as part of the patient's behavior. Throughout this period of assaultiveness and disturbed aggressive impulsivity, the patient remained tidy. He has been maintained on Thorazine with increased dosages since his twelfth birthday, in order to control his hyperactivity. At the time of the last progress report (when Thomas was fourteen years of age), the patient's condition was unchanged: "This 14-year-old patient is still very active; destructive; disturbed;

abusive and assaultive to others." Thomas' intellectual functioning continued to remain within the severely retarded range.

Schulman and Stern (1959) conducted an interesting experiment which indicated that parents were fairly accurate in their estimation of their children's intellectual abilities, thus repudiating the widely-held view that parents are unaware of their children's retardation before seeking professional help.

A study, part of which dealt specifically with the problems of parents of imbeciles and idiots, was carried out by Tizard and Grad (1961). Of those retardates living at home, 31 percent presented no special management problems, 38 percent evidenced some problems, and the remainder exhibited severe problems. Notwithstanding the fact that more than half of the parents were satisfied with the medical advice and treatment that they had received or were receiving, the parents tended to criticize various aspects of community facilities and individual treatment. This finding may perhaps be related to a study by Stern and Longnecker (1962), who found that the expectations of parents of retarded, brain-damaged, and emotionally disturbed children differed from that of parental surrogates. Treatment approaches were different, leading to serious communication problems. It would be worthwhile having a study dealing solely with parental versus institutional attitudes toward the severely retarded to see if the different approach applies here as well.

Quite a different problem in our subgrouping of retardation occurs with the idiot savant. Here, the possibility of specific superiority in retardates leads to interesting speculation as to its origin and its development. Lindsley (1965) reviews the possible interpretations for this occurrence: (1) motivational compensation; (2) ego strength due to early reinforcement of gains; (3) less reflex competition from other behaviors and distractive stimuli; (4) increased reinforcing power of stimuli not involved in deficient behavior; (5) lowered thresholds because of limited sensory capacities; (6) easier career choice making for early specialization; and (7) greater creativity fostered by having less behavior to extinguish. He emphasizes, however, that instead of focusing our energies on explaining away the phenomenon of the idiot savant, we should concentrate on designing prosthetic environments which not only will restore average behavioral functioning for handicapped individuals, but which also may develop special skills to the point of superiority.

The following case history of an idiot savant may be illustrative.

Burton is a nearly fifty-year-old man, with obtained IQs ranging in the mildly retarded category (IQs 54-69). Although there is relatively little information available on his early history, both his parents and an only sibling are reported to have been of normal intelligence. Burton was described as a poorly developed, physically undersized, and fairly well nourished boy who had congenital syphilis and who was blind in his left eye following a corneal ulcer (the eye was later enucleated). He first walked and talked at four years of age, never attended school, and was reportedly cruel and assaultive toward his sister.

The patient was admitted to a State School in New York State at the age of six years, with a diagnosis of "mental deficiency due to syphilis (congenital)." At the time of his admission, he was apparently not toilet trained, was unable to dress or to undress himself, and suffered from a speech defect of unspecified nature. A qualitative description of his behavior was excerpted as follows: "Little cooperation. Sits quietly in chair. After repeated urging, gives an answer. Names colors. Counts 4 pennies. Enumerates objects in pictures." From the beginning of his stay at the State School, Burton was considered a very bright, active, and cooperative boy, who at times, however, became disturbed and noisy. The general picture conveyed by various institutional reports is one of a basically pleasant, engaging, quaint, obedient, serious, careful child with strong independent strivings and a mind of his own, a high degree of imagination, creativity, and ingenuity, and at times a nervous irritability and excitability. The following are excerpts from school reports at the institution which capture the essential flavor of the boy's behavior:

A quaint, very friendly fellow, quite deliberate and serious in manner. Very obedient. In class Burton is very particular to be accurate, placing his material with a nice regard for order and generaly (sic) appearance, according to his childish view. Suggestions from the teacher are well received, yet Burton is not all dependent. Sometimes he finds his material a bit hard to handle, in which case his ingenuity is drafted into service. If one method does not work he tries another.

The word and number work seem especially fascinating. He recognizes about fifty words in script, with or without capitals and a few of these in print. He readily reads and writes numbers beyond 100; I believe he could read and write to 1,000, did he not grow tired, for he has grasped the idea of the 'hundreds' so easily. . . . Burton enjoys combining words in sentences and building new words with phonic cards. Memory is good; the child has learned several songs, his kindergarten prayers, the days of the week and is learning the months of the year. His rhythm response is excellent and there seems an unusual appreciation of music. . . . Burton has a sense of orderliness in the conduct of classes. He likes to have our program carried out according to schedule. . . . In hand works, while he is fairly painstaking, Burton's desire to get things done makes him rather hasty and inaccurate. On rare occasions especially if he has been quite absorbed and has grown a little tired, delay in finishing seems to make him nervous and peevish. Recently he was almost at the point of tears, pushed aside his own word building and that of his neighbor in his irritation. However this disturbance was a matter of a few minutes. Tension broken, Burton turned happily to his work again.

He could count indefinitely, recognized and wrote readily the numbers to and beyond 100, knew some of the number combinations. . . . He was and still is excellent in perception, of color, form, size unless objects are too small for vision. . . . Burton knows all our songs and rhymes, recognizes and names some of the common measures, names the days of the week, months of the year, the holidays and tells the time accurately.

This was a rather unusual little fellow. He had a number of quaint original ideas which (he) expressed in class. His politeness and friendliness was unfailing and he was sweet spirited and helpful. A nervous irritability which was sometimes noted last year did not once appear this past year. Burton was quick of comprehension in his work, industrious and painstaking, had a good memory. Burton was beyond the rest in his ability to develop new words by help of phonics, showed quite a bit of comprehension in this respect. He wrote well—much better than many of more years, and could spell probably more than 100 words. Burton was slow in numbers but met the requirements of the year.

Toward the end of his stay at this particular State School, Burton received a vocational training in one of the hospital wards, assisting in the care of the more severely retarded children, and in messenger work. The patient was transferred from that State School to another State School in New York at the age of twenty-eight (where he still is currently residing). Upon admission, he was fearful, nervous, and tense. In short time, however, he adjusted himself well to the institution and—except for a period of depression owing to apparent loneliness from lack of visits and for regular but controlled states of moodiness—has repeatedly been described as cooperative, obedient, respectful, and friendly. He was eventually given a job as a messenger boy in the Administration Building, which he has held with very good reports to the present time. He can be depended upon, and he causes no trouble.

Early in the course of his stay at this second State School, certain unique and extraordinary skills and talents, vaguely hinted at in the reports at the previous facility but not described as such, manifested themselves; namely, (1) the patient's phenomenal feats of memory including the ability to name almost instantaneously the day of the week on which a given date of a given year falls, without his being able to explain how he does it (calendar calculation ability); and (2) his unusual musical talent which enables him to play with advanced skill and technique such instruments as the piano, organ, xylophone, guitar, harmonica, drums and glockenspiel. The patient has a strong streak of showmanship and his performance in the areas of both memory and music have become well known at the institution. He also likes to draw (with crayons) pictures of houses, some of which are exceedingly elaborate and complex.

Finally, a recent physician's end-of-year report indicates:

In his spare time he likes to watch television and plays with articles made of soft fur. He dresses neatly and is very tidy with his room. He takes care of his daily needs. He gets along very well with the other patients and with attendants. At times patient gets very disturbed and becomes very moody. His weight is maintained at a steady level—107 lbs. Participates in recreational activities and attends Catholic religious services.

Special attention is usually given to the higher grade retarded subjects because it is anticipated that they will exhibit greater receptivity to external stimulation and to therapeutic programs. Zigler (1967) says that the retardate having a low IQ (below 40) is almost invariably of the physiologically defective type and that the cultural-familial retardate is almost invariably mildly retarded (IQ above 50). His two-group approach, therefore, is also a distinction on the basis of degree of retardation. Kelson (1965) also has demonstrated that educable mentally retarded children achieve nonverbal scores in creativity which are not markedly different from those obtained from intellectually average children.

Ellis and Distefano (1959) stated that the mentally retarded have a certain ability to respond to verbal stimulation (verbal praise and urging). Tobias and Gorelick (1960) found that rigid orderliness, which has a detrimental effect on productivity, decreases as the scale of IQs rises, at least with retarded adults. Albee and Pascal (1951) found that dominance and competitiveness and popularity correlated significantly with mental age (.66), whereas no significant relationship exists between both dominance and popularity and physical strength, height, weight, or chronological age. The higher mental age was, therefore, the significant variable. As an example, Benda has even claimed that there was a biological difference between high and low grade retardates.

Kennedy (1966) found that morons, although they do not adhere to the conventional codes of conduct, do not threaten the safety of society by serious crimes. Their educational potentialities are weak, and they often make a confused, contradictory occupational adjustment.

Angelino and Shedd (1956) administered the Rosenzweig Picture-Frustration Study to 102 retarded public school children in order to test the hypothesis that level of intelligence is a factor in the individual's mode of reaction to frustration, and they found that, instead of a different response, the low intelligence group gave a so-called retarded response. The progression was from an extrapunitive to an intropunitive response with advancing age (although the retarded children reached each level nearly two years later than nonretarded children). Similarly, Bialer (1961), working with retarded and nonretarded children, concluded that retarded children were chronologically older than their normal peers at any given level, at least in the conceptualization of success and failure.

Durling and Esen (1956) found that those retardates who scored higher in performance tests were somewhat more likely to have good personality traits, although this is inconclusive. Beier, Gorlow, and Stacey (1951) found that differences in intellect did not insure differences in psychological or environmental needs or press.

On the contrary, theoreticians have shown that a greater awareness of limitations (a negative self-concept) may lead to greater personality disturbance. Churchill and Dingman (1965) showed that high IQ retardates have greater manifest anxiety and do not possess a more likeable personality. Hence, higher intellectual functioning need not mean a better emotional adjustment, but may more likely indicate greater emotional disturbance, which is modified somewhat by the greater likelihood of a favorable prognosis, if psychotherapy or other kinds of environmental stimulation are offered. The emotional factors, because they cut across specific categories of retarded subjects will be discussed at the conclusion of this review of the various subheadings of mental retardation. Whereas we are now taking apart the generalized groupings and major divisions, our task later will be to re-unify these categories to facilitate a broad overview of the problem.

The case of Kathleen, a seventeen-year-old adolescent girl, might serve as illustrative of the behavioral functioning of an institutionalized mildly retarded individual. Kathleen pronounced her first words at eight months of age, and she sat when she was ten months old. The exact ages of feeding and dressing are not reported, though the patient was toilet trained at two years of age. Kathleen reportedly would help around the home, go to the movies and dances, and was able to get along as well in the community as her siblings. She was, however, a truant from school. The parents found it difficult to accept the idea that their daughter was retarded. Kathleen began attending school at the age of six years in regular classes and attained the sixth or seventh grade. She reportedly liked school but became tired of it and therefore truanted. In school, Kathleen related well to the teacher and to her peers, with no behavioral problems noted. She was described as generally a sensitive child who was never angry or aggressive. At the age of thirteen, the patient came to the attention of the courts when her parents were charged with neglect and Kathleen with chronic truancy. At that time, the mother was described as a chronic schizophrenic woman. Kathleen's Wechsler-Bellevue IQ then was 62, placing her in the mildly retarded category of intelligence. Placement in a school for the mentally retarded was suggested, and she was admitted to Willowbrook then. She was described as friendly and cooperative, and she understood and spoke clearly, being able to carry on a simple conversation. Her relationship with other patients was good. Kathleen was considered a quiet, well-mannered, and pleasant girl who followed the ward routine nicely. She cared adequately for her personal needs. One year later, she developed temper tantrums at times when she would suspect that other girls had taken some of her clothing. This pattern continued, and three months later it was reported that she liked to tease the other patients for laughs. She would talk a great deal about home and cry when she did not receive a visit. She became defiant at times toward the attendants, answering back and acting resistive to the ward routine. After an interval of six months, she was again considered cheerful, friendly, and cooperative, with no mention of negative behavior. It was then noted that Kathleen showed a normal interest in the opposite sex. She continued to maintain a friendly and cooperative attitude. She liked to please the attendants. At the age of sixteen, Kathleen was assigned to work in the Willowbrook Community Store, an assignment with which she was very pleased. At about this time, a request by the patient's mother for Kathleen's discharge was denied because of the home situation. The patient was then transferred from the Community Store to the Staff Dining Room. Kathleen was rotated from the Staff Dining Room to the Patient's Clinic. The patient's school and prevocational reports indicate that, almost without exception, the patient's performance in class was exemplary. Relatively recently, her Advanced Girls class teacher reported: "constant improvement. . . (Interest) keen. . . varies, often gets the giggles. . . (Interpersonal Relationship) Good. . . Kathleen tries very hard to do what is expected of her. She accepts corrections gracefully." On her seventeenth birthday, her Young Adults report showed: "Constantly improves. . . (Interest) Keen. . . (Conduct) Very Good. . . (Interpersonal Relationship) Very good. . . Respects others as well as self. Excellent Self Control." Her most recent psychological evaluation was performed when she was fifteen years old. She obtained an IQ of 62, and the psychologist noted at that time: "In Kathleen's personality there emerge feelings of guilt concerning aggressive impulses and feelings of insecurity and inadequacy. There is a pattern of constriction and fear of self-expression. Kathleen seems to feel the need to present a 'good' and 'acceptable' picture of herself which she feels to be in conflict with her more basic personality."

Another manner of differentiation of those individuals classified as retarded, then, is that based upon sex. Churchill (1964) differentiates by sex in a study which showed that mildly retarded female admissions were more deviant among women in general (on factors other than IQ) than male admissions are among men in general. Thus, in comparison with mildly retarded males, mildly retarded females displayed more manifest anxiety, and more deviancy in such areas as physical attractiveness and likeability of personality.

Walker (1948) has noted that the homosexual practices of the female retardates appear more potentially dangerous psychologically and also more truly homosexual than those same practices exhibited by male subjects, on account of generally weaker heterosexual attachments on the part of females (both normal and retarded). She also believes that full heterosexual feeling does not develop in retardates with less than moron intelligence.

Fisher (1961) has found intelligence to be the most significant variable in sexual identification for females, but not so for males. In fact, sexual identification for the male retarded child appear similar to those of normals, whereas the female retarded child shows different sexual identifications and different sexual roles than does her normal counterpart. Yet the reverse was true in adulthood, with female retardates more closely approximating normal females and male retardates showing a greater gap between themselves and normal adult males. Brown (1956) also showed that kindergarten boys display greater preference for the same sex, and McCandless (1961) found that, generally, as age increases, so too does the attractability of the opposite sex. Amplifying these findings, in 1960 Fisher again demonstrated experimentally that male children have near-normal male sexual identifications, which is not the case in adulthood. He found that neither a greater degree of retardation nor a greater age increased the frequency with which the male figure was drawn first. He suggested that a degree of minimal intelligence is needed in order to differentiate between the sexes and in order to identify with one's own sex.

Institutionalization also is mentioned as a variable that may have influenced the development of sexual identifications. To test this hypothesis, Clark (1963), using the ITSC on 58 institutionalized female retardates and 58 normal females, found no significant differences in sexual identification between retarded and normal females, although the retarded group were less variable in their sex role preferences (e.g., there were no exclusive masculine sex role preferences among the retarded females although there were some cases of this among the normal females). Yet, Iscoe and McCann (1965) found institutionalization to have adverse effects on the "perception of an emotional continuum." Younger retardates were found to be vastly superior to older retardates on the performance of a task of sorting nine cards from "happiest" to "unhappiest." Since neither mental age nor chronological age was significantly related to performance ability, the effect of prolonged institutionalization was deemed the key factor in explaining these findings. (The younger retardates had been institutionalized for an average of 2.6 years, while the older group had been institutionalized for a much longer average period of time.) Guthrie, Butler, and Gorlow (1963) had foreshadowed this finding.

In the sphere of intellectual functioning per se, however, Zigler (1966) casts doubts as to the utilization of institutionalization, as a variable, since institutions differ from one another, and even in the same institution retardates' pre-institutional histories differ.

An environment which affords a relatively greater amount of stimulation, it is postulated, will allow subjects to maintain their sensitivity to discriminate the subtleties of human expressions. Rose, Smith, and Robles (1964) similarly viewed the mentally retarded (not differentiated according to etiology) as perceptually handicapped—which leads to the various symptoms of hyperactivity, lack of attention, negativism, etc., so characteristic of mental retardation. Because the retarded child is viewed as unable to structure his environment, the need to elicit responses to stimuli in the environment by utilizing concrete situations and by simplifying the environment are viewed as necessary techniques in his therapy. It should be noted that this study does not differentiate between institutionalized and noninstitutionalized children as lacking in environmental stimulation. (See chap. 3 for a fuller discussion of this area.)

With regard to what form this stimulation should take, Tizard (1953) has experimentally demonstrated that both strict supervision and friendly supervision (as against a laissez faire policy) have worked equally well in effecting better behavior and greater productivity in mentally retarded boys (working in sheltered workshop situations), although the more intelligent boys needed the strictest supervision. Directive approaches are thereby indicated. This viewpoint has been buttressed by Sternlicht (1962), who ascertained that the nondirective approach (in group psychotherapy) failed to produce any demonstrable positive behavioral changes. In his comprehensive review of the literature, Sternlicht (1966) concluded that "successful therapeutic results will best be achieved by a combination of a nonverbal and a directive psychotherapeutic approach."

We could go on by further elaborating the many variables which, it is postulated, account for the diverse behavioral manifestations of retarded individuals. Differences in age, in socioeconomic status (Bloom, 1965), and a host of other factors have been raised, and the possibilities of combinations and interrelations stagger the imagination (mathematically). The sociologist Moore has stated that a physicist can formulate the general principle of gravitation, but cannot predict the behavior of a single atom. In order to forecast atomic behavior, he requires statistical probabilities based on large numbers. The analogy with the problem before us is that we are faced with an inadequate numerical sampling, that our studies are not meant to predict the behavior of a single individual, and that our problem is magnified in that we are dealing with human beings. We need knowledge of cause and effect before we can establish dynamic models of personality. Since cases of single and isolated causes followed by single and isolated effects are rare, the effects becoming occasionally causes, we must confine our investigations to amassing data which point in the general direction of personality components. We must not become so involved with differences that we forget similarities. Only through systematized studies and cross-studies can our body of information be augmented. Thus, we should not hesitate to make generalized observations of the personality dynamics of retardates as a whole, while, at the same time, we realize that these observations may exist to a greater or lesser degree in different subgroupings. Until we determine what factor or factors are operant in creating similar behavioral patterns among different categories of retardates, and act to create performance patterns which differ from those of normals of the same cognitive level, we cannot deny either the view that there may be some specific defect inherent in retardation (Luria, 1963; Spitz, 1963; Ellis, 1963; Lewin, 1935; and Kounin, 1941) or the view which holds that the defect may result from motivational and experiential differences, especially the high degree of social deprivation and failure experiences (Zigler, 1961). Perhaps both are operant; at this stage of our knowledge, we really do not know, and therefore cannot make definite conclusions.

What we have observed, although elementary, is the critical difference between normals and retardates, that mentally retarded persons possess a less than normal capacity to acquire information and to utilize it in differing problem-solving situations. The simultaneous weak ego development of the retardate often intensifies the original intellectual impairment. Although the brain damaged have suffered a loss rather than a lack, their difficulties are similar. Just as an individual whose auto has been damaged is like the man who never possessed a vehicle, in that both are denied transportation, so, too, do organic and nonorganic retardates suffer from a similar handicap. How both will cope with their environment—that is, how their personality structure can show adaptability—is often the source of research studies. What often appears as pathology is the retardates' attempt to flee from threatening situations.

Yet, in many ways, the mental retardate's personality is similar to that of the person of normal intelligence. Unless there is evidence of psychosis, he is in contact with reality and can express a wide range of feelings and emotions. The general consensus is that the incidence of severe behavioral disorders, including psychosis, is considerably higher among institutionalized retardates than in the general population. As brief examples, Weaver (1946), in a study of retardates' adjustment to military life, found that 44 percent of males and 38 percent of females became psychiatric or psychosomatic problem cases. Dewan (1948) found 48 percent of Canadian army recruits to be emotionally unstable, as compared to 20 percent of nonretarded recruits.

Solomon (1961) distinguished between the intellectual and emotional aspects of interpersonal relationships. As the result of an investigation with 69 retarded and 81 bright males (CAs 3-59) of the developmental problem of cognitive and emotional factors pertaining to interpersonal relationships, he concluded that retarded persons will be like bright persons in interpersonal situations where intellectual factors do not play a major role (i.e., where feeling aspects are more important), and conversely.

Although his work is entitled "Emotional Problems of the Retarded Child," Davis (1951) speaks of all children's basic needs which, if not satisfied, will lead to the development of emotional problems. He mentions a sense of security, the sense of belonging, love and affection, training and discipline, recreation and play, and a goal in life and a sense of worth as being common to all children. The emotional problems of the retarded child also are viewed as related to the parents' emotional difficulties.

The difference between a retarded child and a normal child, as Michal-Smith (1962) concisely pointed out, is that he is less subject to normal modulation of behavior: "He is prone to act out his impulses without control, or else he is subject to rigid repression. Either of these reactions evoke fear and anxiety leading to the formulation of behavioral patterns which give rise to asocial characteristics. . . . Sooner or later (he) comes to realize that his differences are considered a social and intellectual liability." Because of environmental pressures causing anxiety and emotional disturbance, Michal-Smith suggests psychotherapy to alleviate some of these tensions. In fact, some authors regard emotional difficulties as "inevitable," in some degree, among the mentally retarded. Beier, Gorlow, and Stacey (1951) view emotional disturbance as a necessary part of the constellation of the mentally retarded. Although McLachlan (1955) states that the correlation between emotional disturbance and intellectual deficiency is not invariable, he does indicate that retardation carries with it a lower stress tolerance and inadequate integration, which leads to the mentally retarded's being always "in a state of uncertainty and insecurity." It is suggested that the mentally retarded child suffers much emotional trauma from his disability, but that proper handling can alleviate this condition. Such appropriate handling would include that the retarded child be protected and prepared for those situations where the demands may exceed his capabilities, and that he must be allowed an outlet for the effective release of emotional tensions. "Patience, tolerance, reasonableness, fairness and, above all, consistency in handling these patients are the keystones of success."

Yet, many investigators regard the behavior of the retarded individual as traceable to his intellectual defect, and not otherwise different from that of the non-mentally retarded. For example, Doll (1953) classified the mentally retarded into two subdivisions, one being the "clinically feebleminded" who are socially incompetent, the other being the "borderline normals" who are marginally adequate. The first group, psychodynamically similar to normal children except for various developmental arrests, are said to have relatively simple emotional lives, emotional suppression or regression seldom being encountered, and disturbances becoming apparent only in those suffering from psychosis or severe emotional trauma. The second group, whose psychodynamic processes are comparable to those of normal children, is said to experience the usual psychodynamic disturbances of any deprived childhood, except for experiencing even greater frustration because of their retardation. Aside from this frustration, no further elaboration of unique personality structure is undertaken.

Sarason (1957) stated that the lack of theoretical concern about the personality of the retardate is the result of the assumption that the behavior and development of the retarded child requires no special explanation, and that the same theory applies to all children. Cromwell (1959) agreed, and also mentioned the fact that basic research has been ignored in favor of applied research. Yet, there have been theories formulated on the personality of the retarded. Lewin (1935) formulated a dynamic theory of the retarded, and Kounin (1941) has formulated the rigidity hypothesis; Rotter (1954) has formulated a social learning theory of personality; Birnbaum (1942) stressed that developmental arrest occurs not only in the intellectual sphere but in the total personality of the mentally retarded; and Williams and Belinson (1953) have undertaken an analysis of neurotic behavior in the retarded as resulting from their (inadequate) perceptual development. Kanner (1949) has used the concept of "pseudofeeblemindedness" to explain mental retardation occurring secondary to, and as a symptom of, personality pathology. Kirk and Johnson (1951) have discussed the potential consequences of differential school experiences on the behavioral deviations of retardates, as has Bloom (1965). Mangus (1950) likewise has suggested that school failure can destroy a child's confidence in himself and be a potent determinant of personality maladjustment. In addition, basic personality maladjustments also may be intensified by a series of school failures. McCoy (1963) discovered significant personality differences between academically successful and academically unsuccessful mentally retarded pupils. The successful group of retardates had a greater degree of realistic self-confidence, and their levels of aspiration were higher and more realistic. Dexter (1958) has proposed a social theory of mental retardation, which focuses on the effects upon the retardates of being continually confronted with unattainable goals in an essentially competitive society. Retardates' reactions to success and failure experiences will be elaborated upon further in this book (see chap. 6).

Pearson (1942) has interpreted mental retardation from a psychoanalytic frame of reference, as being basically a defect in ego functioning, which indicates an awareness of the emotional factors in retardation. Goldstein (1959), Frankenstein (1958), Hirsch (1959), Sternlicht (1964), and others have similarly tried to find relationships between personality traits or disorders and mental retardation.

Hirsch (1959) has explained the high frequency of personality disorders among the retarded on the following basis:

Perhaps only by implication there is the suggestion that the retarded child does not function in accordance with the same psychological principles or with the same need systems as the normal child. The knowledge that the intelligence is dulled seems to carry with it the false implication that the retarded child is less sensitive to hurt, less responsive to disappointment, and not in need of gratifications which come with the knowledge that one's efforts are appreciated (p. 639).

Because the retarded person is more limited in his capacity to gratify his basic needs in a socially approved manner in our culture, the author concludes that it would be remarkable if the mentally retarded did not show a heightened susceptibility to personal and social maladjustments. Greene (1945), who made a comparative study of 45 adjusted and 45 maladjusted female institutionalized retardates which pointed to several minor differences between the groups (all needing further research), concluded that the primary variable was the question of "weaning." (A further discussion of the general topic of maladjustment and delinquent behavior is to be found in chap. 5.)

Whether we are trying to determine emotional maladjustment, reaction to stress, or a host of other personality variables, we are immediately faced with a problem that the concept of IQ does not have its counterpart in a numerical personality index. There is no Personality Quotient—just an Intelligence Quotient.

References

Albee, G.W., and Pascal, G.R. A study of competitive behavior in mental defectives. *American Journal of Mental Deficiency*, 1951, 55, 576-581.

Angelino, H., and Shedd, C.L. A study of the reactions to "frustration" of a group of mentally retarded children as measured by the Rosenzweig Picture-Frustration Study. *Psychological Newsletter*, 1956, 8, 49-54.

Bakwin, H. Feeblemindedness and pseudofeeblemindedness. *Journal of Pediatrics*, 1950, 37, 271-280.

Beier, E.G.; Gorlow, L.; and Stacey, C.L. The fantasy life of the mental defective. *American Journal of Mental Deficiency*, 1951, 55, 582-589.

Benda, C.E. *Mongolism and Cretinism*. New York: Grune and Stratton, 1949. (2nd Edition).

Benton, A.L. The concept of pseudofeeblemindedness. *American Medical Association Archives of Neurology and Psychiatry*, 1956, 75, 379-388.

Bialer, I. Conceptualization of success and failure in mentally retarded and normal children. *Journal of Personality*, 1961, 29, 303-320.

Birnbaum, K. The mental defective from the personality approach. *The Nervous Child*, 1942, 2, 21-28.

Blacketer-Simmonds, L.D.A. An investigation into the supposed differences existing between mongols and other mentally defective subjects with regard to certain psychological traits. *Journal of Mental Science*, 1953, 99, 702-719.

Bloom, W. Attitudes of mentally retarded subjects identified by education level, ethnic group, sex, and socio-economic class. *Dissertation Abstracts*, 1965, 25, 5103.

Brown, D.G. Sex role preferences in young children. *Psychological Monographs*, 1956, 70, No. 14.

Chipman, C.E. Undirected activity of a group of adult idiots. *American Journal of Mental Deficiency*, 1940, 45, 228-232.

Churchill, L. Sex differences among mildly retarded admissions to a hospital for the mentally retarded. *American Journal of Mental Deficiency*, 1964, 69, 269-276.

Churchill, L., and Dingman, H.F. Anxiety, physical attractiveness, and likeability of personality in mental retardates. *Psychological Reports*, 1965, 16, 519-523.

Clark, E.T. Sex-role preference in mentally retarded females. *American Journal of Mental Deficiency*, 1963, 68, 433-439.

Cromwell, R.L. A methodological approach to personality research in mental retardation. *American Journal of Mental Deficiency*, 1959, 64, 333-340.

Davis, P. Emotional problems of the retarded child. *Training School Bulletin*, 1951, 48, 50-56.

Dexter, L. A social theory of mental deficiency. *American Journal of Mental Deficiency*, 1958, 62, 920-928.

Dokecki, P.R. Reviews of the literature relative to the behavior potential of the severely retarded. *Training School Bulletin*, 1964, 61, 65-75.

Doll, E.A. Psychodynamics of the mentally retarded. *American Medical Association Archives of Neurology and Psychiatry*, 1953, 70, 121.

Domino, G.; Goldschmid, M.; and Kaplan, M. Personality traits of institutionalized mongoloid girls. *American Journal of Mental Deficiency*, 1964, 68, 498-502.

Durling, D., and Esen, F.M. Irregular test profiles correlated with personality traits. *American Journal of Mental Deficiency*, 1956, 61, 409-412.

Ellis, N.R. The stimulus trace and behavioral inadequacy. In N.R. Ellis (Ed.), *Handbook of mental deficiency*. New York: McGraw-Hill, 1963, pp. 134-158.

Ellis, N.R., and Distefano, M.K. Effects of verbal urging and praise upon rotary pursuit performances in mental defectives. *American Journal of Mental Deficiency*, 1959, 64, 486-490.

Fisher, G.M. Sexual identification in mentally retarded male children and adults. *American Journal of Mental Deficiency*, 1960, 65, 42-45.

_____. Sexual identification in mentally subnormal females. *American Journal of Mental Deficiency*, 1961, 66, 266-269.

Frankenstein, C. Low level of intellectual functioning and dissocial behavior in children. *American Journal of Mental Deficiency*, 1958, 63, 294-303.

Goldstein, K. Abnormal mental conditions in infancy. *Journal of Nervous and Mental Diseases*, 1959, 128, 538-557.

Greene, C.L. A study of personal adjustment in mentally retarded girls. *American Journal of Mental Deficiency*, 1945, 49, 472-476.

Guthrie, G.M.; Butler, A.; and Gorlow, L. Personality differences between institutionalized and non-institutionalized retardates. *American Journal of Mental Deficiency*, 1963, 67, 543-548.

Heber, R. (Ed.) A manual on terminology and classification in mental retardation. *American Journal of Mental Deficiency Monograph Supplement*, 1961.

Hirsch, E. The adaptive significance of commonly described behavior of the mentally retarded. *American Journal of Mental Deficiency*, 1959, 63, 639-646.

Iscoe, I., and McCann, B. Perception of an emotional continuum by older and younger mental retardates. *Journal of Personality and Social Psychology*, 1965, 1, 383-385.

Kanner, L. Child psychiatry; mental deficiency. *American Journal of Psychiatry*, 1949, 105, 526-528.

Kelson, F. An assessment of creativity in the retarded child. *Dissertation Abstracts*, 1965, 26, 3478-3479.

Kennedy, R.J.R. The social adjustment of morons in a Connecticut City: Summary and conclusions. In T.E. Jordan (Ed.), *Perspectives in mental retardation*. Carbondale, Illinois: Southern Illinois University Press, 1966, pp. 339-352.

Kirk, S.A., and Johnson, G.O. *Educating the retarded child*. Boston: Houghton-Mifflin, 1951.

Kounin, J. Experimental studies of rigidity. I. The measurement of rigidity in normal and feebleminded persons. *Character and Personality*, 1941a, 9, 251-273.

_____. Experimental studies of rigidity. II. The explanatory power of the concept of rigidity as applied to feeblemindedness. *Character and Personality*, 1941b, 9, 273-282.

Lewin, K. *A dynamic theory of personality: Selected papers*. New York: McGraw-Hill, 1935.

Lindsley, O.R. Can deficiency produce specific superiority. The challenge of the idiot savant. *Exceptional Children*, 1965, 31, 225-232.

Luria, A.R. Psychological studies of mental deficiency in the Soviet Union. In N.R. Ellis (Ed.), *Handbook of Mental Deficiency*. New York: McGraw-Hill, 1963, pp. 353-387.

Mangus, A.R. Effect of mental and educational retardation on personality development of children. *American Journal of Mental Deficiency*, 1950, 55, 208-212.

McCandless, B.R. *Children and adolescents*. New York: Holt, Rinehart, Winston, 1961.

McCoy, G. Some ego factors associated with academic success and failure of educable mentally retarded pupils. *Exceptional Children*, 1963, 30, 80-84.

McLachlan, D.G. Emotional aspects of the backward child. *American Journal of Mental Deficiency*, 1955, 60, 323-330.

McNeill, W.D.D. Developmental patterns of mongoloid children: A study of certain aspects of their growth and development. *Dissertation Abstracts*, 1955, 15, 86-87.

Michal-Smith, H., and Kastein, S. *The special child: diagnosis, treatment, habilitation*. Seattle: New School for the Special Child, 1962.

Murphy, M.M. Comparison of developmental patterns of three diagnostic groups of middle grade and low grade mental defectives. *American Journal of Mental Deficiency*, 1956, 61, 164-169.

Pearson, G.H.J. The psychopathology of mental defect. *Nervous Child*, 1942, 2, 9-20.

Rose, D.; Smith, R.E.; and Robles, A. Some problems in perceptual handicap of mentally retarded children. *Journal of Genetic Psychology*, 1964, 104, 123-133.

Rotter, J. *Social learning and clinical psychology*. New York: Prentice-Hall, 1954.

Sarason, S.B. Foreword. In C.L. Stacey and M.F. DeMartino (Eds.) *Counseling and psychotherapy with the mentally retarded*. Glencoe, Illinois: Free Press, 1957, pp. 5-7.

Sarason, S.B., and Gladwin, T. Psychological and cultural problems in mental subnormality: A review of research. *Genetic Psychology Monographs*, 1958, 57, 3-290.

Schulman, J.L., and Stern, S. Parents' estimate of the intelligence of retarded children. *American Journal of Mental Deficiency*, 1959, 63, 696-698.

Siipola, E.M., and Hayden, S.D. Exploring eidetic imagery among the retarded. *Perceptual and Motor Skills*, 1965, 21, 275-286.

Silverstein, A.B. An empirical test of the mongoloid stereotype. *American Journal of Mental Deficiency*, 1964, 68, 493-497.

_____. Psychological testing practices in state institutions for the mentally retarded. Undated mimeo paper.

Solomon, P. A developmental study of compassion and tact among intellectually bright and retarded males. *Dissertation Abstracts*, 1961, 21, 2019-2020.

Spitz, H.H. Field theory in mental deficiency. In N.R. Ellis (Ed.), *Handbook of mental deficiency*. New York: McGraw-Hill, 1963, pp. 11-40.

Stein, J.F., and Longanecker, E.D. Patterns of mothering affecting handicapped children in residential treatment. *American Journal of Mental Deficiency*, 1962, 66, 749-758.

Sternlicht, M. *A talk to parents of the mongoloid child*. New York: Staten Island Aid for Retarded Children, 1966.

———. A theoretical model for the psychological treatment of mental retardation. *American Journal of Mental Deficiency*, 1964, 68, 618-622.

———. Client-centered counseling with mental retardates. Paper presented at annual meeting, Eastern Psychological Association, Atlantic City, April, 1962.

———. Psychotherapeutic procedures with the retarded. In N.R. Ellis (Ed.), *International review of research in mental retardation, v. 2*. New York: Academic Press, 1966, pp. 279-354.

Strauss, A.A., and Lehtinen, L. *The psychopathology and the education of the brain-injured child*. Vol. I. New York: Grune and Stratton, 1948.

Tizard, J. Effects of supervision on behavior of mental defectives. *American Journal of Mental Deficiency*, 1953, 58, 143-161.

Tizard, J., and Grad, J.C. *The mentally handicapped and their families*. New York: Oxford, 1961.

Tobias, J., and Gorelick, J. An investigation of "orderliness" as a characteristic of mentally retarded adults. *American Journal of Mental Deficiency*, 1960, 64, 761-764.

Tolman, N.G., and Johnson, A.P. Need for achievement as related to brain injury in mentally retarded children. *American Journal of Mental Deficiency*, 1958, 62, 692-697.

Walker, G.H. Some psychosexual considerations of institutionalized mental defectives. *American Journal of Mental Deficiency*, 1948, 53, 312-317.

Werner, H. Perceptual behavior of brain-injured, mentally defective children: An experimental study by means of the Rorschach technique. *Genetic Psychology Monographs*, 1945, 31, 51-110.

———. Rorschach method applied to two clinical groups of mental defectives. *American Journal of Mental Deficiency*, 1945, 49, 304-306.

Williams, J.R., and Belinson, L. Neurosis in a mental defective. *American Journal of Mental Deficiency*, 1953, 57, 601-612.

Wunsch, W.L. Some characteristics of mongoloids evaluated in a clinic for children with retarded mental development. *American Journal of Mental Deficiency*, 1957, 62, 122-130.

Zigler, E. Familial mental retardation: A continuing dilemma. *Science*, 1967, 155, 292-298.

_____. Research on personality structure in the retardate. In N.R. Ellis (Ed.), *International review of research in mental retardation, v. I.* New York: Academic Press, 1966, pp. 66-108.

_____. Social deprivation and rigidity in the performance of feebleminded children. *Journal of Abnormal and Social Psychology*, 1961, 62, 413-421.

3 Environmental Influences on Personality

An integral consideration in the discussion of the personality development of the retardate, though not treated as such in the previous chapter, is the role which environmental factors play in this development. Such factors may very well be viewed as cardinal forces or prime movers in the retardate's development, although they are traditionally considered to be secondary or shaping influences in his life. We do not feel that any authentic nature-nurture or heredity-environment dichotomy exists in the personality of the retardate. Development might best be considered a combined function of individual maturation and of those various environmental demands, of different intensities, upon the individual at different ages throughout his lifetime. The retardate should be viewed as an ongoing, developing, unfolding organism whose potential and actual developmental attainments are continually defined and redefined at each point in the course of his life in terms of a blending and coalescing of organismic tendencies and environmental circumstances. As Stern (1956) has said in this connection:

The genetic endowment in respect to any one trait has been compared to a rubber band and the trait itself to the length which the rubber band assumes when it is stretched by outside forces. Different people initially may have been given different lengths of unstretched endowment, but the natural forces of the environment may have stretched their expression to equal length, or led to differences in attained length sometimes corresponding to their innate differences and at other times in reverse of the relation (p. 53).

The environmental factors which influence the retardate's personality will be treated according to a variety of separate categories as follows:

1. The Role of the Family: In this category, consideration will be given to those environmental factors which derive from the relationship of the family to the retardate.
2. Deprivation and Isolation: Under this heading, an examination will be made of the effects of emotional deprivation and isolation upon the functioning of the retardate.
3. Institutionalization: In this section, an analysis will be made of the differential effects of institutionalization and community rearing upon the retardate's development.

The Role of the Family

So integral is the role of the family in the personality development of the mental retardate that it becomes an inextricable part of this development. For, as is the case with any child, it is the family—the parents and siblings—which provides the first and most immediate environment and social milieu within which the retardate comes to think, to feel, and to act, a milieu so pervasive, powerful, and complex that its influence lasts far beyond the early years of its existence and helps to shape the personality of the retardate throughout the course of his life. Gorlow, Butler, and Guthrie (1963) experimentally demonstrated the validity of the view that retardates' self-attitudes are ingrained early in life and in the family surroundings. Working with socially deprived children, Deutsch and his coworkers (1967) have found that the child's mental abilities are developed via his experiences with people, and that the child's early social experiences are of the utmost importance.

As Abel and Kinder (1942) have pointed out:

The first social environment the subnormal girl must encounter is that of her home. The home is her chief, if not her only, social milieu until she enters school. But even during her elementary school experiences it is the home that plays a dominant role in guiding and modifying a girl's attitudes and patterns of behavior. When adolescence is reached, the girl extends her social milieu to include the community. She becomes interested in 'going out' with girls and boys and in leading a life more-or-less distinct from that of her home. Even in this respect, however, it is her home background that largely determines the kind of adjustment she will make in the larger community. For instance, an adolescent girl may be fearful of the larger community, continually seeking her home and parental protection, or she may feel antagonistic toward her home to the extent of seeking to escape parental control by defiance, disobedience, or running away, or she may like one parent and feel hostility toward another or feel extreme rivalry toward a sibling. The patterns of behavior in the subnormal girl vary to a great degree, but, regardless of the pattern, it is the home atmosphere that channels her emotional reactions and attitudes in specific directions (p. 27).

In like manner, Towne and Joiner (1966) found that, in answer to the question, "Who are the people you feel are important in your life?", thirteen- to fifteen-year-old special class educable mental retardates named their parents most frequently, followed next by relatives. Also both DeMartino (1954) and Sternlicht (1966) demonstrated that the dreams of institutionalized retardates are replete with motifs of returning home and being reunited with the family unit. These retardates' dreams are studded with words like "father" and "mother" and "brother" and "sister."

The home-familial milieu which is perhaps maximally enhancing is that which will provide the retardate with the kind of controlled and supportive environment which will protect him until such time as he is capable of developing fully his own resources. Adequate "mothering," through its supportive and evocative values, provides the analogue at an affective level for the development of a sense of self and for self-confidence.

Thus, the attitudes which parents assume toward their retarded child and the manner in which they act toward the child play a highly significant role in the retardate's formative development. Considerable light is shed on this subject by a study performed by Graliker, Parmelee, and Koch (1959) which treated the question of the attitudes of parents of mentally retarded children, and, in particular, the initial reactions and concerns of parents to a diagnosis of mental retardation. In this study, the parents of a group of infant children diagnosed as mentally retarded were interviewed by a social worker, who allowed them adequate opportunity to express their doubts, anxieties, and concerns regarding the diagnosis of retardation. The results of the study indicated three major areas of subjective parental reactions: (1) they asked about the cause of the retardation (a finding confirmed by Concell, 1966); (2) they frankly rejected the child with shame or guilt; and (3) they were worried about how and what to tell relatives.

Those who were concerned with the cause of the retardation (33 percent of all of the parents) especially wanted to know if the condition was hereditary. "Was it something I did?" was a common question as well, as the mothers worried about the possibility that incidents occurring during the pregnancy might have been causative factors, such as a plane trip, furniture moving, or a minor automobile accident. A smaller group of parents expressed anxiety in terms of: "Why did it happen to us?"

Those who rejected the child (43%) expressed this rejection in various ways: "I try to love her more now that I know she is retarded"; "Something like this is a slap in the face"; or "I remember how sweet he was before I knew he was retarded." Six parents verbally expressed embarrassment at the physical appearance of the child. In two instances the rejection was so complete that the children were placed in a foster home shortly after birth.

Those who expressed concern about what and how to tell relatives (30%) in some cases initiated discussion concerning the effect on siblings of the presence of a retarded child in the home. Of these, a few worried that friends might no longer come to the home or would make fun of the retarded child, thus hurting the siblings. Some even projected concern into the siblings' adolescent period with questions about dating and marriage. Usually these fears were magnified unrealistically. Condell (1966) confirmed the finding that parents of retardates exhibit an inordinate amount of concern and anxiety about the future of their children. One of the present authors (M.S.) also has come across parents who never went out together, as they felt that "no babysitter can take care of my son" or "He's too wild for anyone to handle." (We were able to replace these fears with more realistic attitudes, via parents group counseling. In one such group, a particularly articulate parent commented that "Frank discussion by parents with similar problems is very beneficial.")

It is the cluster of guilt, rejection, and shame, as revealed by the aforementioned study (Graliker, Parmelee, and Koch, 1959) which forms the nucleus of parental reaction and attitude toward a retarded offspring. And it is this nucleus which creates a situation in which the retarded child comes to feel the influences of the parental orientation. The feelings of guilt which the parents harbor begin to express themselves in a syndrome of overprotection and infantilization by which the retarded child is continuously kept in a state of babyhood, a situation which permits the parents to regard the child as a helpless infant and thus to mask the terrible reality and to hold it in a once-removed state, thereby preventing any exposure of the child's deficits. In addition, any illness of the child (e.g., upper respiratory infections of mongoloids) will enhance this oversolicitous feature of the overprotective behavior. This pattern of overprotection elicits from the retarded child a corresponding pattern of overdependence, which has the effect of inhibiting even that limited amount of development of which the child is capable. The process becomes a viciously circular one, for the more he is protected, the more the retarded child becomes dependent, and the more he becomes dependent, the greater is the need to protect him further. Thus, the typical parental attitude of guilt toward a retarded child furnishes an additional factor in the development of the retardate, one which aggravates and exaggerates the very retardation itself. Furthermore, the love and affection which the parents display toward their retarded child may have in them the remnants of guilt which can have a deleterious effect upon the retardate's personality. As Tredgold and Soddy (1963) have pointed out in this connection: "Some defectives may even receive an impression, dimly, that their mother's love is not objective, and this impression may serve to increase what inferiority feelings they already have. An anxious love, on the part of the mother, may do much to exacerbate the defective's disability (p. 413)."

At the same time that a parent maintains an attitude of overprotection deriving from guilt, he or she might develop, too, a feeling of hostility toward, and rejection of, the child. With some parents, this reaction dominates their thoughts and feelings. In the most extreme cases, a frank and definite repudiation of the child is expressed, though this is not the most common reaction. More often the rejection is of a more subtle and masked variety, in the form of a denial of the retardation in an overcompensating parental reaction. As Tredgold and Soddy (1963) point out:

No amount of reasoning, demonstration or explanation will alter their attitude and the attempt is not only useless but may actually aggravate the difficulty. History taking can be quite unreal, for the doctor may learn that the child sat up at 3 months, stood at 6 months, walked at 9 months, and spoke in sentences at 12 months, or other equally unlikely 'facts' that are given quite ingenuously by the parents, in some of whom there appears to be no limit to the capacity for self-deception and for false memory formation. Statements and conclusions of the doctor are disputed even before the sentence is spoken and the doctor will gain an impression, not without reason, that some of the blame for the child's condition is being projected on to him. The doctor will not be alone in this, for everyone who attempts to help will find himself involved in the hatred which these unfortunate parents are projecting (p. 418).

An extreme form of such parental denial and overcompensation is the case cited in the literature by Coleman (1950) of a mother who held the belief that developmental retardation in actuality indicated unusual mental superiority. "One mother," writes Coleman, "whose nine-year-old son had been diagnosed by several psychologists as mentally deficient, developed the firm belief that her son was a member of a new species which matured at a slow rate and would in the long run achieve a higher level of mental development (p. 82)."

The father of a retardate may also harbor strong hostile feelings toward his offspring, especially if marital relationships have been poor. The father may view his retarded child's birth as a confirmation of fantasies of sexual inadequacy, and hold the birth as a blow to his own procreative powers. One father, immediately after institutionalizing his seven-year-old son, commented that "Now I can be a man again."

In connection with the foregoing discussion of parental reactions to retarded offspring, it is to be noted that the divorce rate among parents of retarded children is approximately three times that of other parents and the suicide rate for the former is almost twice that of the national average.

In addition to the basic reactions and attitudes of parents to a retarded child as already discussed, one must consider the effects on the offspring of the actual childrearing practices in which such parents engage. Various studies have thrown light on this question. In one such study, Kent and Davis (1957) found that different types of parental discipline are related to different child intelligence levels. What the authors did was to divide the parents of a group of children into four categories of familial discipline: (1) Demanding parents, which were those who set such high standards that the child's weakness was not taken into account sufficiently. These parents provided good opportunities for the child to learn in a stimulating home atmosphere, but they expected that the child would conform to a model of what he thought they should be. The model the parents set was inflexible, and they became intolerant of any departure from it. (2) Overanxious parents, which were those who were ambitious for their child and who become unceasingly anxious out of fear that he might fall short of what they expected. Such parents, because of their apprehension and uncertainty, tended to be inconsistent in their use of rewards and punishments, acting in an indulgent manner on some occasions and in an intolerant way on other occasions. This pattern had the effect of sapping the child's confidence. (3) Normal parents, which were those who were tolerant and patient, but at the same time firm. They enjoyed their children and acted affectionately toward them. (4) Unconcerned parents, which were those who remained content if their child stayed out of trouble and made no demands on them. These parents were haphazard and inconsistent in their application of punishment. The authors administered an intelligence test to the children of these parents and found that the IQ's of the children of the demanding parents averaged 124, of the overanxious parents 107, of the normal parents 110, and of the unconcerned parents 97. The children of demanding parents thus were shown to be significantly brighter than the children of normal parents, while the children of unconcerned parents were significantly less bright than the children of normal parents. Such a finding would suggest that an intellectually stimulating, driving, and demanding attitude on the part of parents, at the possible expense of a balanced emotional growth, acts to enhance the intellectual development of a child. On the other hand, it appears that an unconcerned and disinterested parental attitude would have the effect of inhibiting and retarding a child's intellectual capabilities. The significance of such findings for the problem of child-rearing of retardates is considerable. Since intellectual inhibition and retardation are by definition the functional problems of the mental retardate, any environmental regimen or technique which can enhance and improve the intellectual functioning of the retardate thus assumes signal importance. At the same time, however, the possible deleterious effects of overdemandingness upon the overall personality of the retardate, in contrast with its suggested enhancing effects upon intelligence as such, call for a careful examination of the total state of affairs and a more global appraisal of the situation. It appears that studies are needed which will consider the influences of parental discipline not merely upon the intellectual performance of the retardate, but rather upon his whole emotional, personal, and social functioning as well. It is not enough to be concerned with the retardate's intelligence per se, for such circumscribed concern can exaggerate and distort the behavioral picture and produce isolated, artificial, and unbalanced functioning.

Pertinent to this consideration is a paper by Greber (1952) which advances the following general thesis on the interrelationship of parent attitudes and retarded child adjustment:

On the one hand, the parents' own personality problems are brought into the open by the child's difficulties, their feelings are intensified, and their attitudes therefore have more impact upon the child's development. On the other hand, a mentally retarded child is less equipped, due to lack of intelligence and lack of other resources, to understand the parents' attitudes. The more difficulties the parents have in accepting their mentally retarded child, the harder it will be for the child to accept himself and to make a social adjustment within his limited capacities (p. 476).

An example of the interrelationship of parental attitudes and retarded child adjustment is provided by Thorne and Andrews (1946), in the following description of the reaction of a fourteen-year-old institutionalized retarded boy to a pattern of rejection by his adoptive parents:

J. keeps asking why he does not hear from his father; he senses the rejecting attitudes but cannot understand it. He writes every month to friends and relatives but never receives any replies.

He developed a very unhealthy personality reaction to his rejection characterized by intense emotional instability, incorrigibility, aggressiveness toward other children and paranoid attitudes. In school he is disrespectful, impertinent and disturbs the other children by laughing boisterously at their mistakes. Told the school psychologist that his actions did not matter because he had no folks and would never be released from the school anyway (p. 416).

It is just such a state of despair into which a retardate may ultimately slip, when he finds that he has been abandoned by those whom he might have called his loved ones. Such a development serves as a grim tribute to the mighty role which the family plays in the life of the retardate. At the same time, it points to the beneficial and healthful contribution which parents can make to their retarded child by a simple attitude of acceptance and love.

Then, too, the process of the retardate's growing into adulthood may confront parents, especially those who have defended themselves against the realities of the situation, with new concerns and anxieties, particularly with reference to overall self-sufficiency and sexual functioning.

Finally, the role of the retardate as a member of the family unit also must be considered. The retardate may serve to coalesce a family unit or he may act as a divisive force. Normally, the latter would terminate with an institutional placement. On the positive side, the retardate may serve as a companion for a widowed and/or lonely mother, or as a liaison person between members of the family group. He also may act to continually reinforce parental fantasies of youth and virility, by permitting them to play the role of parents of an ever-young child. In many of these cases, however, the retardate may be forced to play a role that is not of his own choosing or necessarily in his best interests. This is especially true in the case of essentially masochistic parents, who will utilize their retarded child in the service of their neurotic needs for martyrdom.

Deprivation and Isolation

It has been the general psychological finding that emotional and social deprivation and isolation during the formative years have a deeply adverse and deleterious effect, often irreversible, upon the entire growth and development of children. Parent-child communication is thought to influence the child's socialization rather directly. (See chap. 6 for an additional discussion of this area.) This observation has come from a host of sources, ranging over a great number of years and a wide variety of settings. It has particular significance for our present discussion, for it provides one large set of possible external factors which could play a part in the ontogenesis of a retarded individual.

Classic among the observations on the severely harmful effects of early deprivation and isolation, and perhaps the most dramatic, are the (largely anecdotal) accounts which have been offered in the literature, over the centuries, of so-called "wild children" who allegedly had lived for several years in isolation or in company with animals and who, as a result of such rearing, adopted infrahuman traits. As Anastasi and Foley (1949) have observed: "When a child is brought up in contact with animals, striking similarity to the behavior of those animals is exhibited, and such behavior proves difficult to eradicate once it has become firmly established. Subsequent educational efforts are inadequate to undo the effects of early nurture (p. 189)."

Perhaps the most celebrated of these cases is the one described so graphically by the French physician, Itard (1932), of Victor, the so-called "wild boy of Aveyron," who was captured in a forest in France in 1799, after supposedly managing to survive in the woods for years without any human contact. He was described as a degraded being who was human only in shape and who trotted and grunted like the beasts of the field. Attempts to train Victor, which utilized many ingenious techniques, ended in almost total failure. The effects of the boy's lack of early human contact and socialization were evidently too firmly implanted and established to be undone by even the most efficient and sustained training efforts.

Similarly, Gesell (1941) presented a case of a feral girl who was found living in a wolf's den and who displayed in her behavior an affinity with wolves. It was extremely difficult for this girl to develop into a normally functioning human being despite the great love and care provided her by an Indian missionary in whose house she was placed. At the time of her death, after twelve years with the missionary's family, the child was still not quite human. Again, the relative permanence of the early isolation effects appears to have been demonstrated.

These testimonies to the strength and permanence of the effects of early isolation from human contact are amplified by numerous accounts of other feral children reported in the literature. The following are a representative sample of the salient features of three of thirty such cases reviewed by Singh and Zingg (1942), and summarized by Dennis (1951):

1. A Wolf-Boy of India: He was isolated at an estimated three years of age, having been led by his mother to the field from which he was stolen. The boy was discovered at nine years of age, at which time he was described as ferocious, biting at his captors, eating nothing but raw flesh, dipping his face in the water to drink, going about on all fours, and tearing off his clothes. He never learned to speak, and generally showed little improvement.

2. A Leopard-Boy of India: He was isolated at an estimated two years of age and discovered at an estimated five years of age. At the time of discovery, the boy

ran on all fours and would bite at people and at raw flesh. He eventually learned to walk, to eat vegetables, and to be friendly.

3. A Bear-Girl of India: She was isolated at an estimated age of less than three years and discovered at the estimated age of three years. At the time of discovery, the girl acted in a ferocious manner, attempting to bite and to scratch, running on all fours, growling like a bear, and eating and drinking like a bear. She eventually learned to walk, to eat, and to drink like a human being. The girl would laugh often and loudly, but did not learn to use or to understand language.

The extreme and infrahuman nature of these cases serves to dramatize the effects of early isolation and deprivation by pointing up the radical kinds of behavior among human beings which can be produced in the absence of normal human contact and environmental stimulation. Similar kinds of behavior have been produced by conditions which lack the infrahuman and perhaps feral quality of the previously described cases, but which still retain the conditions of extreme social isolation and deprivation. Such a case has been recorded by Davis (1947) who described the behavior of an illegitimate girl, Anna, who was isolated in an attic for the first five years of her life. At the time the child was found, "she had no glimmering of speech, absolutely no ability to walk, no sense of gesture, not the least capacity to feed herself even when the food was put in front of her, and no comprehension of cleanliness. She was so apathetic that it was hard to tell whether or not she could hear (p. 434)." Nearly two years after she had been discovered, Anna "had progressed . . . to the point where she could walk, understand simple commands, feed herself, achieve some neatness, remember people, etc. But she still did not speak (indicating the importance of early verbal content) and, though she was much more like a normal infant of something over one year of age in mentality, she was far from normal for her age (p. 433)." Approximately two years after that, it was reported that Anna "could bounce and catch a ball and was said to conform to group socialization, though as a follower rather than a leader. Toilet habits were firmly established. Food habits were normal, except that she still used a spoon as her sole implement. She could dress herself except for fastening her clothes. Most remarkable of all, she had finally begun to develop speech. She was characterized as being at about the two-year level in this regard. She could call attendants by name and bring in one when she was asked to. She had a few complete sentences to express her wants (p. 434)." A final report on the girl made about one year later pictured only a slight advance over the previous one: "Anna could follow directions, string beads, identify a few colors, build with blocks, and differentiate between attractive and unattractive pictures. She had a good sense of rhythm and loved a doll. She talked mainly in phrases but would repeat words and try to carry on a conversation. She was clean about clothing. She habitually washed her hands and brushed her teeth. She would try to help other children. She walked well and could run fairly well, though clumsily. Although easily excited, she had a pleasant disposition (p. 434)." It should be noted that Anna represented a marginal case, because she had been discovered before six years of age, while she was still young enough to allow for a degree of plasticity in development. Thus, it appears, as Davis (1947) has pointed out, that while the girl's early isolation may have played a major role in her subsequent slow development, it is necessary at the same time to entertain the hypothesis that there may have been a congenital predisposition to mental retardation.

Another case similar to that of Anna, described by Mason (1942) and by Maxfield (Undated), bears on this point. The girl, Isabelle, was discovered when she was approximately six and one-half years old. Like Anna, she was an illegitimate child and was kept in seclusion for that reason. Her mother was a deaf mute, and it appears that she and Isabelle had spent most of their time together in a dark room secluded from the rest of the family. As a result, the child had no opportunity to develop speech. Communication with her mother was restricted to gesturing. Isabelle behaved toward strangers almost in the manner of a wild animal, displaying a great deal of fear and hostility. She would typically make a strange croaking sound. Her behavior in many ways was that of an infant. As described by Mason (1942):

She was apparently utterly unaware of relationships of any kind. When presented with a ball for the first time, she held it in the palm of her hand, then reached out and stroked my face with it. Such behavior is comparable to that of a child of six months. . . . The general impression was that she was wholly uneducable and that any attempt to teach her to speak, after so long period of silence, would meet with failure (p. 299).

Through an elaborate and intensive program of training, however, Isabelle made remarkable progress. Davis (1947) writes in his account of the case:

Gradually she began to respond, . . . and after the first hurdles had at last been overcome, a curious thing happened. She went through the usual stages of learning characteristic of the years from one to six not only in proper succession but far more rapidly than normal. In a little over two months after her first vocalization she was putting sentences together. Nine months after that she could identify words and sentences on the printed page, could write well, and add to ten, and could retell a story after hearing it. Seven months beyond this point she had a vocabulary of 1,500-2,000 words and was asking complicated questions. Starting from an educational level of between one and three years (depending on what aspect one considers), she had reached a normal level by the time she was eight and a half years old. In short, she covered in two years the stages of learning that ordinarily require six. . . . The speed with which she reached the normal level of mental development seems analogous to the recovery of body weight in a growing child after an illness, the recovery being achieved by an extra fast rate of growth for a period after the illness until normal weight for the given age is again attained (p. 436).

It thus becomes clear that the history of Isabelle's development subsequent to discovery, and following isolation, is quite different from that of the earlier discussed case, Anna, despite the fact that in both cases there was an exceedingly low, almost blank, intellectual development at the time of discovery. Whereas Isabelle achieved a normal mentality within two years, Anna was still markedly inadequate after four and one-half years. Such contrasting development in two otherwise similar cases of early isolation points to the possible operation of factors other than the isolation itself in the subsequent development of the two girls. In particular, it suggests that Anna might have had a lower initial capacity than Isabelle. In addition, it must be recognized that Anna never received the protracted and maternal attention and training which Isabelle received. Both of these considerations—the initial capacity and the subsequent experience—serve to place into proper perspective the actual role which the environmental factor of isolation played in the inhibited and retarded development of the two children. Isolation did indeed exert its effect, but not in a vacuum or without other modifying influences.

What is of ultimate significance for our present discussion is the fact that a situation which in actuality represents a state of mental retardation in its more severe form can arise out of conditions in which a child is deprived of all of those experiences, large and small, which are part-and-parcel of the total human experience. As such, the fact of this environmental retardation can throw light on the very nature and meaning of mental retardation, in terms of the blending and coalescing of an individual's organismic tendencies and his environmental circumstances mentioned at the beginning of the present chapter. If a human child can assume the basic and largely irreversible traits characteristic of a wolf or a leopard or a bear as a result of an early exclusive contact with the animal, it appears by definition that the environment of a human being, at least under extreme circumstances, can shape and mold the development of the human being in the most radical, comprehensive, and total way, to the point not merely of producing a mentally retarded individual, but even of creating another kind of creature. Such a phenomenon attests to the compelling power of the environment as a causative agent in the development of mental retardation. At the same time, however, the term "environment" should not be construed in some magical or mystical way as though it were a free-floating, nebulous, and unanchored entity—the "out-there" factor as it were—but rather as a word which has special reference to the social milieu and the interpersonal relationships which are available to a developing individual. Nor, as we have seen in the cases of the two isolated girls, does the compelling shaping power of the environment suggest that the mind of a newborn child is a "tabula rasa" or blank slate, to be written on by experience. Rather, an individual should be conceived of as a being who comes into the world with certain vague and undefined impulses whose definition and elaboration are made according to a blending process by which circumscribed limits are set on one's innate tendencies, such that these tendencies are molded in this way or that, and to one degree or another. A given human being placed from earliest times in a purely animal environment is perforce exposed to an exclusively infrahuman experience in which he comes to see and to know only those acts which his animal contacts perform. In the absence of human postures and modes of locomotion, he will not automatically develop human sitting, standing, and walking behaviors. In the absence of civilized feeding, bathing, and toileting procedures, he will not and indeed cannot utilize those implements which humans employ to feed, to bathe, and to toilet themselves. In the absence of speech and symbolism, he will not instinctively begin to use language and to comprehend the world about him in an abstract way. In these terms, the human infant can be seen as an organism who has the given inborn potential to develop these abilities and behaviors if they are properly elicited, but in whom such achievements will lie dormant and eventually be prevented from developing at all in the absence of adequate environmental stimulation. The psychological traits and characteristics which human beings prototypically assume are thus to be viewed not as "necessary" but rather as "possible" developments which find their full expression in the normal and healthy human environment. Accordingly, anything less than a normal and healthy human environment can inhibit and even destroy the full development of such human traits and characteristics. In these terms, the mental retardate, in many cases, can be considered to a large degree as the product of a series of circumstances in which his human environment was something less than normal and healthy, and by which he was therefore inhibited in the full expression of his innate impulses and drives. For, if extreme conditions of isolation and deprivation can produce such severely and unusually retarded behaviors as those of the feral, animal-like children, it appears reasonable to assume that other, more moderate conditions of isolation and deprivation might equally produce retarded behaviors, though in a more attenuated form and to a milder degree.

Institutionalization

That the aforementioned situation can in fact exist is attested to by the many studies which have shown the detrimental effects of emotionally impoverished environments with their lack of communication, affectional relationships, and social participation, upon the overall development of the mental retardate. Home care nearly always is preferable to institutional care. Zigler (1966) has inferred that, because institutionalized retardates have been (relatively) deprived of adult approval and attention, they are more strongly motivated to obtain this, and that they possess greater negative reactive tendencies as a consequence of their earlier and relatively frequent punitive relationships with adults.

These studies have prototypically utilized an institutionalization vs. noninstitutionalization paradigm as a general model for representing emotional and social deprivation and isolation (the institution) on the one hand, and emotional and social enrichment and stimulation (the home) on the other hand. Such a differential comparison is based simply on the widely accepted and tenable observation that some degree of social deprivation, partly because of certain inherent factors and partly because of certain existing realities, is in fact to a large degree a constituent condition of institutions and residential facilities for the care and treatment of children. (Retrospective studies also have been employed in this context.) It is well known, for example, that over a period of months there are frequent changes in the staff caring for the child in an institution, thereby depriving the child of the opportunity for continuous, intensive, or intimate contact with specific adults. The retardate thus is unable to develop a set of consistent expectancies toward any one person. Human relationships, therefore, become vague and transitory, in what the child comes gradually to perceive as an unstable, unauthentic, and emotionally threatening world. The fear of loss becomes an imminent and perpetual reality for the institutionalized child. No sooner has he formed an incipiently close and warm relationship with a mother figure than he loses her as a part of the ever-continuing turnover reality of institutions. In addition, as Gesell and Amatruda (1947) have pointed out, there is the problem of the inconsistency with which an institutional child is handled by different attendants, such that the child is often stimulated at psychologically improper times, thereby developing "an enfeebled sense of security and a blurred sense of identity."

The problem of institutionalization as an environmental factor in the personality functioning of the retardate might thus be thought of as a particular case or as an offshoot of the general question of deprivation and isolation. At the same time, owing to the systematic and specialized treatment it has received in the research literature and to the pervasiveness of the problem in the actual lives of mental retardates, institutionalization may be properly treated as a subject in its own right, with certain problems and considerations peculiar to it.

Most prominent among the studies which have investigated this problem and have brought it to light as a matter of signal importance in the personality development of the retardate are those of Spitz (1945). What Spitz did was to compare children from an adequate hereditary background who were placed in an environmentally sterile nursery with those from a poor hereditary background who were placed in an environmentally enriched nursery in which they saw other infants and in which mothers and other surrogates gave them more than routine attention. Spitz found that the children in the sterile nursery situation, though far superior mentally to those in the enriched nursery situation at the beginning, were far inferior to them by the end of the first year. The "sterile" group had fallen significantly in their performance on an infant scale, while the "enriched" group had gained slightly. A follow-up study by Spitz (1946) of the children in the "sterile" group indicated that the intellectual damage which they had suffered in the environmentally impoverished atmosphere was irreversible.

In an investigation of an infant nursery group comparable to the one investigated by Spitz, Pasamanick (1946) found the same phenomenon of rapid and extreme retardation as did Spitz. Contrary to the findings of Spitz, however, the effects proved to be reversible when the affected children were given more individual attention.

Corresponding results are reported by Levy (1947) who has found that the longer a group had remained in a nursery ward (as contrasted with a boarding or foster home situation), the more retarded they showed themselves to be, as measured by a composite index of general aptitude. Similar results have been demonstrated with children from other cultural backgrounds. In a study of Chinese infants, Hsu (1946) found that the longer the infants had been in a baby ward, the lower their developmental quotient was likely to be. In a more recent investigation, Dennis (1960) found that children residing in public institutions in Teheran (in Iran) were strikingly retarded in their motor development as compared with those residing in a private institution in the same city. The children in the public institutions, who received minimal environmental stimulation owing to overcrowded and understaffed conditions, sat, crawled, stood, and walked at a considerably later age than did those children who were brought up in the private institution, which provided extensive attention, fondling and stimulation. McKinney and Keele (1963) found that increased mothering caused significant changes in institutionalized retardates: the retardates' verbal behavior improved, and their general behavior became more purposeful and goal oriented, there being a decrease in the amount of asocial behavior exhibited. (The increased mothering was provided by twelve mildly retarded mother surrogates, who each spent at least four hours a day with two institutionalized severely retarded boys, five days a week, for a period of four weeks.)

Concurring findings concerning the generally retarding effects on children of institutionalization, with its concomitant absence of stimulation and mother love, have come from a variety of investigators. Studies reviewed by Bowlby (1951) that dealt with the effects of maternal deprivation revealed that total deprivation of maternal care has far-reaching, detrimental, and possibly irreversible effects on a child's entire development. In a follow-up study of individuals who had spent their first two or three years of life in an institution, Beres and Obers (1950), who followed up children who had spent their earliest years in an institution, found mental retardation, though in some cases temporary and with many exceptions, to be one possible effect of institutionalization. An investigation by Sternlicht and Siegel (1968), which utilized a patient sample of children, adolescents, and adults drawn from the world's largest institutionalized population of mental retardates (Willowbrook State School in Staten Island, New York), illustrated that institutionalization has a depressing effect upon intellectual functioning, the effect being most marked with younger patients, especially low IQ (IQs 30-49) male children. The authors suggested that these results may have been secured because of a lack of adequate attention, affection, and stimulation that these institutionalized children received, as well as because "retarded children are still in an intellectually formative phase of development." In a comparison of educable children in public school special classes with a comparable group in an institutional setting, Reynolds and Stunkard (1960) found that the institutionalized group was inferior in academic achievement to the non-institutionalized one. Brower and Brower (1947) reported that institutionalization has particularly negative effects upon those retardates whose mental retardation is the consequence of external or traumatic factors (as against those whose retardation is caused by hereditary or constitutional factors).

Various studies on speech and language development by Badt (1958), Haggerty (1959), Lyle (1959), Papania (1954), and Rheingold and Bayley (1959) all have found that institutionalized subjects generally demonstrate a lower level of development than comparable noninstitutionalized subjects. In a summary of pertinent studies, Clarke and Clarke (1960) concluded that gross deprivation produces permanent adverse effects, although individuals differ considerably in their reaction to, and potential recovery from, milder types of deprivation. In his examination and review of the literature, Yarrow (1961) found that in cases where sensory deprivation associated with institutionalization took place before the child was one year old, severe intellectual damage was likely to result, although the irreversibility of such damage was considered questionable.

In a study concerned particularly with mongoloid patients, Centerwall and Centerwall (1960) compared a group of thirty-two hospitalized mongoloid children who had been placed in private institutions soon after birth with a group of thirty-two hospitalized mongoloid children who had spent the first two and one-half years of life at home. They found that intellectual and social functioning was significantly higher in the home-reared group, presumably as a consequence of the differential care received during the early years of life. In a further study of mongoloids, Stedman, Eichorn, Griffin, and Gooch (1962) compared a group of very young mongoloid children who had been placed in an enriched institutional environment with a matched group of home-reared mongoloid children. It was their finding, too, that the home-reared group demonstrated a higher intellectual and social maturity than did the hospital-reared group. A study by Shotwell and Shipe (1964) produced similar findings: a group of twenty-five mongoloid children reared at home for at least the first two years of their life was found to be intellectually and socially superior to another group of seventeen mongoloid children who had been placed in private boarding facilities shortly after birth. Further, this superiority was of a persistent nature. They concluded that institutional placement during the earliest years of life adversely affects the development of mongoloid children.

More specific to the question of the effects of institutionalization upon the child's personality, rather than upon his mentality as such, are the studies by Dentler and Mackler (1964), Gorlow, Butler, and Guthrie (1963), Guthrie, Butler, and Gorlow (1963), and Lowery (1940). Working on the hypothesis that institutionalization will modify the social status and interpersonal relations of incoming residents, Dentler and Mackler (1964) determined the status of a group of twenty-nine newly-institutionalized mildly retarded boys (CAs 6-12), by asking each boy a series of questions about all of the other boys, e.g., "Which boys would you most like to play with in the Day Hall?" Group status, they found, initially correlated positively with social imitation, mental ability, and appropriate conduct. After more than a month of institutionalization, however, the abler boys experienced a decline in their status, presumably because of the more severe restrictions placed on them by the attendants. The authors concluded that "the effect of the institution is to control social relations by restricting activity and so modify group structure as to make relative ability, social or mental, a liability."

Gorlow, Butler, and Guthrie (1963) administered the Laurelton Self-Attitude Scale to 164 mildly retarded institutionalized young women, and found that those retardates who had been separated from their parents at an early age expressed more negative self-attitudes. In a comparison of institutionalized and noninstitutionalized retarded girls, Guthrie, Butler, and Gorlow (1963) noted that the institutionalized girls were adjusting more poorly: they had greater negative attitudes, less respect for themselves, and lowered frustration tolerances.

Vogel, Kun, and Meshorer (1967; 1968) ascertained that institutional "environmental enrichment programs" facilitate the acquisition of particular types of coping adjustments (i.e., personal skills), rather than the further development of intellectual resources per se (e.g., MA or IQ). They also found that intellectual prowess decreased markedly without parental visits, but much less so when retardates visited their parental homes during the year.

Lowrey (1940) reported on his psychiatric observations of a group of children living in boarding homes who had been reared in an institution for the first three years of their lives. On the basis of his observations, Lowrey concluded that these children had developed an "isolation" type of personality, which was characterized by unsocial behavior, aggressive hostility, the absence of patterns for the giving and receiving of affection, an inability to understand and to accept limitations and restrictions, and a great deal of insecurity in adapting to their environment.

In a much-cited series of controlled experimental investigations which focused upon the parameters of personality which Lowrey had considered, Goldfarb (1943a, 1943b, 1943c, 1944a, 1944b) studied a group of children who had entered the same baby institution in their early months, had remained in the institution until approximately three years of age, and had then been transferred to foster homes for care. These "institution" children were compared with a control group of "foster" children, whose total life experience had been with foster families in addition to a very brief period of time with their own families. The two groups were equated on the basis of age, sex, and, as closely as possible, total number of years of dependence. In an initial investigation, the children placed in foster homes after babyhood rearing in institutions demonstrated a clearly greater frequency of problem behavior than did those children who had had continuous foster home experience. The institution children typically displayed problems which involved the overt expression of anxiety (restlessness, hyperactivity, inability to concentrate, etc.), the overt expression of aggression (temper display, impudence, destructiveness, cruelty, etc.), and emotional impoverishment. Goldfarb concluded that the institution children were less secure, more isolated from other people, and less able to enter into meaningful relationships. In addition, the institution children showed more frequent speech retardation, school deficiency, and mental retardation. In a subsequent study, Goldfarb (1944b) demonstrated that, owing to their deviant behavior, the institution children were predisposed to frequent foster home replacement, in contrast with the almost total absence of such replacement among the foster children.

In a further exploration of the problem in the form of an intensive experimental, observational, and genetic study of a group of adolescents with institutional experience in infancy, Goldfarb (1943a, 1943b, 1944a) found it possible to formulate a more elaborate statement of the psychology of the institutional child. The institution group of adolescents and the foster home group with which they were contrasted had both been in foster homes. These foster homes were equivalent in such subjective factors as the degree of acceptance and assimilation by the foster family and in such objective home factors as children's facilities, economic status, cultural status, social status, occupational status, and educational status. It was Goldfarb's finding that the institution group were more retarded mentally and were considerably more immature in perceptual reaction and in level of conceptual performance. In addition, they more frequently showed problems such as restlessness, hyperactivity, inability to concentrate, lack of popularity with children, poor school achievement, fearfulness, and excessive craving for affection. These institution subjects were shown to be deficient in drive and to be marked by an unusual degree of apathy or emptiness of emotional response. On the basis of the aforementioned studies and a later one of similar design, Goldfarb (1945) concluded:

There is cumulative evidence that an extensive period of deprivation of babies in an infant institution is profoundly detrimental to their psychological growth. There is also evidence that the pernicious effects of the early experience persist even in the face of careful placement in selected foster homes, casework supervision and, in some cases, psychiatric treatment. The extreme deprivation experience of the institution children has apparently resulted in a quasi-constitutional fixation on the most primitive levels of conceptual and emotional behavior. . . . The experimental studies of institutional deprivation in infancy confirm conspicuous lack of development in emotional organization, social relationship and the ability to conceptualize in the institution children. In addition, the generalized passivity of personality is so dominant that the child is no longer in a position to assimilate new sources of stimulation and new relationships as these may be found in the personal and material worlds. Paucity of emotional and intellectual reactions is consequently characteristically maintained (p. 32).

The situation thus described by Goldfarb seems to reduce itself largely to the fact that in institutions there is a de facto absence of perhaps the most essential ingredient in the healthy psychological development of the human infant, namely, mother love. Under normal circumstances, an intimate and warm attachment to the mother is part-and-parcel of the infant experience and is ordinarily characterized by a reciprocating acknowledgment of the individual wills and drives of both parent and child. The mother quickly learns that the child has an individual will of his own and a capacity for influencing his own living routine. As Goldfarb (1945) has stressed, the existence of a relationship and the nature of this relationship with the mother are the cornerstones of developing identifications. The warm and loving contact between mother and child exists on a continuous and sustained basis, the contact serving as a source of constant stimulation for the child. As Goldfarb (1945) points out, the child is fondled and handled physically a great deal. The child is talked to and lullabies are sung to him. Both his verbal and his motor response are given immediate recognition, and a mutual communication begins to develop. He is encouraged to babble, to form sounds and then put together words, to sit, to stand, and to walk. The child is presented with a myriad of colorful toys and playthings and is constantly introduced to a whole houseful of interesting objects as well as people. He is encouraged to execute various life tasks and activities, and to respond to difficulties and to frustrations in a way which is satisfying to his parents, whom he loves and wants to please. And further, the child comes to assume a sense of functional autonomy and to learn that he may be active in regulating his own life, and in ordering his environment in accordance with his own emerging needs and desires. It is this total pattern of development, sustained and nourished instinctively by the warmth of mother love, which is wanting in the life of the institutionalized infant and which therefore can act so adversely and deleteriously to inhibit and to retard the growth of such a child.

In fact, as Allen (1949) has shown, the major reason given by institutionalized girls for "eloping" was either a complete lack of family contacts or an insufficient number of such contacts. A study performed by Pustel, Sternlicht, and Siegel (1968) has indicated that institutionalized retardates "brutally" perceived the negative and hostile influences of the institution. In some respects, they viewed the institution as "a punishing monster, perhaps similar to the 'punishing' parents who have 'deserted' them." By way of dramatically illustrating this feeling, the following is a letter exactly as received from a twenty-four-year-old man with a (Wechsler Adult Intelligence Scale) Full Scale IQ of 63, who was institutionalized at Willowbrook State School:

Doctor Sternlicht could you please see a doctor about me. Please I want get help real Bad I want to go on Familie care and I can't wait hear any longer. I came hear around 1950 or 1960 and that has been a long time now and I don't want to be hear any long if to stay hear any more I might run a way and I don't to do that but if I have to I will do. will you Please try and help me. Please Doctor Sternlicht thats all I am asking for not to much from you Just this ok Please.

The role of the institution in mental retardation, however, currently is undergoing change in a positive direction. The modern conceptualization of the residential facility is that it will serve as the dynamic center for a wide spectrum of services for the retarded, supplementing expanding community programs, evolving specialized programs for care and training, and attempting in every way possible to minimize the very need for institutionalization. In this connection, a promising concept has recently made its appearance in the literature under the name of temporary institutionalization. According to a view advanced by Sternlicht and Deutsch (1971), the residential facility for the retarded can be seen

not merely as a permanent repository for the highly dependent, severely retarded individual, but also as a temporary refuge for the retardate living in the community who is indeed capable of meaningful self-realization but who finds himself momentarily in a psychological quandary. Such an individual, perhaps confused and emotionally disjointed in the face of a world whose lack of boundaries has granted him more freedom than he himself can tolerate, may find within the setting of an institution the temporary shelter, protection, and structure necessary to restore a measure of cohesion and strength to his growing but fragmented personality. The institution would offer a respite from the trials and tribulations of a complex existence, a respite during which the retardate could take hold of himself before having to face the further challenges of the normal world. The value of temporary institutionalization would thus be two-fold: first, the institution would act to reduce psychological pressures by allowing the retardate to live within a community of peers whose demands upon him would be no greater than the demands he would make upon himself; and secondly, the institution would be able to offer the retardate an individually tailored program designed to permit him to realize his inner potentialities and to come to terms with himself (p. 37).

References

Abel, T.M., and Kinder, E.F. *The subnormal adolescent girl*. New York: Columbia University, 1942.

Allen, R.M. Why some girls "run away." *American Journal of Mental Deficiency*, 1949, 53, 438-440.

Anastasi, A., and Foley, J.P., Jr. *Differential psychology*. (Rev. ed.) New York: Macmillan, 1949.

Badt, M.I. Levels of abstraction in vocabulary definitions of mentally retarded children. *American Journal of Mental Deficiency*, 1958, 63, 241-246.

Beres, D., and Obers, S.J. The effects of extreme deprivation in infancy on psychic structure in adolescence. *Psychoanalytic Study of the Child*, 1950, 5, 212-235.

Bowlby, J. (Ed.) Maternal care and mental health. *W.H.O. Monograph*, 1951, No. 2.

Brower, J.F., and Brower, D. The relation between temporal judgment and social competence in the feebleminded. *American Journal of Mental Deficiency*, 1947, 51, 619-623.

Centerwall, S.A., and Centerwall, W.R. A study of children with mongolism reared in the home compared to those reared away from the home. *Pediatrics*, 1960, 25, 678-685.

Clarke, A.D.B., and Clarke, A.M. Some recent advances in the study of early deprivation. *Journal of Child Psychology and Psychiatry*, 1960, 1, 26-36.

Coleman, J.C. *Abnormal psychology and modern life*. Chicago: Scott, Foresman, 1950.

Condell, J.F. Parental attitudes toward mental retardation. *American Journal of Mental Deficiency*, 1966, 71, 85-92.

Davis, K. Final note on a case of extreme isolation. *American Journal of Sociology*, 1947, 52, 432-437.

DeMartino, M.F. Some characteristics of the manifest dream content of mental defectives. *Journal of Clinical Psychology*, 1954, 10, 175-178.

Dennis, W. A further analysis of reports of wild children. *Child Development*, 1951, 22, 153-158.

———. Causes of retardation among institutional children. *Journal of Genetic Psychology*, 1960, 96, 47-59.

Dentler, R.A., and Mackler, B. Effects on sociometric status of institutional pressure to adjust among retarded children. *British Journal of Social and Clinical Psychology*, 1964, 3, 81-89.

Deutsch, M., et al. *The disadvantaged child*. New York: Basic Books, 1967.

Gesell, A. *Wolf child and human child*. New York: Harper, 1941.

Gesell, A., and Amatruda, C.A. *Developmental diagnosis*. (2nd ed.) New York: Hoeber, 1947.

Goldfarb, W. Infant rearing and problem behavior. *American Journal of Orthopsychiatry*, 1943a, 13, 249-265.

———. The effects of early institutional care on adolescent personality. *Journal of Experimental Education*, 1943b, 12, 106-129.

———. The effects of early institutional care on adolescent personality, (Graphic Rorschach results). *Child Development*, 1943c, 14, 213-223.

———. Infant rearing as a factor in foster home placement. *American Journal of Orthopsychiatry*, 1944a, 14, 162-166.

———. The effects of early institutional care on adolescent personality. (Rorschach results.) *American Journal of Orthopsychiatry*, 1944b, 14, 441-447.

_____. Effects of psychological deprivation in infancy and subsequent stimulation. *American Journal of Psychiatry*, 1945, 102, 18-33.

Gorlow, L.; Butler, A.; and Guthrie, G.M. Correlates of self-attitudes of retardates. *American Journal of Mental Deficiency*, 1963, 67, 549-555.

Graliker, B.V.; Parmelee, A.H.; and Koch, R. Attitude study of parents of mentally retarded children. II. Initial reactions and concerns of parents to a diagnosis of mental retardation. *Pediatrics*, 1959, 23, 819-821.

Grebler, A.M. Parental attitudes toward mentally retarded children. *American Journal of Mental Deficiency*, 1952, 56, 475-483.

Guthrie, G.M., Butler, A.; and Gorlow, L. Personality differences between institutionalized and non-institutionalized retardates. *American Journal of Mental Deficiency*, 1963, 67, 543-548.

Haggerty, A.D. The effects of long-term hospitalization or institutionalization upon the language development of children. *Journal of Genetic Psychology*, 1959, 94, 205-209.

Hsu, E.H. On the application of Viennese Infant Scale to Peiping babies. *Journal of Genetic Psychology*, 1946, 69, 217-220.

Itard, J.M. *The wild boy of Aveyron*. New York: Century, 1932.

Kent, N., and Davis, D.R. Discipline in the home and intellectual development. *British Journal of Medical Psychology*, 1957, 30, 194-201.

Levy, R.J. Effects of institutional versus boarding home care on a group of infants. *Journal of Persoanlity*, 1947, 15, 233-241.

Lowrey, L.G. Personality distortion and early institutional care. *American Journal of Orthopsychiatry*, 1940, 10, 576-585.

Lyle, J.G. The effects of an institution environment upon the verbal development of imbecile children. *Journal of Mental Deficiency Research*, 1959, 3, 122-128.

Mason, M.K. Learning to speak after six and one-half years of silence. *Journal of Speech Disorders*, 1942, 7, 295-304.

Maxfield, F.N. What happens when the social environment of a child approaches zero. Unpublished manuscript.

McKinney, J.P., and Keele, T. Effects of increased mothering on the behavior of severely retarded boys. *American Journal of Mental Deficiency*, 1963, 67, 556-562.

Papania, N. A qualitative analysis of vocabulary responses of institutionalized mentally retarded children. *Journal of Clinical Psychology*, 1954, 10, 361-365.

Pasamanick, B. A comparative study of the behavioral development of Negro infants. *Journal of Genetic Psychology*, 1946, 69, 3-44.

Pustel, G.; Sternlicht, M.; and Siegel, L. Institutionalized retardates' reactions to authority figures: God and monster drawings. *Journal of Psychology*, 1968, 68, 299-303.

Reynolds, M., and Stunkard, C. A comparative study of day class versus institutionalized educable retardates. Cooperative research project No. 192, University of Minnesota, 1960.

Rheingold, H.L., and Bayley, N. The later effects of an experimental modification of mothering. *Child Development*, 1959, 30, 363-372.

Shotwell, A.M., and Shipe, D. Effect of out-of-home care on the intellectual and social development of mongoloid children. *American Journal of Mental Deficiency*, 1964, 68, 693-699.

Singh, J.A.L., and Zingg, R.M. *Wolf-children and feral man*. New York: Harper, 1942.

Spitz, R.A. Hospitalism. *Psychoanalytic Study of the Child*, 1945, 1, 53-74.

———. Hospitalism. A follow-up report on investigation described in Volume I, 1945. *Psychoanalytic Study of the Child*, 1946, 2, 113-117.

Stedman, D.J.; Eichorn, D.H.; Griffin, J.; and Gooch, B. A comparative study of growth and developmental trends of institutionalized and non-institutionalized retarded children. Paper presented at the meeting of the American Association on Mental Deficiency, May, 1962.

Stern, C. Hereditary factors affecting adoption. In M. Schapiro (Ed.) *A study of adoption practice*. New York: Child Welfare League of America, 1956, pp. 47-58.

Sternlicht, M. Dreaming in adolescent and adult institutionalized mental retardates. *Psychiatric Quarterly Supplement*, 1966, 40, Part 1, 97-99.

Sternlicht, M., and Deutsch, M. The value of temporary institutionalization in habilitating the mentally retarded. *Mental Retardation*, 1971, 9 (3), 37-38.

Sternlicht, M., and Siegel, L. Institutional residence and intellectual functioning. *Journal of Mental Deficiency Research*, 1968, 12, 119-127.

Thorne, F.C., and Andrews, J.S. Unworthy parental attitudes toward mental defectives. *American Journal of Mental Deficiency*, 1946, 50, 411-418.

Towne, R.C., and Joiner, L.M. *The effects of special class placement on the self-concept-of-ability of the educable mentally retarded child*. East Lansing, Michigan: Michigan State University, 1966.

Tredgold, R.F., and Soddy, K. *A textbook of mental deficiency (subnormality)*. Baltimore: Williams & Wilkins, 1963.

Vogel, W.; Kun, K.J.; and Meshorer, E. Effects of environmental enrichment and environmental deprivation on cognitive functioning in institutionalized retardates. *Journal of Consulting Psychology*, 1967, 31, 570-576.

———. Changes in adaptive behavior in institutionalized retardates in response to environmental enrichment or deprivation. *Journal of Consulting and Clinical Psychology*, 1968, 32, 76-82.

Yarrow, L. Maternal deprivation: Toward an empirical and conceptual reevaluation. *Psychological Bulletin*, 1961, 58, 459-490.

Zigler, E. Research on personality structure in the retardate. In N.R. Ellis (Ed.), *International review of research in mental retardation, v. 1*. New York: Academic Press, 1966, pp. 77-108.

4 Self-Concept and Personality Traits

In this chapter, attention will be directed to what are perhaps the central core considerations in the psychological examination of the personality of the mental retardate: namely, his self-concept and his personality traits. For it is the very concept of "self"—i.e., the sum total of all of the characteristics a person attributes to himself and the positive and negative values he attaches to these characteristics—that lies at the root of the mental retardate's emotional functioning. This self-concept provides the kernel for understanding his unique personality, his various mechanisms for effecting and sustaining an adequate relationship to the world, and the manifold traits which become an integral part of his personality makeup. It also can be viewed as a kind of catalytic agent in the retardate's overall adjustment: a positive self-concept will facilitate appropriate behavioral adjustments, and conversely. Notwithstanding this, comparatively little attention has been expended in exploring the personality factors of retardates per se, or in the intrapsychic mechanisms involved in the formation of their self-concepts. Perhaps, as Guskin (1963) has suggested, this may not be so much due to lack of interest as to the technical difficulties involved in an area, which, because of its very nature, is concerned primarily with organismic variables which cannot be accurately measured by any of our currently existing instruments.

The self-concept of the retardate will be examined from a variety of vantage points, with the aim of providing a comprehensive and parallactic view of the nature of the retardate's self-concept and its role in his total personality functioning. Toward this end, an analysis will be made of two basic and wide-ranging personality traits of the retardate: namely, hostility and rigidity, under which many of the more particular traits and characteristics can be subsumed. The operation of "self" processes in these subsuming areas will be analyzed as a means of gaining insight into the essence of the retardate's personality. Finally, an examination of the attitudes of retardates will be made in order to provide a greater "content" analysis of the feelings, desires, and anxieties of the retardate from the retardate's own point of view.

The Dynamic Structure of the Personality of the Retardate

Expressed in psychoanalytic terms, the main defect in the personality of the mental retardate lies in the structure of the ego, which is that portion of the

57

mental life of an individual that is concerned with testing reality and bringing unconscious impulses into harmony with the demands of this reality. There is a concomitant defect in the structure of the superego as well, since the superego is that portion of the mental life which develops originally out of the ego itself and becomes the seat of what is roughly known as conscience. The superego of the retardate is therefore not so amenable to the demands of reality as is the superego of an individual with normal intelligence. In addition, the retardate's superego structure tends to be either excessively permissive or excessively strict, and values are derived in terms of externally derived absolutes. Therefore, some intervention is warranted in assisting retardates in developing truly effective moral and ethical judgments. On the other hand, the id, that portion of the mental life from which the instinctual impulses of an individual emanate, usually remains intact in most retardates and therefore does not differ from the id of intellectually normal people (Pearson, 1942).

The defect which takes place in the organization of the ego results in a relative failure of the defense mechanisms of repression and inhibition, such that the retardate has great difficulty in developing social control of instinctual aggressive and hostile impulses emanating from the id. Such impulses tend to be expressed in an uninhibited manner, and those controls that are eventually established operate on an infantile and relatively ineffective level. By virtue of this situation, the retardate becomes less the master and more the servant of his own inner feelings, needs, and drives. Accordingly, the orientation he assumes toward his world and toward others is a relatively passive, helpless, and dependent one. But the effects of the retardate's crippled ego are more far reaching than that. As has been pointed out by Green (1961), in his discussion of the ego structure of the adolescent retardate, the limited ego resources that are available to the retardate extend into all realms of functioning, including the synthesizing function, the ability to communicate meaningfully with others, the ability to substitute future gratifications for immediate pleasures, the capacity for conceptualization, the use of adaptive and coping skills, reality testing, judgment, general fund of information, organized self-image, and some degree of empathic awareness of others. Retardates are only rarely capable of establishing and sustaining true and stable love relationships. This is because the ego defect interferes with the love relationship between the child and his parents, and, as a result, the mentally retarded child does not have the same security in his parents' love as does the normal child. Such negative child-rearing practices as domination, rejection, and severe punishment also will result in a crippled self-concept. In any case, retardates, because they have fewer experiences of love, are less likely to be wholly adequate in their everyday functioning. Hence, any effective treatment program for the retarded must take into consideration not only the need to develop ego skills and enhance the self-image, but also that the need for love and acceptance is especially vital and all-embracing.

The resulting picture points to a conception of mental retardation as a clinical syndrome, rather than merely as an intellectual defect or brain disease per se, a view which has been expounded in Webster's (1963) study of the retarded, which reviewed 159 cases of mentally retarded children. According to this view, which appears to provide the most adequate and meaningful conception of the retardate, the mental retardation syndrome regularly includes significant disturbances in emotional development which involve an impairment in the differentiation of ego functions. Despite the fact that sufficient differentiation takes place in the retardate to pass developmental stages at a rather consistent rate, close observation reveals that in many ways there is only a superficial resemblance to normal emotional development. The advancing phases of ego differentiation, according to Webster (1963), involve a smaller segment of the ego and differ in quality from the maturation of a nonretarded individual. Some of this impairment in ego function is concealed from the casual observer by virtue of those functions which are imitative in nature or which are learned via rote conditioning. This poor differentiation of ego functions is observed in a variety of areas, including modification of instinctual impulses, reality orientation, object relations, and the achievement of autonomy.

The Nature of the Self-Concept of the Retardate

The splintered and crippled character of the retardate's ego has manifold ramifications in the total personality structure of the retardate, the most important and pivotal of which is the special quality which the self-concept of the retardate assumes and the effect that it has on his overall functioning. In order to gain a proper understanding and appreciation of the retardate's unique self-concept, it must be recognized that the retardate's conception of his own retardation is usually so emotionally charged that it renders him incapable of accepting his limitations and working with them. Such a self-concept develops historically out of early negative experiences that act to humiliate and to alienate the retardate. Owing to his limited intellectual abilities, the mentally retarded person, in constant competition with his intellectually normal peers, is likely to fail in much of his goal-directed activity. Having experienced a disproportionately great number of failures and only a minimal number of successes in a wide variety of life situations, the retardate comes to hold a rather low level of expectancy for the successful attainment of goals, and his self-concept becomes a not wholly realistic one. Such low expectancy itself acts to decrease the retardate's performance still further, since expectancy is one of the factors that operate to set the general level of potential in an individual's performance. The resulting lowered performance leads to yet further failure and to consequent lower expectancies in a viciously circular process. Thus, the experience of failure, per se, compounds the situation and creates an additional factor in lowered performance above and beyond the actual intellectual deficit itself. The retardate also grows to distrust his own problem-solving capabilities, and tends to rely upon others to solve his problems for him. He may defensively compensate for this by overconfidence, by consistently overestimating himself on measures of either current or future performance. That is, there is a significant disparity between what the retardate acknowledges he can or will accomplish and actual performance criteria.

Developing concomitantly with these negative experiences is a process by which the retardation appears to the retardate to be the kind of phenomenon it has been to other persons: namely, something odd and repulsive, something that causes people to treat him differently by means of ridicule and rejection. In these terms, the self-image of the retardate in a society which places emphasis on intellectual aptitude and achievement is likely to be negative because what has been described as the "looking-glass self" principle operates in the situation, so that the retardate learns from his social contacts and experiences to look down upon and to distrust himself. Society assigns him a lower status and role, which favors the acquisition of different types of behavioral patterns and reactions. In this regard Anastasi (1958) indicates that the influence of social stereotype may modify a person's own self-concept and his subsequent behavioral development. "What people expect of someone may be an important factor in determining his behavior (p. 126)." Thus, because he differs in such a way as to be regarded negatively by the people with whom he spends the greater part of his life, the retardate comes to develop an image of himself which extends beyond the specific areas of actual incompetence or hostility and permeates most of his behavior, especially in the sphere of interpersonal relationships, creating secondary emotional problems. Further, there is a consistently positive correlation between intellectual level and the direction of self-appraisal.

Thus, because of traumatic experiences to which he is continually exposed, the retardate becomes fearful about the retardation itself. Although dimly aware of some all-encompassing peculiarity which manifests itself whenever he makes a move and which sets him apart from others, the reality of his difference is unacceptable to his ego. He continually tries to escape from the painful truth. The retardate's primary defense against the anxiety which develops is one of denial. As Edgerton (1967) has phrased it, the retardate wraps himself in a "cloak of competence," and he seems unable to accept the fact of his defensiveness. Such denial leads the retarded individual into situations and activities that he cannot manage, and, as a result, he must marshal further defenses to cope with the situation. He may develop compensatory reactions of self-worth based upon pretensions of excessive success and occasionally unrealistic estimations of superiority in relation to his peers. The retardate is confronted by his inadequacy and difference whenever he attempts to act in an independent and autonomous and self-sustaining way. Because of his tendency to thrust awareness of his inadequacy and difference from his consciousness, feelings in this area continue to perpetuate themselves and to rankle underneath, at an unconscious level. As Bomse

(1958) has demonstrated, mentally retarded adolescents are concerned with a significantly greater number of problems about themselves and about their relationships with others than are nonretarded adolescents. Thus, both excessive exposure to failure with resulting feelings of inadequacy, on the one hand, and excessive protection from them, on the other hand, result in an unrealistic and unreliable (Ringness, 1961) self-estimate by the retardate (often in the form of a gross overestimation), a tendency to underperform, and a self-concept in which success or failure, and consequently one's status, is perceived as independent of one's own efforts. As a result of the foregoing factors which operate in his personality and experience, the retardate finds himself in a situation in which he feels both a manifest sense of inadequacy and self-denial and a latent sense of resentment and frustration, as well as a strong need for self-protection. Indeed, much psychotherapeutic work is directed toward modifying these feelings, as well as toward the establishment of an adequate self-concept.

The Retardate's Ideal-Self

Owing to the uniquely limiting situation which develops with respect to his image and conception of himself, the retardate comes to place great importance on his "ideal-self," i.e., the sum total of the person's view of what he wishes he were or thinks he ought to be. The retardate has a particular need to strengthen himself by identifying with stronger persons and to cling to these persons with great tenacity. Because of his special life situation, the retarded individual tends to select more "fortunate" and "desirable" individuals as ideals in order to attain the social, economic, and personal status which he finds that he is unable to attain by himself. As a result of this tendency, a condition is created in which there arises a considerable discrepancy between the self-concept which a retardate develops, on the one hand, and the ideal-self which he forms, on the other hand, such that the retardate tends to formulate a somewhat unrealistic level of aspiration for himself. The unattainability of the goals he has set for himself produces an unsatisfying and frustrating state of affairs for the retardate, who from time to time comes to feel the impact of the discrepancy between his imagined being and the reality of his limiting life situation.

A study by Kniss, et al. (1962), utilizing 79 institutionalized mildly retarded female young adults, found that their subjects viewed the ideal-self in terms of general personal worth and physical health, and in terms of specific ways of getting along with others, e.g., by acting in a socially conforming manner and by maintaining emotional control. However, while their conceptualization of ideal-self may not be grossly distorted, retardates actually exhibit a rather negative ideal self-concept, as Curtis (1964) has demonstrated.

Hostility

From the dissatisfaction and the frustration experienced by the retardate because of the discrepancy and conflict between his self-concept and his ideal-self, there is set up a pattern of underlying hostility and anger directed both at himself and at the outside world. Owing to the defect in the organization of the retardate's ego mentioned earlier, the defense mechanisms of repression and inhibition fail to operate properly, and consequently the retardate experiences great difficulty in developing effective social control of aggressive impulses. The situation is thus ripe for the releasing of aggressive impulses, since both the seeds of hostility are planted and the mechanisms of repression and inhibition are weakened. Basically, hostility may be viewed as either a reaction to a frustrating situation or a defense against anxiety-producing or anxiety-laden experiences.

The hostility born of frustration in the retardate can thus be unleashed by environmental situations which tend to exaggerate and to accentuate his difficulties and limitations. To the extent that he is surrounded by accepting and understanding adults, the retardate may find himself able to make an adequate emotional adjustment. To the extent, however, that significant adult figures are inconsistent in their attitudes, are overly demanding, are undependable, and are nonunderstanding and nonsupportive of his efforts, the retardate's needs emerge with greater urgency, his frustration becomes magnified and aggravated, and his hostility intensifies. When he finds that the demands made upon him are either confusing or impossible to meet, and when his necessarily limited accomplishments remain unappreciated or even become ridiculed, it is understandable that feelings of negativism, resentment, and anger would come to the fore. What is important to recognize in this connection, and in fact as a keynote in our entire discussion of the retardate's personality, is that the personality trait in question is not a structural entity in the retardate's personality system, per se, but is rather the expression of a functional attempt by the retardate to cope with and to deal with certain life situations. This attempt represents not any special or pathological characteristic peculiar to the makeup of retarded individuals, but rather that normal and healthy tendency in every individual to maintain his integrity and worth as a human being, to effect an integration of his self and his personality, and ultimately to achieve a realization of his inner potentialities. It is precisely the limitation and weakness of his ego-structure, as discussed earlier, which creates difficulties for the retardate when he attempts to come to terms with his environment and which produces, therefore, certain traits or symptoms which appear to have a pathognomic character, but which, in reality, are the expression of the retardate's efforts to meet environmental demands. Thus, the hostility and aggression of the retardate, so often marked by hyperactivity and destructiveness, can be understood not merely as the result of organic or structural factors, but rather as an expression of the retardate's psychological anxiety in certain situations. For example, one of the major difficulties that retardates face in an employment situation is getting along well with co-workers; often the retardate will get into an argument, and hostile behavior is most likely to ensue. (A full discussion of this problem will be found in chap. 8.)

As a clearly delineated case in point, we might cite a clinical description of a mentally retarded child offered by Hirsch (1959), which highlights, in a circumscribed psychological situation, the kinds of processes which we have outlined in our discussion:

Jerry, age 12, was brought to the Clinic to have the degree of his retardation evaluated. The psychologist, aware of the retardation, began testing at the six-year level of the Stanford-Binet Test. Even at this level, however, Jerry (who later was found to have a mental age of four) experienced great difficulty. When the psychologist nevertheless persisted in his attempt to administer six-year items, Jerry, who until this point had remained quietly seated in his chair, became immensely active, destructive and uncontained. He threw test items on the floor, broke dictaphone cylinders, attempted to rip the curtains, and to bite, hit and kick the psychologist. All this behavior was accompanied by tense, uncontrolled giggling. Jerry had to be physically restrained to control his destructiveness. It was decided then to start with another examiner, who administered Merrill-Palmer performance items, starting at the 18-month level. Jerry enjoyed doing these tasks and completed them without indulging in hyperactive provocative behavior. As the tasks became more difficult, he once again became teasingly hyperactive (p. 641).

The patient's aggressive behavior in this clinical situation is interpreted as an attempt to destroy the structure which the first psychologist tried to impose. Through hyperactivity and destructiveness, he maintained control of the threatening external situation. His aggressive, hyperactive behavior represented an emergency reaction at finding himself in a novel situation in which he was being asked to do things which he was unable to do. The notion that his behavior had such motivational meaning was suggested by the modifications in the patient's behavior which took place when certain psychological stresses were lightened. The patient's hyperactivity, anger, and tension were associated with his experience and continued expectation of failure. The first psychologist came to symbolize the patient's defeat, so that the patient responded with aggression, even on tasks which he might, and later did, handle with little difficulty.

The kinds of processes observed in this situation in miniature may occur similarly in any of the myriad situations in which the retardate finds himself in the course of his daily existence. Thus, hostile and aggressive behavior in the retardate, at home, in the community, or in an institutional setting, can be seen as a reaction by the retardate to the feeling that impossible demands are being made upon him. (Normally, parents will not tolerate intense externally-directed aggressivity, and this is an important factor in accounting for institutionalization.) When such demands are sufficiently relaxed, one can expect an accompanying change in the retardate's behavior in the direction of decreased hostility, negativism, and aggression, and increased friendliness, openness, and calmness.

Rigidity

Of all the traits which are commonly ascribed to the personality of the mental retardate, perhaps the most familiar and universal, as well as the most widely discussed and examined in the literature, is that which has generally been characterized as "rigidity," together with its many particular manifestations in the forms of "perseveration," "concreteness," "stereotypy," "imitation," "echolalia," and "distractibility." The term "rigidity" is used here in a broadly descriptive way to refer to behaviors which are inflexible and resistant to change, even in the face of alterations in environmental demands, such that the behaviors in question are inadequate, in that they do not correspond to the existing situation.

As with other personality traits of the retardate, rigidity can be viewed as a manifestation of the retardate's lack of ego-structure. The processes which are put into motion continue automatically, without being related either to the ego as the center of consciousness or to the changing conditions of the milieu. Under such conditions, satisfaction is derived from the fact of repetition, by means of which the content of the area of the unknown is artificially limited, thereby becoming known. With repetition, the danger is minimized that something new, unknown, and thus threatening might occur. As a result of such narrowing of the boundaries of that which is known and manageable, the retardate is able to create for himself the illusion or image of ego strength vital to him in his effort to preserve and to perpetuate the integrity of his personality (English and Pearson, 1945). Again, as with other traits, what is important to note, as Goldstein (1943) has done so well, is that the rigidity of the mental retardate is not a special type of disease. Rather it is to be viewed as the result of a discrepancy between the demands of the environment and the capacities of the individual. That rigidity is not a special pathological phenomenon can be seen in the fact that such rigidity occurs at times in normal individuals as well. The difference between the two lies in the nature of the environmental demands which are exerted: in normal individuals, rigidity is the consequence of the imposition of "abnormal" demands; whereas in retarded individuals, rigidity is the consequence of the discrepancy between "normal" demands and limited capacities. Thus, rigidity is a more widespread and frequent phenomenon among retardates because a catastrophic or severely anxious and disorganized condition results more easily from "normal" environmental demands with which the retardate cannot cope, but which would create no undue difficulty for the normal individual.

The rigidity of the retardate typically involves an inability or reluctance to shift from one type of activity to another. The following excerpt from a discussion by Abel and Kinder (1942) of the subnormal adolescent girl describes and elucidates this behavior:

Sometimes a teacher complains of a girl who had been very successful in one type of work, such as hemstitching, but when transferred to a new task, such as featherstitching, becomes 'mulish' and wants to keep on doing the original task. This type of behavior . . . is of frequent occurrence among subnormals. Rigidity is not due to the difficulty of the new task, but results from the fact that it is not easy for a subnormal individual to shift from one type of work to another even though the new task may be simpler than the old. Featherstitching with a coarse needle and thread is obviously easier to master than very fine hemstitching. But the subnormal is more 'perseverative' than the normal; she cannot break away from work she has been doing and turn to something new. This characteristic may help her stay on a monotonous job; the repetitive activity is not only agreeable and easy for her, but she seems to be almost under compulsion to keep it up.

The kind of observation made by Abel and Kinder, pointing up the lack of shifting ability in the retardate, has received considerable experimental treatment and elaboration in a large number of laboratory investigations which have utilized the "shifting" paradigm as a general model for the study of rigidity (Lewin, 1936; Kounin, 1941; Plenderleith, 1956; Stevenson and Zigler, 1957). These experiments, while almost universally attesting to the fact of rigidity in the mental retardate, have at the same time raised certain pertinent theoretical questions concerning the particular nature of such rigidity. The ensuing controversy which has surrounded these experiments will be highlighted here insofar as it is important for our understanding of the rigidity phenomenon as a personality trait of the retardate.

The existing research on the phenomenon derives largely from a psychological formulation of rigidity advanced originally by Kurt Lewin (1936), a personality theorist who developed a dynamic theory of retardation (or "feeblemindedness" as he referred to it) based on his own abstract concept of "rigidity." According to his theory, an individual is conceptualized as a dynamic system, with differences among individuals derivable from certain factors including the structure of the total system, the material and state of the system, and its meaningful content. The first two of these factors play the most important role in Lewin's theory of retardation. With respect to the structure of the system, the retarded individual is viewed as being less differentiated, i.e., having fewer of what are called "regions," than a normal individual of the same chronological age. Thus, in terms of structure, the retarded individual resembles a normal, nonretarded younger individual. Owing to this lesser degree of differentiation, the retarded individual, according to the theory, will manifest more rigid behavior over a wide range of tasks than will the normal individual of the same chronological age. With respect to the material and state of the system, it is postulated that even though a retarded individual corresponds in degree of differentiation to a normal younger individual, these individuals are not otherwise entirely similar. That is, the system of the retarded individual is considered to be characterized by a greater stiffness and smaller capacity for dynamic rearrangement than is the system of the normal individual, i.e., the boundaries between the regions in the retarded individual are less permeable, thereby making the total system less fluid and more rigid. Owing to this rigidity within the system, the retarded individual, according to the theory, will manifest more rigid behaviors over a wide range of tasks than will the chronologically younger normal individual possessing an equal degree of differentiation.

In support of his theoretical position on the rigidity of the retarded, Lewin presented a considerable amount of observational and anecdotal material, as well as the findings of one of his own experiments. The experimental procedure consisted in having groups of normal and retarded children draw moon faces until they were satiated on this activity. The persistence, i.e., the longer satiation time, displayed by the ten-year-old retarded children as compared with that displayed by the ten-year-old normal children was considered to be evidence of the greater rigidity of the retarded.

However, the criticism has been raised that this study involved comparisons between groups of individuals differing in their mental ages and thus varying in their degrees of differentiation. The situation was therefore confounded by the fact that the greater persistence of the retarded group could be attributed to their lessened differentiation as well as to the lessened fluidity between regions of their system.

Noting this confounding factor in Lewin's satiation study, Kounin (1941) conducted an experiment in which he controlled for the degree of differentiation by holding constant the mental age of the subjects. Three groups of subjects were employed in a drawing satiation activity—older retarded individuals, younger retarded individuals, and normal individuals. The normals, as expected, showed the least persistence, the young retardates a greater persistence, and the older retardates the greatest persistence. Thus, with mental age as representative of degree of differentiation held constant, the older and/or more retarded an individual is, the more will his behavior be characterized by dynamic rigidity, i.e., by rigidity in the boundaries between regions of his system.

At the same time, however, a question arose concerning the possibility that a variety of other factors, motivational in nature, and including such feelings as fear of failure and conflicts raised by the experimental situation, might have given rise to those behaviors which were labelled as rigid in the retardate. More recently, the consideration of such motivational factors has formed the basis of a modified approach to the problem by maintaining that it is in fact motivational factors rather than inherent rigidity, per se, that results in the greater incidence of rigid behaviors in the retarded. This approach appears to provide a fruitful and meaningful conceptualization of the phenomenon of rigidity as a personality trait of the retardate, and one that is in accord with the present view concerning the adaptive, functional, organismic, nonpathognomic character of the retardate's personality traits.

One such motivational variable which can be seen as a determinant in the rigid performances of retardates is their high expectancy of failure. This failure expectancy, as discussed earlier in the chapter, is an outgrowth of a lifetime characterized by confrontations with tasks with which the retarded are not intellectually equipped to deal. As a result of this situation, the retardate comes to develop a style and pattern in his approach to solving problems in which he is oriented much more toward the avoidance of failure than toward the achievement of success. Studies by Cromwell (1963) and Gardner (1958) have lent support to this notion by demonstrating, through the utilization of externally imposed failure in certain laboratory task situations, that retardates perform better following success and more poorly following failure as compared with normals. At the same time, however, other investigators (Heber, 1957; Gardner, 1957) have found conflicting results which confound the picture and suggest the need for further refinement of the experimental situation. Beyond this consideration, a major problem involved in the success-failure experiments—as in so many experiments in other areas which involve the test of the validity of certain clinical and experimental concepts—concerns the very nature of the experimental paradigm and the essential character of the laboratory situation employed in these studies. The experimental manipulations typically involve very simple, circumscribed experiences of success and failure which do not appear to constitute an adequate experimental analogue of the lengthy and repeated history of failure which the retardate experiences in the course of his life. Thus, whereas expectation of failure seems indeed to be a typical pattern for retardates in their daily lives, it may not be feasible or possible to demonstrate such behavior in isolated and artificially constructed laboratory situations. Such a consideration further suggests the severe limitation and general inadequacy of attempts to understand and to explain the personality functioning of retardates ultimately by purely experimental means. One must rather gain and sustain a meaningful phenomenological conception of the retardate through clinical observation without necessary recourse to so-called experimental validation. Only in this way can one do justice to the principle that it is the total personality of the retardate, operating in real-life situations, which is of ultimate concern in a study of the retardate's personality functioning. Accordingly, the phenomenon of rigidity in the retardate can best be understood, as we have tried to understand it, through an entirely molar, organismic, phenomenological, experiential treatment of the trait as an expression of basic personality processes operating within the individual.

Another motivational variable which is viewed as a possible factor in the retardate's rigidity, and one which is related to his expectation of failure, is that which is characterized as "outer-directedness," or, as we should like to call it, "other-directedness." Several recent studies (Green and Zigler, 1962; Zigler, Hodgden, and Stevenson, 1958; Shepps and Zigler, 1962) have suggested that the great number of failures which the retardate experiences in the course of his development give rise to a style and pattern of approaching problems which is characterized by an other-directed orientation to the world. Because of his exposure to repeated failure, the retardate comes to distrust his own solutions to problems and therefore seeks to be guided in his behavior by others in his immediate environment. This orientation of other-directedness in the retardate results in behavior marked by an oversensitivity to external models, with a consequent lack of spontaneity and creativity. Such other-directedness thus seems to serve as an explanation of the high suggestibility so often observed in, and ascribed to, the retardate. In this connection, it appears that retarded children are more sensitive to verbal cues from adults and peers than are normal children. A study by Zigler, Hodgden, and Stevenson (1958) found that retarded children tend to terminate their performance on experimental games following a suggestion from the experimenter that they might do so, whereas normal children tend to ignore such suggestions, stopping instead of their own volition. In addition, there is some evidence (Green and Zigler, 1962) that noninstitutionalized retardates are more other-directed than institutionalized retardates, a difference which is understandable if one considers that the noninstitutionalized retardate, living in an environment that is not adjusted and geared to his intellectual shortcomings, probably experiences more failure in his life than does the institutionalized retardate. However, there do not seem to be any significant differences in this area between organic and familial retardates of the same MA (Shepps and Zigler, 1962).

The attitude of other-directedness also may be viewed as a factor in another type of behavior, namely distractibility, which, though outwardly the opposite in appearance from rigidity, can actually be viewed dynamically and functionally as one of its particular manifestations. In these terms, other-directedness would, in the course of the life of a retardate, generalize to a multiplicity of external stimuli. Through this generalization, the retardate comes to attend to a wide variety of stimuli impinging on him since such behavior has been conducive to more successful problem solving. It can be expected that this style of behavior would be abandoned relatively early in the development of the normal individual, but would be perpetuated by the retarded individual because of the inordinate amount of failure the latter experiences when he relies on his own resources. This style of behavior, then, is what one would characterize as distractibility. According to the present interpretation, such distractibility is to be viewed not as an inherent characteristic of the retardate, but rather as a reflection of a style of problem-solving behavior which is the outgrowth of a particular kind of historical experience with failure. A related explanation of distractibility as a particular form of rigidity, one offered by Goldstein (1943), considers distractibility a function of the retarded individual's inability to cope adequately with any one task with which he is confronted. Goldstein's own description of the phenomenon best explicates this interpretation. Of retarded individuals, he writes:

Under certain conditions it is as difficult to call their attention to some things, as it is to detach them from others, or they pass from one object to another without fixating upon any one of them. Apparently they are attracted by stimuli of which the normal may not be aware. If a picture with many details is presented to such a patient, he may not be able to react in the correct way to the essential content, but he may react soon to one peculiarity and then to another, and so on. Very often, the peculiarities are not at all important, sometimes they are even not recognized by the normal. Many of the so-called illusions or misinterpretations of patients are due to their abnormal reactions to stimuli to which the normal does not react at all because they are not important for the present task. The sick individual is always in distress because he feels he cannot cope with the given situation in a normal manner, and tries to do something to escape this distress. Therefore, he reacts to that part of the task with which he is able to cope with his remaining capacity and sticks to that in a rigid way. But under certain conditions he seems to feel that he has not fulfilled the task correctly, particularly if he is told so. Then he gives up this reaction, I think because continuing it does not help him in overcoming the distress. He tries again and may now become attached to another part of the situation to which he is able to react, and again may feel that he is not performing quite correctly. Thus, he is shifted passively from one situational part to another, to all those with which he can cope. So he appears abnormally distractible. This abnormal distractibility presents a sequel to the same functional condition which underlies rigidity. Which one of the phenomena occurs depends upon whether or not the individual is sufficiently able to cope with the task (p. 215).

Thus, what appears to be a trait of distractibility, per se, in the retardate can more adequately be explained as an inability to cope with demands of the environment. Distractibility, therefore, can be treated as any of the other particular manifestations of rigidity, in the forms of perseveration, concreteness, stereotypy, imitation, and echolalia.

Still another factor which might act as a possible determinant of rigidity in the retardate is the inordinate amount of social deprivation which the retardate experiences in the course of his life history. Specifically, it has been hypothesized that the greater the amount of social deprivation experienced by a retarded child, the greater will be his motivation to interact with an adult, making such interaction and any adult approval or support that accompanies it more rewarding and reinforcing for his responses than for the responses of a retarded child who has experienced a lesser amount of social deprivation. In other words, the rigid behavior observed in retarded individuals is to be viewed as a product of greater motivation to maintain interaction with an adult and to secure approval from him through compliance and persistence. This greater motivation is in turn related to the greater social deprivation which retarded individuals experience, especially institutionalized retardates.

Support for this hypothesis is provided in a study performed by Zigler (1961), who examined the relationship between the degree of social deprivation experienced and the amount of rigidity manifested within an institutionalized retarded population. On the basis of independent ratings which were made of the degree of social deprivation in their preinstitutional history, sixty retarded children were divided into two groups: high socially deprived and low socially deprived. The two groups did not differ significantly on the other relevant variables: chronological age, mental age, and length of institutionalization. The study employed an instruction-initiated satiation game, involvement in which can be utilized as a measure of an individual's persistence and compliance. It was found that the more socially deprived retardates spent a greater amount of time on the game and that they more frequently made the maximum number of responses allowed by the game, both of which are indications of greater persistence and compliance. These findings thus offer evidence that the institutionalized retarded individual's higher motivation to interact with an adult is related to the greater preinstitutional social deprivation such individuals have experienced. In these terms, therefore, persistence is to be seen not as a function of cognitive rigidity in the retardate, but rather as a behavioral manifestation of compliance by the retardate in his effort to gain approval and support. Again, the so-called rigid behavior in question becomes an adaptive, functional, dynamic phenomenon rather than a structural entity per se.

Two Personality Studies

In an effort to offer a greater "content" analysis of the personality traits of the retardate, the authors should like to present the findings of two personality studies which have investigated the actual feelings, desires, anxieties, attitudes, and values of the retardate from the retardate's own point of view. These studies—one by Stacey (1955) which employed a personality inventory in an exploration of the worries of retarded adolescent girls and the other by Sternlicht (1967) which utilized a projective technique in an investigation of the values of both male and female adolescent retardates—offer a suggestive phenomenological picture of the retardate's personal world as he himself sees it.

The Stacey Study

In the study conducted by Stacey (1955), an analysis was made of the worries of a group of 79 mildly retarded institutionalized adolescent girls in order to discover their specific and general problems. The analysis of the response of these girls revealed how certain areas of worries had been selected as causing special anxiety to these girls whereas others were considered to be of minor importance. The inventory used in the study was based on that employed by Pinter and Lev (1940) in their study of the worries of young school children, with certain modifications which take into account the particular situations within the institution which might be a potential source of worry to the retarded girls. A total of fifty items comprised the questionnaire used by Stacey, each item calling for a choice of one of three responses: "often," "sometimes," or "never." The response chosen by the retarded adolescent girl indicated the degree to which she worried about a given item. The items were divided so that they fell into one of eight broad categories: School (e.g., Failing a test); Family (e.g., Not having a good home); Personal Health and Well Being (e.g., Getting sick); Personal Adequacy (e.g., Growing up); Social Adequacy (e.g., Losing your friends); Economic (e.g., Not having enough spending money); Punishment (e.g., Attendants punishing you); and Imaginary or Unreasonable (e.g., Something sad happening to you).

The results indicated that for this group of subnormal adolescent girls the highest ranking category of worry was that of the family, a finding which points to the strength of the emotional ties which retardates have with their families. The school was only slightly below the family in rank as a source of concern for these girls. Their achievement in the various vocational classes which they attended was of great importance to them. Of lower rank were concerns related to personal adequacy, social adequacy, economic problems, and imaginary or unreasonable items, in that order. The percentages for the categories of personal health and well being and punishment showed that items in these areas played a much less important role in the worries of the girls than did other categories. The average percentages of those answering "sometimes" or "often" by categories were as follows:

Category	Percentage
Family	80
School	77
Personal Adequacy	66
Social Adequacy	62
Economic	57
Imaginary or Unreasonable	53
Personal Health and Well Being	39
Punishment	26

Source: Adapted from Stacey (1955).

The Sternlicht Study

In the study conducted by Sternlicht (1967), an examination was made of the values of a group of sixty mildly retarded adolescent males and females derived from responses given on a sentence-completion test. A series of thirty sentence-completion items were specially selected from all the items that comprise the Willowbrook Sentence Completion Test because they were judged to be particularly relevant to the retardate's world of perceptions, attitudes, and values. The items were divided so that they fell into one of five broad categories: Relationship to Significant Others (e.g., "My father"); The Emotions and the Self (e.g., "I want"); Conduct, Behavior, and Morality (e.g., "The worst thing anyone can do is"); Institutional Views and Attitudes (e.g., "The attendants here at Willowbrook"); and General Views and Attitudes (e.g., "Most People").

The results indicated the following. In their relationship with other people who were emotionally significant in their lives, particularly loved ones, retardates of both sexes saw their mother in a slightly more favorable light than they did their father in terms of what they perceived their parents' inherent qualities to be, in terms of what their parents did for them, and in terms of how their parents loved them. When analyzed further, however, certain differences of emphasis appeared between males and females. In her favorable views of the mother, the female laid greater stress on what her mother did for her, whereas the male tended to place the emphasis more on the mother's own inherent positive qualities. When they were probed further by the projective method employed, it was found that retardates viewed their peers, both of the same and of the opposite sex, as their best friends slightly more often than they viewed their own parents and family as their best friends. A very small percentage of the retardates, all males, conceived of God as their best friend. The emotional and motivational life of the retardate, according to the study, presented a number of basic prevailing themes, one of the most pervasive of which was the repeated desire for, longing after, and concern over parents and family. At the same time, however, when considering specifically with whom they would rather be, females chose friends of theirs equally as often as they chose their parents, whereas males overwhelmingly selected their parents over their friends. Very high also in the retardate's motivational hierarchy was the desire for material goods, of the variety that the retardate could utilize in the moment, notably food, clothing, and playthings. Still another basic theme that emerged in the general motivational picture of the retardate was his deep concern over the idea of being good, with an accompanying fear of his own hostility and aggression. The idea of being good had additional implications for the retardate for he or she viewed it quite often as a prerequisite condition for the receiving of love from others. The retardate considered his own show or feeling of love for others to be less important than his behavior and deportment as a condition for gaining another's affection. This finding was seen as consistent with the retardate's generally rather childlike and passive orientation to the world. On the subject of love itself, the retardate perceived the phenomenon most often in a generalized and wholesome way, viewing it in its more physical and romantic sense to a lesser degree. At the other end of the motivational continuum, the phenomenon of hate was experienced slightly more often by the retardate in connection with other people, rather than directed toward objects, experiences, or situations, or toward tendencies within himself. In the area of conduct, behavior, and morality, being good, per se, and avoiding one's own strong hostility and aggression in particular, were among the most important elements in the system of values of the retardate. Stealing and lying also were viewed as rather serious violations of good conduct and morality, and, to a lesser degree, using bad or foul language. The retardate's view of life within the institution was by and large a positive one. Similarly, the retardate's view of life in general was predominantly positive. His thoughts about the future were exclusively positive and happy thoughts.

References

Abel, T.M., and Kinder, E.F., *The subnormal adolescent girl*, New York: Columbia University Press, 1942.

Anastasi, A. *Differential psychology*. Third Edition. New York: Macmillan, 1958.

Bomse, G.C. A study to determine the degree of similarity of personality problem awareness between normal and mentally retarded children. *Dissertation Abstracts*, 1958, 18, 1844.

Cromwell, R.L. A social learning approach to mental retardation. In N.R. Ellis (Ed.), *Handbook of mental deficiency*. New York: McGraw-Hill, 1963. Pp. 41-91.

Curtis, L.T. A comparative analysis of the self-concept of the adolescent mentally retarded in relation to certain groups of adolescents. *Dissertation Abstracts*, 1964, 25, 2846-2847.

Edgerton, R.B. *The cloak of competence (stigma in the lives of the mentally retarded)*. Berkeley: University of California, 1967.

English, O.S., and Pearson, G.H.J. *Emotional problems of living*. London: W.W. Norton, 1945.

Gardner, W. Reactions of intellectually normal and retarded boys after experimentally induced failure. Unpublished doctoral dissertation, Peabody College for Teachers, 1958.

Gardner, W.I. Effects of interpolated success and failure on motor task performance in mental defectives. Paper presented at the meeting of the Southeastern Psychological Association, Nashville, Tennessee, 1957.

Goldstein, K. Concerning rigidity. *Character & Personality*, 1943, 11, 209-226.

Green, C.G., and Zigler, E. Social deprivation and the performance of retarded and normal children on satiation type tasks. *Child Development*, 1962, 33, 499-508.

Green, S.L. The ego structure of the adolescent retardate: Psychological principles for clinical application. *International Records of Medicine*, 1961, 174, 205-211.

Guskin, S. Social psychologies of mental deficiencies. In N.R. Ellis (Ed.) *Handbook of mental deficiency*. New York: McGraw-Hill, 1963. Pp. 325-352.

Heber, R. Expectancy and expectancy changes in normal and mentally retarded boys. Unpublished doctoral dissertation, Peabody College for Teachers, 1957.

Hirsch, E.A. The adaptive significance of commonly described behavior of the mentally retarded. *American Journal of Mental Deficiency*, 1959, 63, 639-646.

Kniss, J.T.; Butler, A.; Gorlow, L.; and Guthrie, G.M. Ideal self patterns of female retardates. *American Journal of Mental Deficiency*, 1962, 67, 245-249.

Kounin, J. Experimental studies of rigidity. I. The measurement of rigidity in normal and feebleminded persons. *Character & Personality*, 1941a, 9, 251-273.

———. Experimental studies of rigidity. II. The explanatory power of the concept of rigidity as applied to feeblemindedness. *Character & Personality*, 1941b, 9, 273-282.

Lewin, K. *A dynamic theory of personality*, New York: McGraw-Hill, 1936.

Pearson, G. The psychopathology of mental defect. *Nervous Child*, 1942, 2, 9-20.

Pinter, R., and Lev, J. Worries of school children. *Journal of Genetic Psychology*, 1940, 56, 67-76.

Plenderleith, M. Discrimination learning and discrimination reversal learning in normal and feebleminded children. *Journal of Genetic Psychology*, 1956, 88, 107-112.

Ringness, T.A. Self concept of children of low, average and high intelligence. *American Journal of Mental Deficiency*, 1961, 65, 453-461.

Shepps, R., and Zigler, E. Social deprivation and rigidity in the performance of organic and familial retardates. *American Journal of Mental Deficiency*, 1962, 67, 262-268.

Stacey, C.L. Worries of subnormal adolescent girls. *Exceptional Children*, 1955, 21, 184-186.

Sternlicht, M. Adolescent retardates' values, as gleaned from sentence-completion responses. Paper presented at the meeting of the Eastern Psychological Association, Boston, April, 1967.

Stevenson, H., and Zigler, E. Discrimination learning and rigidity in normal and feebleminded individuals. *Journal of Personality*, 1957, 25, 699-711.

Webster, T.G. Problems of emotional development in young retarded children. *American Journal of Psychiatry*, 1963, 120, 37-43.

Zigler, E. Social deprivation and rigidity in the performance of feebleminded children. *Journal of Abnormal and Social Psychology*, 1961, 62, 413-421.

Zigler, E.F.; Hodgden, L.; and Stevenson, H.W. The effect of support and nonsupport on the performance of normal and feebleminded children. *Journal of Personality*, 1958, 26, 106-122.

5 Deviant Behavior

Our discussion of deviant behavior in the mental retardate will include those aspects of the retardate's behavior which can be thought of as either abnormal or antisocial, in the sense of being at variance with, opposed to, or disruptive of the generally accepted standards of conduct in our society. Such discussion will consider in particular two crucial questions:

A. The relationship between mental retardation and criminal and delinquent behavior; and

B. The relationship between mental retardation and emotional disturbance.

Treatment of these questions will be directed toward pinpointing and highlighting those aspects of the problem which will illuminate the nature of the mental retardate.

The Relationship Between Mental Retardation and Criminal and Delinquent Behavior

In order to gain a comprehensive view of the problem of criminal behavior among the retarded, and its implications for our understanding of the retardate's personality functioning, it is necessary to provide a brief historical perspective and orientation. As has been pointed out elsewhere (Wallin, 1955), over the years there has been a decided modification in the thinking of workers in the field concerning the relationship between mental retardation and criminality. Whereas at one time, about the beginning of this century, authorities placed exaggerated emphasis upon the role of subnormal intelligence in criminal, delinquent, and antisocial behavior, the more recent tendency has been to underplay and to minimize the factor of low intelligence in criminality and delinquency. An example of the early prevailing view which captures the flavor of the extreme position held by professional workers in the field is the following excerpt from an address by Walter E. Fernald—a former medical superintendent of the Massachusetts School for the Feebleminded—delivered before the Massachusetts Medical Society in 1912:

Every feeble-minded person, especially the high grade imbecile, is a potential criminal needing only the proper environment and opportunity for the development and expression of his criminal tendencies. . . . Feebleminded women are almost invariably immoral. . . . It has been truly said that feeblemindedness is the mother of crime, pauperism, and degeneracy. (Quoted by Wallin, 1956, pp. 78-79.)

This rather extreme, exaggerated, and striking statement about the alleged criminal nature of the personality of the retardate thus represents one pole at the end of a continuum along which one may find a series of representative views expressing varying degrees of belief in the existence of a positive relationship between retardation and criminality. The range of divergent views on the matter is reflected in the following sampling of observations and opinions of some leading authorities on the subject: Chassell (1935), after comprehensively surveying the literature, concluded that "the relation is positive but low"; Healy and Bronner (1936), in their classic treatment of the problem, wrote: "intellectual level (does) not, in general, distinguish the delinquent from his non-delinquent sibling, though (it) may have importance . . . in the individual case"; Exner (1939), a noted authority on the subject, held that the correlation between mental retardation and delinquency was barely significant and by no means implied a cause and effect relationship; Stein (reported in Davies, 1959), a psychiatrist to the Chicago Juvenile Court, in a study of 705 juvenile delinquents seen by him in 1947, stated that his findings indicated that in all probability the distribution of intelligence among juveniles labelled delinquents was the same as, if not higher than, for non-delinquents; Burt (1948), in his study of the young delinquent, stated: ". . . my own percentage . . . reveals among the delinquent population a proportion of mental defectives five times as great as among the school population at large. Mental defect, beyond all controversy, therefore, is a notable factor in the production of crime"; and Pearce (1949), in a report at the Scientific Conference held in London, observed: "A great deal is known about the influence of intelligence in juvenile delinquency. It seems definite that the intelligence of the average delinquent is considerably less than that of his non-delinquent neighbor." Representing the more up-to-date and modern position, in line with the thinking of the present authors concerning the functional, non-pathognomic character of the retardate's personality, is the following view advanced by Philips (1966): "It is important to note that delinquent, perverse, and antisocial behavior is no more frequent in the retarded population than in the general population. Delinquent acts are determined, not by intellectual abilities, but more likely by social, economic, cultural, and, most of all, family attitudes (p. 117)." Bowman and Young (1959) hold that the delinquent retardate does not differ significantly from those "sociopathic personalities" found so regularly in prisons and reformatories. "He is not delinquent because he is mentally retarded." One of the present authors (M.R.D.) has found, in the course of his psychodiagnostic evaluation of a large cross-section of all the adult males incarcerated in state penal institutions throughout the Commonwealth of Pennsylvania between 1961 and 1963, that the IQs of the inmates hovered about or slightly below the norm for the population at large, with only a very small percentage falling into the "defective delinquent" category. The number of inmates who presented themselves as authentically and primarily mentally retarded was negligible.

As a "horrible" example, however, of the way in which an individual can become recorded on a police blotter as a delinquent is the case of John. One of the present authors (M.S.) had been giving John, a seventeen-year-old mildly retarded adolescent living in the community, intensive remedial reading tutoring; he was nearly a total nonreader. One evening, he went out with a date to a Greenwich Village (in New York City) bistro. Having to go to the lavatory, he found himself confronted by two signs reading "Hens" and "Roosters." Because "Hens" is so similar to "mens" in configuration, he entered that room. The women in there screamed, the police were called, and poor John was booked on a delinquency charge!

Whereas the views of authorities diverge widely on the question of the relationship between retardation and criminality, it is not the purpose of the present discussion to resolve the controversy. Rather, the purpose of the present discussion is to identify and to delineate some of the possible personality factors that could act to produce deviant, antisocial behavior in the retardate. Concerning the question of the relationship between retardation and criminality per se, it will serve the present purpose merely to review the systematic research which has treated this relationship and to note some of the possible limitations in any attempt to determine or to establish such a relationship. Among the earliest investigations of the relationship between retardation and criminality during this century were those of Goddard (1912) who tested a group of incarcerated delinquents, using the relatively limited and crude psychological instruments of his day. He found that 50 percent of the incarcerated delinquents he tested were mentally retarded. Goddard thus was led to the belief that low intelligence was the principal cause of antisocial behavior. Since the investigations of Goddard, a multitude of studies have been conducted on the role of intelligence in criminal behavior. Notwithstanding this, no absolute conclusions can be reached on the basis of all of the evidence adduced. The early research on the intelligence level of delinquents, though varying to some degree, generally yielded a mean IQ score for delinquents that was between 15 and 20 points below that of the general population. In addition, the incidence of delinquents classified as mentally retarded was five to ten times greater than that of the general population. It thus appeared that delinquents were significantly of lower intelligence than the general population. In 1931, Sutherland conducted a survey of 340 separate reports of the IQs of 150,000 delinquent and adult offenders for the period 1910 through 1928, and he found an unusually high percentage of juvenile delinquents classified as mentally retarded. In 1935, Chassell reported 24 separate instances in which mental retardation was compared in delinquent and nondelinquent samples between 1913 and 1926, and she found that in 22 of the instances the percentage of mentally retarded cases was higher among the delinquents. Typical of the mean IQs in early studies of delinquent samples were a 71 found by Snyder (1931), an 82 by Beane (1931), and an 80 by McClure (1933). Typical of the percentages of mental retardates in delinquent samples were 23 percent found by Merrill (1926), 13 percent by Rogers and Austin (1934), and 13.1 percent by Glueck and Glueck (1934).

In evaluating these findings, however, one must take cultural and social factors into consideration, since such factors can play an important role in determining intellectual performance (Neff, 1938; and Jones, 1946). In this connection, a study was performed by Maller (1937), who examined the intelligence test results from New York City schools and compared them with the rate of delinquency for the area in which each school was located. The results of the study indicated a negative relationship between intelligence test scores and delinquency rates throughout the various areas of the city, and thus suggested that the cultural and social conditions which characterized the high delinquency areas had an adverse or detrimental effect upon the intellectual development and functioning of all of the children living in these areas. In a similar kind of investigation, Lichtenstein and Brown (1938) studied 658 grade school children living in a high delinquency area in Chicago and found a mean IQ of 90.6 with just under 10 percent of the group producing IQs below 70. On the basis of these findings, the conclusion was drawn that a high percentage of lower IQ children is typical for geographical areas from which delinquents come.

In an effort to control for the possible effects of the kinds of cultural, social, economic, and geographical factors highlighted by the aforementioned studies, a number of investigators over the years have employed matching techniques and procedures in their studies of the relationship between retardation and criminality. Unfortunately, the findings have been inconclusive. In a study which matched delinquent and nondelinquent individuals for the factors of age and social class, Burt (1948) reported a higher incidence of mental retardation among the delinquents. On the other hand, Baker, Decker, and Hill (1929) matched delinquents and nondelinquents for the factors of age, nationality, and neighborhood, and found only a small difference in IQ scores between the two groups. In a more precise and refined attempt to control for extraneous factors, other studies have utilized the matching of siblings with similarly inconclusive results. In a study by Shulman (1929), which involved the matching of 28 pairs of siblings, a mean difference of 11 IQ points was obtained in favor of the nondelinquents. On the other hand, a study by Ackerly (1933), involving a sample of 30 matched pairs of delinquent and nondelinquent siblings, found no significant differences between the two groups. Nevertheless, despite conflicting evidence concerning the intelligence of delinquents and nondelinquents, it is generally agreed by those reviewing the research in this area, such as Rouke (1950), Woodward (1955), and Caplan (1965), that with proper control of the extraneous factors operating in the situation, there is a negligible difference, if any, between the intellectual level of delinquents and that of nondelinquents. As Caplan (1965) has pointed out, however, this does not eliminate the problem as an area of meaningful and fruitful investigation in the future. Neither does it preclude the possibility that a certain interdependence exists between mental retardation and criminality and delinquency. It is possible, as Caplan (1965) has further suggested, that the problem has to be redefined and different investigative techniques and procedures employed.

The Role of the Retardate's Personality Structure in Deviant Behavior

In order to understand the personality factors involved in deviant retardate behavior—which is the primary aim of the present section—one must utilize the frame of reference of the previous chapter: namely, the self-concept of the retardate, with its theoretical constituents, the id, ego, and superego. In particular, attention must be focused upon the nature and the development of the superego, for, as was mentioned in the previous chapter, the superego is that portion of the mental life which becomes the seat of what is roughly known as conscience and which, in the retardate, becomes defective in its structure, since it develops originally out of the retardate's impaired ego. As a result, the superego of the retardate is not so amenable to the demands of reality as is the superego of an individual with normal intelligence. Concomitantly, the defect which takes place in the organization of the ego results in a relative failure of the defense mechanisms of repression and inhibition, such that the retardate has great difficulty in developing social control of instinctual aggressive impulses emanating from the id. The retarded, deprived child may fail to develop needed inner controls against immediate drive gratifications either because of the unavailability of a suitable parental model for internalization or because of a lack of adequate awareness of the self or because of inadequate positive rewards for internalization when such controls may have been manifested.

By virtue of this situation, the retardate becomes less the master and more the servant of his own inner feelings, needs, and drives. He is thus rendered powerless to cope with any serious struggle between instinctual forces and the demands of reality. He thus becomes characterized as a suspicious, egocentric, immature, selfish, socially inadequate, volatile individual.

With such a situation as background, the stage is set for the development of propensities and tendencies in the retardate toward behaviors which, because of their somewhat uncontrolled and impulsive character, would tend to come into conflict with the accepted standards of conduct of the community, and thus to be labelled as deviant and antisocial.

The combined ego and superego impairment which is part of the retardate's psychological makeup acts in a special way to produce occasional deviant behavior in the retardate. What it does specifically is to give rise to a defect in the guilt anticipation function or as it is referred to by Redl and Wineman (1951), "a disturbance of the job of 'giving value danger signals' (p. 239)." Whereas an individual of normal intelligence would feel some pangs of conscience in a given situation even before he or she decided in what way to act, the mentally retarded individual would have only a very dim awareness that what he or she was about to do might not be a good or desirable kind of behavior because of his inability to foresee the future consequences of his current actions. It is this lack of anticipatory and moral abstracting capacity which keeps the retardate inordinately anchored to the immediately palpable events and situations of his life, and which can therefore create the kind of splitting of total situations that leads to the performance of improper and deviant acts. It is just such an impairment of the abstract attitude which one is actually describing when he characterizes the mental retardate in terms of his inability to utilize and to exercise effective judgment. In these terms, the retardate can be seen not as a clinical entity with certain innate pathological tendencies toward criminal or deviant behavior, but rather as an individual with certain shortcomings and impairments in the mental apparatus which normally enables one to abstract himself properly from his environment and to gain a global and comprehensive and sustained view of his life situation. Because of the retardate's weakness in conscience, he will act out his drives with fewer scruples than others.

In a similar consideration of the problem, Tredgold and Soddy (1963) note: ". . . the subnormal's faulty perception is not only of the state of the law, nor of the moral wrongness of the act, but also of its full significance including the significance to other people (p. 252)." They go on to furnish a rather extreme and incredible example of such defective perception of the real nature of an act in the classical case of the imbecile who cut off a man's head as he was asleep, saying in explanation that he thought it would be fun to see what his victim would say when he woke up and found that his head was missing. "Undoubtedly many subnormals commit acts," Tredgold and Soddy continue, "which they know to be wrong, in that they know they will be disapproved of by their fellows, at least in the concrete form of trouble with the police. Thus in some degree it may be held that they understand the *nature*, i.e., the criminal nature of what they are doing. On the other hand, they are very far from understanding the full *quality* of their acts—the ultimate chain of consequences, the harm they may do to other people and the moral significance (p. 252)."

Such consideration of the retardate's limited understanding and appreciation of the full significance of his acts does not mean to suggest that the problem of deviant and antisocial behavior in the retardate is thereby diminished or its dangers minimized. On the contrary, the problem can become perhaps an all the more serious and acute one for the very reason that what is involved is a weakness or defect or impairment in the mental life which remains in many ways less tractable and less subject to circumscribed therapeutic change. And since it is both the ego and the superego which are impaired in their effective functioning, the problem assumes an even more complex and manifold character. As Redl and Wineman (1951) have pointed out, were only the superego involved, the problem would be comparatively simple. Many normal children in fact can show isolated disturbances of their superego which can be treated through reeducation and counseling. In the retardate, however, a deficient superego happens to coexist with a deficient ego, thereby compounding and confounding the clinical picture. Thus, a retarded individual is especially prone to committing deviant acts because he will be subject to weak and ineffective functioning not only in the realm of conscience and values but in the realm of judgment and common sense as well. It is the latter deficit, in fact, which creates perhaps the more immediate and pervasive of the retardate's problems in the area of deviant and antisocial conduct. Since the primary function of the ego is to become aware of the existing reality and to adjust to it, one of the particular ego functions involved in achieving this end is to become aware of certain limitations imposed by the reality situation and to give appropriate anxiety warning signals should an individual's behavioral urges threaten to come into conflict with these limitations, thereby delaying any impulsive actions. Thus, even if an individual has a weakness or deficiency in his superego functioning, with a resulting lack of value identification, he can still be expected to have his ego make a careful assessment and appraisal of a given situation in order to determine what the real risks would be if he were to attempt an illegal or immoral act. With the retardate, however, such reality assessment and appraisal are lacking, so that in the absence of a strong superego there is no existing ego check on prospective improper behavior.

A poorly developed ("weak") ego also can give rise to strong feelings of inferiority per se (especially when there also are concomitant feelings of rejection), which may lead the retardate to stealing as a symbolic means of "buying" popularity, thereby permitting him to gain some status and to alleviate his inferiority feelings. Another way in which the retardate may accomplish the same results would be to secure some type of outstanding achievement, and an easy means of attaining such an "outstanding achievement" might very well be via some spectacular act of destruction or desecration.

Inextricably connected with a weak ego assessment function in the retardate is a similarly weak ego control function, such that the retardate has great difficulty in suppressing certain instinctual impulses and drives emanating from the id. This lack of instinct control gives rise to a familiar condition in the retardate which is commonly referred to as "low frustration tolerance" and which consists in the retardate's inability to withhold or to postpone gratification of his immediate and momentary needs and desires. This means that a particular retardate, when exposed to a situation which might be frustrating, may not allow himself to be frustrated, but may insist upon a total gratification of the full reservoir of impulses waiting to be released. Were the retardate to be required by external circumstances to control his impulses, he might soon find himself in a state of disorganization, confusion, and catastrophic reaction owing to the fact that his weak ego would be helpless in the face of the aggression, fear, and inordinate discomfort produced by the environmental frustrations. Budoff and Liebowitz (1964) demonstrated that borderline and mildly retarded institutionalized adolescents with a lowered stress (frustration) tolerance exhibited poorer behavioral controls and poorer adjustment in general than did those with a greater tolerance for stress. Pollock (1945) also found that retardates were very poorly equipped to withstand stress, especially when the stress was of any unusual duration. It might be noted, in this connection, that such low frustration tolerance, by virtue of which the retardate does not allow frustration to build within himself, could serve as a partial explanation of the failure of a number of recent experimental studies to differentiate between delinquent and nondelinquent retardates in terms of certain projective measures of aggression in personality functioning. Sternlicht and Silverg (1965), for example, found no significant differences in fantasy aggression or in fantasy punishment on the Thematic Apperception Test between overtly aggressive and nonaggressive institutionalized mentally retarded adolescents. Similarly, Sternlicht (1966), in an expanded study using the same delinquent and docile populations, found no significant differences between the two groups in fantasy aggression as measured by an entire battery of projective techniques. Such lack of correspondence between overt aggression and fantasy aggression might be understandable, since the operation of the former could to a large extent preclude the existence of the latter. The greater a retardate's tendency to gratify the full reservoir of his impulses and to discharge his accompanying hostility in daily overt behavior, the smaller will be the residual impulse and hostility which might be tapped in the form of fantasy aggression on a projective technique. Foreman (1962) also noted less overt aggressivity with older age and greater length of institutionalization.

The following description by Redl and Wineman (1951) of the behavior of a group of juvenile delinquents highlights the impulsivity and lack of frustration tolerance so characteristic of retardates:

They were especially low in their ability to block any ongoing impulse push for even short periods of time, and the helplessness of their ego in view of even mild doses of frustration—produced aggression or fear was pathetic to watch. Even in the midst of a happily enjoyed game the slightest addition to be met or mild frustration to be added would throw the whole group into wild bursts of unstructured bickering, fighting, disorganization, and griping. Even small quantities of limitation, no matter how wisely imposed, and how realistically designed, would bring forth temper outbursts which, in other children, would only happen as a result of exposure to extreme threat or mishandling (pp. 91-92).

Redl and Wineman also cite the following incident as a case in point:

The kids burst out of the station wagon in their usual exuberant mood and barged madly up the steps into the house. Luckily, this time the door was open so the usual pounding, kicking of doors, etc., wasn't necessary. I was in my office tied up in a phone call and the door was closed. Mike yelled for me, shouting something about his jack knife which I was keeping in the drawer for him. I put my hand over the receiver and said 'OK, come on in.' But the lock had slipped on the door and he could not open it. Before I even had a chance to excuse myself from my phone conversation, and say 'Just a minute, I'll be back' he was pounding on the door, kicking it, calling me a 'sonofabitch' repetitively. I opened the door and gave him his knife. Even this failed to quiet his furor and, when I commented on the obvious fact that I hadn't even meant to make him wait, that the lock had slipped, all I got was a snarling, contemptuous 'Shit' (p. 92).

Milner (1949) has outlined the way in which sexual frustration may become a rather frequent cause of institutional aggressive acting-out behavior, especially among the "brighter" patients. Acting-out hostile behavior is likely to be a direct reaction to frustrated physical desires, and assaultive acts may arise from heterosexual or homosexual jealousy, or violent means may be employed to intimidate an unwilling homosexual partner. Such sexual frustrations may be greater in the case of female retardates, owing to the additional thwarting of "the maternal and home-making instincts." In general, Milner feels that the retarded are nearly ten times more likely to perpetrate sexual offenses than is the nonretarded criminal population. Some confirmation for this latter view has been offered by Boslow and Kaudel (1965), who found that retarded offenders had a higher proportion of sexual assaults and crimes than did nonretarded offenders, and by Foale (1956), who found many mentally retarded females to be prostitutes (because of an inability to cope with their sexual drives).

It thus is not difficult to see how such a lack of frustration tolerance, given the proper external circumstances, could lead the retardate into a situation in which his behavior would come to assume an antisocial, delinquent, or criminal character. If, for example, he were furnished with certain material, tangible lures and temptations, how easily might the retardate commit an impulsive act of robbery or burglary in order to satisfy his momentary desires. Or were he the object of a sexual enticement, how naturally he might be led into imprudent behavior in order to gratify his pressing sexual needs and drives. Or were he subjected to excessive restriction on his behavior or severe threat to his well being, how quickly he might respond out of fear and impulse with assaultive and destructive behavior. And, in many ways, owing to his life situation, the retardate is in fact more easily exposed than is the normal individual to the kinds of circumstances which would tend to evoke such behavior. As Dexter (1958) has pointed out, for example, in his discussion of the retardate:

In a society where people in a given category are restricted in role, made fun of, looked down upon, and subjected to great obstacles, the people in that category are likely to learn to feel considerable self-doubt may express itself in helplessness, lack of ambition, or erratic, impulsive, and highly negative behavior—'kicking out' at a world in which 'the generalized other'—the typical or model other person as they have experienced him—has frustrated, bewildered, or oppressed him. These undesirable or antisocial types of conduct are not *per se* the result of any particular abnormality, low status position, or deviation from conventional conduct; they are rather responses to the way people are treated who are regarded as abnormal, of low status, or undesirably unconventional (p. 924).

Similarly, in courts of law the burden of guilt falls upon the retardate. While a child would probably be excused for a crime because of an insufficient knowledge of the nature and content of his actions, this same consideration is not offered the retardate, unless he is deemed to be "without intelligence from nativity." Hinkle (1961) feels that a retardate should not be held fully responsible for his actions, and that the courts should plan a treatment program "to fit the offender rather than the offense." In other words, a court decision should be based not merely on overt behavior, but also should take into account the psychodynamics which led to such deviant behavior.

The Relationship Between Mental Retardation and Emotional Disturbance

As was the case with the question of criminality and delinquency, in order to gain a comprehensive view of the problem of emotional disturbance among the retarded, together with its import for our general understanding of the retardate's personality, it is necessary to provide some kind of perspective and framework. The prevailing views concerning the relationship between mental retardation and emotional disturbance are mixed and multifarious, which is not unreasonable in view of the very complex, fluid, and wide-ranging nature of the subject matter, and in view of the different retarded populations being studied. The term "emotional disturbance" itself is a far-reaching and global one, embracing a multitude of sins as it were, with the result that what one writer may be addressing himself to in his treatment of the problem may be quite different in character, though undelineated as such, from what another writer is considering. One writer, for example, while using the term emotional disturbance or the like, might be referring to neurotic behavior, whereas another might be considering psychotic symptomatology. Even in cases in which these appellations are given, one cannot readily know the exact demarcations of terms such as "neurosis" and "psychosis" as the writer intends them in the absence of clearly delineated diagnostic criteria.

The picture is further complicated by the inherent difficulties encountered when one attempts to distinguish between mentally retarded behavior per se, and emotionally disturbed behavior per se, since a good deal of the former can be considered to fuse, to merge, and to overlap with the latter. (Because the term "emotionally disturbed" is in such common usage, we will maintain that vogue; however, it should be understood that what we really are referring to is not emotionally disturbed behavior, but rather emotionally disturbing behavior, i.e., behavior that is disturbing to someone.) As has been pointed out by Garfield (1963):

Although such terms as mental retardation and psychosis are used to refer to different types of behavior, the distinction is not always easy to make. This problem is particularly evident in the appraisal of disturbed behavior in children. Varying interpretations are possible for many reasons: the child's development is incomplete, similar or overlapping symptoms may be noted in different disorders, communication on the part of the child is frequently limited, and diagnostic techniques are far from adequate. As a result, one encounters variations in the diagnostic and theoretical views pertaining to disturbed behavior in children. An example of this is the psychotic child who functions intellectually at what appears to be a retarded level. One person may view this pattern as reflecting a condition of mental retardation, whereas another may interpret it as a temporary impairment of intellectual functioning, secondary to psychosis. In one instance the child is considered retarded and in the other he is diagnosed as psychotic. . . . Another aspect of this problem is reflected in the term pseudofeeblemindedness, which has been used in the past to denote individuals who appeared to be retarded or were diagnosed as retarded, but who were found on later examinations not to be retarded. . . . There is also the related problem of the accuracy and comparability of diagnosis, since different centers and investigators may vary considerably in their diagnostic procedures and criteria (pp. 574-575).

Many other workers (e.g., Angus (1948); Arthur (1947); Cassel (1957); Garfield, Wilcott, and Milgram (1961); Menolascino (1965a, 1965c); Molish (1958); Papageorgis (1963); and Schachter, Meyer, and Loomis (1962)) also have commented upon the difficulties involved in arriving at adequate differential diagnostic assessments in this sphere. Not only is there ambiguity in the diagnostic criteria utilized per se, but, as has been noted above, there also exists a relative lack of (differentiating) sophistication and discrimination among the evaluative procedures and techniques that are employed. As a consequence of these difficulties, misdiagnoses are likely to occur (e.g., the notion of "pseudofeeblemindedness"). Differential diagnosis represents an attempt to isolate and to specify all of the relevant variables in a given retarded person's case. An adequate evaluation of the retarded is essential, for it is on the basis of such evaluations that far-reaching and significant decisions about him are made, such as which type of placement may be most appropriate and what types of therapeutic and/ or educational procedures are to be used (e.g., which would be most effective and efficient).

Thus, it appears that we are confronted by a situation in which the independent and mutually exclusive character which is tacitly assumed for the categories which we are treating—mental retardation and emotional disturbance—is in fact in the first instance not actually established. For our purposes, however, emotional disturbance will be used in a very broad sense to refer to any emotional features of the retardate's life which interfere with his adaptive behavior.

With these difficulties noted, the present discussion will deal with the question of emotional disturbance among mental retardates by suggesting the possible factors in, and features of, the retardate's personality structure which might predispose the retardate to disturbances and disorders of an emotional nature.

Emotional Disturbance versus Criminality
as Deviant Behaviors

As with the problem of delinquency and criminality, treatment of the relationship between mental retardation and emotional disturbance must derive from a consideration of the personality structure of the retardate, with its constituent defects, impairments, and weaknesses. The very same forces and factors which lead in one case to antisocial and unlawful behavior in a retarded individual can give rise in another case to emotionally disturbed and abnormal behavior in a different individual. The form which the deviant behavior will assume—the antisocially delinquent or the emotionally disturbed—is dependent upon the psychological makeup of the particular person, his functional patterns and tendencies, his religious values, and upon the particular situational context of the behavior itself. (Certain value systems, as Hoffman (1965) has shown, may be a virtual necessity for some degrees of continuing stability.) This point is highlighted and elaborated by Abel and Kinder (1942) in their discussion of the female adolescent retardate:

Both forms of maladjustment, psychopathological behavior and delinquencies, may appear in the same individual, as happens when the outward and visible signs of the psychopathological mental functioning happen to be antisocial acts, such as compulsive stealing in the case of kleptomania, damaging property or injuring others due to delusional trends, and a greatly exaggerated resistance to authority. From the point of view of psychiatry the differentiation between delinquent and psychopathological behavior is highly artificial, since both forms of maladjustment express the revolt of an organism against an intolerable situation, either within or external to itself. But, from the point of view of the society dealing with the individual deviate, the two types of maladjustment are essentially different, since only delinquency is an offense against legal codes (pp. 134-135).

What is important to bear in mind is that in both cases it is the relationship between the retarded individual's ego and his needs and drives which lies at the core of the problem. In particular, the emotional disturbances and disorders of a retarded individual can be traced to the impending threat to his ego which is posed by certain situations and experiences together with the defenses which the retardate marshals in order to meet and to cope with the threat. The particular symptomatology which develops out of this process varies from one retarded individual to another and depends upon the specific character and style of the coping behavior and mechanisms employed. The overt symptomatology displayed, however, may have little or no reference to the degree of existing mental retardation per se, as Humphrey (1940) has suggested. Similarly, Plesset (1941) maintains that any psychotic condition that could occur in a nonretarded individual also could occur in a retardate, and the present writers have dealt with a sufficiently large number of retardates to convince themselves that any psychopathological manifestations exhibited by retardates may also be seen in nonretardates. Some degree of emotional difficulties in retardates almost always is related to adverse psychological pressures and unsatisfactory home relationships.

Bender (1959) postulates that children (i.e., retardates) who have not developed adequately intellectually and in their ego functions may display autistic behavior. Bender does not view "autism" as either mental illness or psychosis, but rather as a primitive form of behavior. In such (autistic) behavior, a part of the normal developmental process may persist and become exacerbated via the utilization of withdrawal behavior (viewed in this light as a defense against "disorganization and anxiety").

Incidence of Emotional Disturbance Associated
with Mental Retardation

There is a general consensus in the literature and among workers in the field that some emotional (personality) disturbance is basic in true mental retardation, and in part, may be manifested by that mental retardation. The incidence of severe behavior disorders, including mental illness, is higher among mental retardates than in the general population; this incidence is considerably higher among institutionalized retardates. In fact, Wyers and Tarjan (1949) assert that the institutionalization of the mildly mentally retarded is generally caused by emotional disturbances. Emotional disturbance, second only to the mental retardation itself, is probably the major cause of institutionalization of mental retardates in general.

All of the minor or major behavioral disorders and other forms of psychiatric difficulties can and do occur in combination with mental retardation. Menolascino (1965a), who investigated 616 potentially retarded children (CAs less than 8-0) over a six-year period, found that approximately 25 percent of the group were both mentally retarded and emotionally disturbed. In a study of 578 institutionalized retardates, LaVeck and de la Cruz (1964) found behavioral reactions in 27.2 percent of the group, severe neurotic reactions in 1.2 percent, and psychoses in 5.2 percent. They also discovered that the nonorganically damaged retardates evidenced the greatest number of behavioral reactions. Woodward (1963) noted a greater incidence of behavior disorders among those severely retarded children who had (pre-institutionalization) derived from an adverse environmental situation, with concomitant negative material or emotional circumstances. O'Connor (1951), who intensively evaluated 104 mildly retarded boys, found that 43 percent of his subjects were unstable, and 12 percent neurotic. Feldman (1946) felt that the dynamics involved in the development of neurotic conditions were essentially similar in retarded adults and nonretarded ones.

Despert and Pierce (1946), in evaluating bright (nonretarded) preschoolers, discovered a definite and positive correlation between emotional adjustment and intellectual functioning. Pollock (1945), on the basis of state hospital admissions, found similar results: the rate of mental illness varied inversely with degree of intelligence (e.g., the higher the intellectual level, the less the rate of mental illness). He concluded that "the general rate of incidence of mental illness is higher among subnormal persons than among the general population." Dewan (1948), who examined the records of over 3,000 army recruits who had gone through an induction center over a fifteen-month period, also discovered that the rate of incidence of neuroses and other types of emotional difficulties declines as the degree of intellectual prowess advances. The highest incidence of emotional instability was found among those recruits who were diagnosed as mentally retarded: 48 percent of the retarded recruits were emotionally unstable, as against 20 percent of the nonretarded recruits. Beier (1964), after a review of the relationship between behavioral disturbances and mental retardation, concluded that "As the age and intelligence level increase, there is also an increase in the clarity of definition of the behavioral disturbances . . . (which) is especially true of the psychoses."

The type of emotional disturbance most common among institutionalized retardates (especially adolescents), according to Angus (1948), is one of severe interest contraction, where the retardate refuses to participate in communal activities, where he is shy and seclusive, and where most of his time is spent in fantasizing, in daydreaming.

The schizophrenic type of reaction is the most frequently found psychosis among the mentally retarded. Plesset (1941), after reviewing the case records of retardates, found that the functional psychoses do not generally occur in persons with an IQ of less than 50. He proposed a two-fold classification: "mental deficiency with psychotic episode," and "mental deficiency with psychosis"—the former being transitory in nature, the latter being more prolonged, with progressive deterioration occurring. Goldberg and Soper (1963) performed an intensive review of the files of 1,216 suspected retarded children, who were seen at the Children's Psychiatric Research Institute in London, Ontario (Canada). They found a high incidence of psychotic symptoms among these retarded children, with 62 of the group, or 5.1 percent, also being diagnosed as overtly psychotic, exhibiting especially impaired relations with people.

LeVann (1950) found a wide range of isolated schizophrenic symptomatology in profoundly retarded persons and the typical "demented schizophrenic." Wortis (1958) outlined the differential dynamics involved in the various types of schizophrenic symptomatologies evidenced by mentally retarded children.

Dynamic Factors in the Emotionally Disturbed
Behavior of the Retardate

Retardates seem to be more prone to the development of (sometimes high levels of) manifest anxiety than are nonretarded persons. Cochran and Cleland (1963), utilizing the Children's Manifest Anxiety Scale (CMAS), found that retarded adolescents exhibited a greater degree of anxiety than did nonretarded adolescents, and that the anxiety was caused by variables other than those associated with the developmental stresses typical of the adolescent period. They thus confirmed the thesis that there exists "more anxiety tension in the buildup of the retardate." Similarly, Knights (1963), employing the Test Anxiety Scale for Children and the Defensiveness Scale for Children with retarded and nonretarded children, ascertained that retarded children evidence more anxiety and more defensiveness than do nonretardates. While no direct correlation between anxiety and overt aggression in retardates has been obtained (Lipman, 1959), anxiety does appear to have an impairing effect upon academic achievement, at least with mildly retarded adolescents, according to a study by Wiener, Crawford, and Snyder (1960). The retardate's ego's capacity to withstand attacks of anxiety is somewhat diminished as well.

One of the most familiar defensive patterns which a retardate might develop in the face of anxiety, in the face of continuing danger and threat to his ego, is the behavioral pattern of denial and/or withdrawal. Chazan (1965) found a pattern of withdrawal to be correlated with physical deficit in the retardate, and positive but weak parental discipline. The entire life experience of the retardate is in many ways tailor-made to the development of just such a pattern. Because he is an ego-crippled individual suffering from feelings of inferiority and shame, withdrawal tendencies are a predictable consequence. As has been pointed out by Chapman (1965) in his discussion of the problem, emotional withdrawal is produced by life experiences which make an individual afraid of relationships with people. The coldness, the criticism, and the indifference of hostile and rejecting parents, which so often is the pattern of life during the early years of a retardate's upbringing, leave the retardate with apprehensions of similar treatment from the world at large. This process of generalization, as Chapman (1965) suggests, has a viciously circular and insidiously lethal effect upon the personality of the retardate. The more he is exposed and the more he is subject to the emotional rejection by significant people in his life, the more the retardate comes automatically to expect such rejection from others, and the more he insulates himself from an increasingly cold and alien world by throwing a protective shell about his vulnerable and already battered ego. The retardate's propensities toward "other-directedness," as discussed in the previous chapter, tend to sharpen his sensitivities to others in the initial phases of the process, so that he senses disapproval quickly and feels criticism keenly. His antennae, as it were, are sharply tuned to catch the signals of emotional acceptance or rejection by those about him. This sensitivity, combined with the retardate's vulnerability to hostility, rejection, and disapproval, causes the retarded individual to flee from interpersonal experiences which he comes to associate with negative feelings. Such flight from the world, if sufficiently persistent and sustained, can begin to take on serious proportions. Carried to its most extreme and severe end, such emotional withdrawal comes to assume a full-blown pathological character in the form of a psychosis, and more particularly a schizophrenic reaction in the retardate. It is at this point that a retarded individual becomes what we can legitimately identify as an emotionally disturbed individual as well.

A good description of the characteristic appearance and behavior of a retardate with a schizophrenic overlay is provided in the following passage by Rohan (1946), who offers several concrete examples as well:

The hall-marks of the schizophrenic group are emotional withdrawal and oddities of behavior. It is sometimes very difficult to conjecture what the original intelligence might have been if the schizophrenic state had not supervened. It has probably affected every level of defect from the barely subnormal to the imbecile group. Schizophrenics are commonly mute and apathetic; they may attend to themselves, and for the rest of the time remain inert and vacant; they respond to advances with a smile and a muttered yes. The less retarded ones can be taught to carry on the simpler processes of domestic cleaning, brush making, dishcloth knitting, etc. They are usually slovenly, and regardless of their personal appearances. They mix passively with the other patients, of whom they are often the butts or dupes. It is not an easy matter to know where to place these patients, as their liability to phases of disorderly excitement, to impulsive striking out and to repeated absconding precludes them from being kept with the quieter or lower grade patients to whom they more naturally belong. Others are manneristic in various ways.

Sidney, aged 22, is quite a high-grade patient who goes out of his way to address one in an exaggeratedly affected and boisterous manner with much laughter. He soon becomes disconnected, jerky and embarrassed in his speech. He is really unsettled and anxious, and confesses that he never feels at ease with his fellow patients.

Marjorie, aged 28, who is very demented, remains with mouth pursed and frequently with limbs crossed and has constant bouts of vigorously rubbing her hair (p. 552).

What should be noted, as a repeated theme throughout our discussion of the retardate's personality, is that the development of such an extreme state as schizophrenia is not an inherent or structural component of the retardate's personality, but rather an expression of an ongoing process in which the retardate makes a functional attempt to cope with his reality as he sees and experiences it. Philips (1966) touches upon this point in the following discussion of the widespread misconception that the maladaptive behavior of the retardate is a function of his retardation per se, rather than of his interpersonal relationships:

The constitutional endowment of any child is not the only factor determining his ability to learn and to develop. The child may have ultimate limitations in his capacity to develop, but his life experiences may interfere with the fullest development of this innate potential. Organic defect resulting from injury, metabolic abnormality, congenital anomaly, infection, and so forth may limit the level of function. However, emotional disorder developing from such experiences as emotional deprivation, frustration, separation, traumatic experiences, and the like also may inhibit or distort function. . . . The child, then, who is retarded because of organic defect may also evidence emotional disorder that interferes with his maximal development. We recognize that although deficiency or disease may be a major contributing stress, the child's emotional disorder probably is not an organically inevitable concomitant of his defect, but is, rather, a function of the same kinds of processes that give rise to emotional disorder in children who have no definable 'disease'. . . .

Thus, disturbed behavior in the retarded is not primarily the result of limited intellectual capacities, but is related to delayed, disordered personality functions and interpersonal relationships with meaningful people in the environment (pp. 112-113).

The weakness of the retardate's ego makes it all the more difficult for him to effect a satisfactory adjustment in the face of existential hardships and negative experiences, and thus causes him to become prone to rely on a more phantasied and ineffectual resolution of the situation than would be the case with an individual of normal intelligence. Since emotionally disturbed behavior among the retarded does not differ in its basic etiological nature from emotionally disturbed behavior among the rest of the intellectual population, one should expect that the retarded would display the same variety and range of psychopathology as do the intellectually normal (c.f., Plesset, 1941). That such is in fact the case is attested to by reports in the literature and by the daily experiences of psychiatric and psychological practitioners in the field whose case materials are wide ranging, running the gamut of psychopathology, including transient, psychoneurotic, character, personality, psychosomatic, and psychotic disorders. The following examples provided by Philips (1966) serve to show concretely the kind of diversity which exists in the repertoire of the psychopathology of retardates:

Jimmy, a three-year-old boy with mongolism, was impulsive and assaultive to his peers, difficult to manage at school, and almost impossible to control at home. A local nursery school for the retarded was ready to expel him—a decision never made with any other child in the history of the school. The father, a former prominent athlete, maintained unrealistic expectations and felt his son would be slow but could finish high school and work in his business. He discussed with pride his son's 'cute' and 'all boy' impulsivity and destructiveness.

Helen, a seventeen-year-old adolescent, was socially isolated and withdrawn in her behavior. Her IQ was 68 and her school repeatedly reported that she could do better in her work, but was withdrawn and disturbed. Her mother spent all of her free time with Helen, fearful that her daughter would get into trouble, that perhaps she would be sexually attacked or be induced to troublesome behavior. Helen developed a phobia about being touched. She avoided crowds, bathed frequently, and washed her hands throughout the day (p. 114).

Such diversity of emotional disorder among retardates, while a reflection of the universal nature of the psychodynamic processes involved, is at the same time an expression of certain personality traits which, as discussed in the previous chapter, are exaggerated in the retardate, owing to the weakness of his ego structure. The earlier discussed pattern of withdrawal, leading ultimately to a psychotic, and particularly a schizophrenic reaction, is but one of the mechanisms by which the retardate can defend his fragile ego in the face of danger, a mechanism which may be especially utilized by mongoloids (Rollen, 1946). In this connection, however, Menolascino (1965b) found the occurrence of psychotic disorders in mongoloids to be less than in other types of mental retardation.

A defense mechanism equally as common among retardates as the earlier discussed denial and/or withdrawal is one which is characterized by a pattern of depression as described by Chapman (1965). This pattern is marked by the retardate's preoccupation with feelings that he suffers from extreme shortcomings, failures, and inadequacies. In his profound state of melancholy, the retardate feels overridingly worthless and guilty, believing that neither he nor anyone else can remedy his shortcomings and the helplessness of his situation. A sense of inferiority pervades his existence and leads him to worry about what he believes to be his past failures and to fear what he anticipates will be his future failures. Success in an activity or task takes on only transitory meaning. On the other hand, a failure in a given isolated situation will assume exaggerated meaning and significance in his total life perception, owing to his repeated experiences of having been punished by his environment because of his inadequacies.

The problems of the depressed retardate, as can be derived from Chapman's (1965) discussion of the question, arise in formative relationships with significant people in his life which leave him with underlying doubts about his essential worth and ability, reinforced time and again by the harsh and bewildering realities of his unique life situation. Again it is the repeated rejection or punishment by frustrated parents and a callous world at large which leads the retardate into his pattern of felt inadequacy, unworthiness, self-depreciation and depression. The depressed retardate feels that the people about him unmistakably see his inadequacies and either shun him or pity him because of them. As a result, he believes that he is unable to relate to others satisfactorily and that this problem will persist and remain with him throughout his life. Consequently he hesitates even to try. The retardate then comes to withdraw from people and to spend a great deal of time sitting by himself, perhaps staring out the window or languidly going through the motions of performing some minor task. He might neglect his physical grooming and general appearance, suffer a loss of appetite, and cry on occasion. In certain cases, an angry sullenness is superimposed upon the retardate's depression, such that he is easily made irritable and may be subject to angry outbursts on occasion. It may develop, too, that the retardate's feelings of worthlessness and depression become so poignant and pervasive that he feels that life is simply not worth living and that suicide may thus be the only solution. In general, however, as Gardner (1967) has shown, there is little likelihood of the retardate developing really severe depressive reactions (e.g., the incidence of depressive psychoses in retardates is quite low). Berman (1967) has presented some evidence to suggest that retardates may defend themselves against depressive feelings by externalizing their anger, thereby presenting overtly antisocial behavior.

Another symptomatological pattern adopted by retardates, perhaps less severe and extreme in its ultimate expression than the pattern of depression, is that of compulsion-obsession, as Chapman (1965) has outlined it. It is in this pattern of defense of the ego that the retardate typically becomes obsessed with certain morbid and threatening thoughts, and accordingly feels compelled to perform certain ritualistic acts in an effort to rid himself of the thoughts. In particular, the compulsivity of the retardate assumes the form of excessive preoccupation with orderliness, cleanliness, and conscientiousness. He becomes tense and diligent in his work, but he often loses track of large objectives while fussing meticulously over many tiny details. There is a mechanical quality in the compulsive retardate's relationships with other people, and though he is conscientious and sincere in his relationships with others, he lacks a warm, informal give-and-take in his dealings with them. These characteristics of compulsiveness are themselves not unexpected in the retardate since his basic trait of rigidity, discussed in the previous chapter, provides a firm base for the development of obsessive and compulsive behaviors. It is only when these behaviors take on an exaggerated and aggravated character, interfering with the total functioning of the retardate, that we can recognize them as phenomena of psychopathology or emotional disturbance.

The pathological quality of an obsession or compulsion in the retardate is identified by its much greater persistence, its extremely anxious and distressing urgency, and generally its manifold appearance in the daily life of the retardate. A retarded individual with pathologically obsessional and compulsive trends might typically harbor the persistent and terrible fear that his parents are not safe or well, and he might feel the recurrent need to touch or place certain objects in a certain way for no functionally explicable reason. These thoughts and acts express both the retardate's profound sense of insecurity and disorganization in his personal world and his anxiety-stricken attempts to protect his ego in the face of this insecurity and disorganization. Nurcombe and Parker (1963), who studied three cases of "idiot savant," noted that these types of retardates, all of whom they considered autistic, employed obsessional defenses extensively to recover from the autistic reaction, and they also exhibited repetitive motor phenomena (i.e., compulsive behavior).

An additional dynamic factor in the formation of compulsive and obsessive behavior patterns is the retardate's guilt reaction to his pent-up feelings of hostility (as discussed in the previous chapter). The retardate, who is struggling with a mass of harbored hostile emotions which he is unable to face consciously and directly, may find such hostility rising to the surface in the form of obsessional thoughts of violence and death and he may devise certain compulsive acts which serve to undo or to control these unacceptable thoughts. The etiology of obsessive and compulsive personality disturbance in the retardate often lies in the hostility engendered by the parents' pattern of coldness and rejection in the formative period of the retardate's life. Such hostility persists in the retardate's personality at an unconscious and unavailable level, revealing itself only in the substitute and devious expressions of obsessional thoughts and compulsive acts. Foulds (1945) ascertained that retardates whose characteristic reactions to frustration were of an intropunitive nature were most likely to exhibit obsessional trends.

These several basic patterns of psychopathology among retardates—withdrawal, depression, and compulsion-obsession—are offered as a representative sample and dynamic guide rather than as an exhaustive encyclopedia of emotional disorders among retardates. The question of which defense mechanism or pattern will be chosen by a particular retardate remains unanswered as such. As Williams and Belinson (1953) have said:

. . . the Ego adopts that pattern of symptoms which for it will allow for gratification of needs with least expenditure of effort, or with least anticipated loss in integration. Several broad behavior patterns lie open for selection, such as the normal, psychopathic, neurotic and psychotic. Counting all the subtypes of these, we find that the possible mechanisms to choose from are numerous indeed. The ultimate question in dynamics, then, becomes: What are the factors determining the Ego's choice? Or, how does the individual Ego go about deciding what mechanism will give satisfaction with least risk in loss of integration? We are no ways near the answer to these questions (p. 612).

A phenomenon that deserves mention in the context of our general discussion of deviant behavior is suicide. While the subject has received virtually no attention in the literature of the mentally retarded over the years, a very recent study by Sternlicht, Pustel, and Deutsch (1970) has offered a broad and detailed picture of the phenomenon and has advanced a theory of retardate suicide which is useful to our understanding of deviant behavior in the retarded. According to this theory:

Suicide in the mental retardate is the one possible remaining act in a life which has been over-run and enervated by an unrelenting series of psychological misfortunes: the rejection by parents; the intellectual inadequacy exacerbated by the intolerance of an alien world of normals; the hostility born of this double rejection; the guilt that is heir to hostility; the confusions and the anxiety in the face of all these unwanted feelings; and the deep dependence that is the almost un-avoidable consequence of living in the first place in a world which seems always to be one step ahead. By attempting suicide, the retardate is both 'having his cake and eating it too' as it were: he flees from an intolerable and hatred reality, at the same time as he gains his revenge upon it through a simple manipulation. For the moment at least, he is the master of his fate. Suicide is the retardate's moment of mournful glory. It is what remains of personal expression in a life which has otherwise been robbed of it. When all else has failed, suicide is, ironically enough, the last remaining proof that he is in fact a living and active human being (p. 9).

Mental Retardation as a Symptom of Emotional Disturbance

Carrying consideration of the problem one step further, a number of writers in the field (Axline, 1949; Eisenberg, 1958; Harris, 1928; Kanner, 1952; Marcotte, 1947; and Sloan, 1947) have explored the role of emotional disturbance in the very etiology of mental retardation. In these terms, mental retardation itself is seen as a symptom of emotional disturbance. The rationale and basic orientation of this conception of the problem is set forth briefly in the following statement by Eisenberg (1958):

The interdependence of emotion and intelligence is a fundamental fact of human behavior, at the psychological and biological levels of integration. We should no longer wonder at the evidence of dysfunction in either in the presence of disorder in the other, but rather ask: By what mechanism has it occurred in the particular case and by what means may it be remedied? (p. 119)

Goldberg and Soper (1963) suggested that there may be an overlap between childhood psychosis and mental retardation, while Honig (1966) has equated mental retardation (as against mental deficiency) with emotional retardation, as he believes that emotional retardation always precedes intellectual retardation.

According to a further elaborated theoretical formulation of the problem by Sternlicht (1964), mental retardation owing to primary emotional maladjustment may be seen as one of a variety of symptoms or analogues as follows:

1. A symptom of schizoid withdrawal.
2. A symptom of schizophrenic regression, with consequent loss of learned material and loss of adult self-image.
3. A symptom of psychotic ideation, interfering with communication with the examiner, and consequent autistic responses.
4. A symptom of neurotic self-defeating behavior, with consequent secondary gains.
5. A symptom of neurotic rebellion, e.g., against an oppressively over-intellectualized home.

6. A symptom of general anxiety and distractibility.
7. An analogue to a conversion hysteria, with partial functional "paralysis" of neuro-intellectual capacities.
8. The possibility of a psychosomatic analogue, wherein suppressed emotional conflicts cause an 'overload' effect on various organs, in this case the central nervous system.
9. Any combination of the above (p. 620).

Thus, emotional disturbance may be seen not only as a phenomenon which is superimposed or overlaid upon mental retardation, but as a possible cause of the retardation itself. The upshot of this consideration appears to be the need for a more integrated, holistic, and organismic conception of the problem which views the retardate as a whole, ongoing, phenomenological being in which there is no isolated entity "mental retardation," on the one hand, and "emotional disturbance," on the other hand.

References

Abel, T.M., and Kinder, E.F. *The subnormal adolescent girl*. New York: Columbia University, 1942.

Ackerly, S. Rebellion and its relation to delinquency and neurosis in sixty adolescents. *American Journal of Orthopsychiatry*, 1933, 3, 146-158.

Angus, L.R. Schizophrenic and schizoid conditions in students in a special school. *American Journal of Mental Deficiency*, 1948, 53, 227-238.

Arthur, G. Pseudo-feeblemindedness. *American Journal of Mental Deficiency*, 1947, 52, 137.

Axline, V. Mental Deficiency—Symptom or disease. *Journal of Consulting Psychology*, 1949, 13, 313-327.

Baker, H.J.; Decker, F.H.; and Hill, A.S. A study of juvenile theft. *Journal of Educational Research*, 1929, 20, 81-87.

Beane, J.C. A survey of 300 delinquent girls, *Journal of Juvenile Research*, 1931, 15, 198-208.

Beier, D.C. Behavioral disturbances in the mentally retarded. In H.A. Stevens and R. Heber (Eds.). *Mental Retardation*. Chicago: University of Chicago, 1964, pp. 453-487.

Bender. L. Autism in children with mental deficiency. *American Journal of Mental Deficiency*, 1959, 64, 81-86.

Berman, M.I. Mental retardation and depression. *Mental Retardation*, 1967, 5(6), 19-21.

Boslow, H.M., and Kandel, A. Psychiatric aspects of dangerous behavior: The retarded offender. *American Journal of Psychiatry*, 1965, 122, 646-652.

Bowman, P.W., and Young, I.H. Disciplinary problems of the mentally retarded. *Mental Hospitals*, 1959, 10 (5), 14-16.

Budoff, M., and Liebowitz, J. Tolerance for stress among institutionalized mildly retarded adolescents. *Journal of Consulting Psychology*, 1964, 28, 333-341.

Burt, C. *The young delinquent*. London: University Press of London, 1948.

Caplan, N.S. Intellectual functioning. In H.C. Quay (Ed.). *Juvenile delinquency: research and theory*. Princeton: Van Nostrand, 1965.

Cassel, R.H. Differentiation between the mental defective with psychosis and the childhood schizophrenic functioning as a mental defective. *American Journal of Mental Deficiency*, 1957, 62, 103-107.

Chapman, A.H. *Management of emotional problems of children and adolescents*. Philadelphia: J.B. Lippincott, 1965.

Chapman, L.G., and Pathman, J.H. Errors in the diagnosis of mental deficiency in schizophrenia. *Journal of Consulting Psychology*, 1959, 23, 432-434.

Chassell, C. *The relation between morality and intellect*. New York: Columbia University, 1935.

Chazan, M. Factors associated with maladjustment in educationally subnormal children. *British Journal of Educational Psychology*, 1965, 35, 277-285.

Cochran, S.L., and Cleland, C.C. Manifest anxiety of retardates and normals matched as to academic achievement. *American Journal of Mental Deficiency*, 1963, 67, 539-542.

Cutts, R.A. Differentiation between pseudo-mental defectives with emotional disorders and mental defectives with emotional disturbances. *American Journal of Mental Deficiency*, 1957, 61, 761-772.

Davies, S.P. *The mentally retarded in society*. New York: Columbia University, 1935.

Despert, J.L., and Pierce, H.O. The relation of emotional adjustment to intellectual functions. *Genetic Psychology Monographs*, 1946, 34, 3-56.

Dewan, J.G. Intelligence and emotional stability. *American Journal of Psychiatry*, 1948, 104, 548-555.

Dexter, L.A. A social theory of mental deficiency. *American Journal of Mental Deficiency*, 1958, 62, 920-928.

Eisenberg, L. Emotional determinants of mental deficiency. *American Medical Association Archives of Neurology and Psychiatry*, 1958, 80, 114-121.

Exner, F. *Kriminalbiologie in ihsen grundzugen*. Hamburg: Hanseatische Verlag., 1939.

Feldman, F. Psychoneuroses in the mentally retarded. *American Journal of Mental Deficiency*, 1946, 51, 247-254.

Foale, M. The special difficulties of the high grade mental defective adolescent. *American Journal of Mental Deficiency*, 1956, 60, 867-877.

Foreman, M.E. Predicting behavioral problems among institutionalized mental retardates. *American Journal of Mental Deficiency*, 1962, 66, 580-588.

Foulds, G. Frustration types among mental defective juvenile delinquents. *British Journal of Psychology*, 1945, 36, 29-32.

Gardner, W.I. Occurrence of severe depressive reactions in the mentally retarded. *American Journal of Psychiatry*, 1967, 124, 386-388.

98

Garfield, S.L. Abnormal behavior and mental deficiency. In N.R. Ellis (Ed.). *Handbook of mental deficiency*. New York: McGraw-Hill, 1963.

Garfield, S.L.; Wilcott, J.B.; and Milgram, N.A. Emotional disturbance and suspected mental deficiency. *American Journal of Mental Deficiency*, 1961, 66, 23-29.

Glueck, S., and Glueck, E.T. *One thousand juvenile delinquents*. Cambridge: Harvard University, 1934.

Goddard, H.H. *Juvenile delinquency*, New York: Dodd, Mead, 1921.

Goldberg, B., and Soper, H. Childhood psychosis or mental retardation: A diagnostic dilemma. *Canadian Medical Association Journal*, 1963, 89, 1015-1019.

Harris, H. Mental deficiency and maladjustment. *British Journal of Medical Psychology*, 1928, 8, 285-315.

Healy, W., and Bronner, A.F. *New light on delinquency and its treatment*. New Haven: Yale University, 1936.

Hinkle, V.R. Criminal responsibility of the mentally retarded. *American Journal of Mental Deficiency*, 1961, 65, 434-439.

Hoffman, J.L. Mental retardation, religious values, and psychiatric universals. *American Journal of Psychiatry*, 1965, 121, 885-889.

Honig, A. Subnormal functioning in mental illness. *Psychoanalytic Review*, 1966, 53, 112-133.

Humphreys, E.J. Psychopathic personality among the mentally defective. *Psychiatric Quarterly*, 1940, 14, 231-247.

Jones, H.E. Environmental influences on mental development. In L. Carmichael (Ed.). *Manual of child psychology*. New York: Wiley, 1946.

Kanner, L. Emotional interference with intellectual functioning. *American Journal of Mental Deficiency*, 1952, 56, 701-707.

Knights, R.M. Test anxiety and defensiveness in institutionalized and noninstitutionalized normal and retarded children. *Child Development*, 1963, 34, 1019-1026.

LaVeck, G.D., and de la Cruz, F. Medical advances in prevention of mental retardation. In J. Hellmuth (Ed.). *The special child in century 21*. Seattle: Special Child Publications, 1964, pp. 23-46.

LeVann, L.J. A concept of schizophrenia in the lower grade mental defective. *American Journal of Mental Deficiency*, 1950, 54, 469-472.

Lichtenstein, M., and Brown, A.W. Intelligence and achievement of children in a delinquency area. *Journal of Juvenile Research*, 1938, 22, 1-25.

Lipman, R.S. Some test correlates of behavioral aggression in institutionalized retardates with particular reference to the Rosenzweig P-F Study. *American Journal of Mental Deficiency*, 1959, 63, 1038-1045.

Marcotte, J.E.A. Mental deficiency in behavioral problems. *American Journal of Mental Deficiency*, 1947, 51, 407-419.

Maller, J.B. Juvenile delinquency in New York: A summary of a comprehensive report. *Journal of Psychology*, 1937, 3, 1-25.

McClure, W.E. Intelligence of 600 juvenile delinquents. *Journal of Juvenile Research*, 1933, 17, 35-43.

Menolascino, F.J. Emotional disturbance and mental retardation. *American Journal of Mental Deficiency*, 1965a, 70, 248-256.

_____. Psychiatric aspects of Mongolism. *American Journal of Mental Deficiency*, 1965b, 69, 653-660.

_____. Psychosis of childhood: Experiences of a mental retardation pilot project. *American Journal of Mental Deficiency*, 1965c, 70, 83-92.

Merrill, M. Mental differences among juvenile delinquents. *Journal of Delinquency*, 1926, 10, 415-427.

Milner, K.O. Delinquent types of mentally defective persons. *Journal of Mental Science*, 1949, 95, 842-859.

Molish, H.B. Contributions of projective tests to problems of psychological diagnosis in mental deficiency. *American Journal of Mental Deficiency*, 1958, 63, 282-293.

Neff, W.S. Socio-economic status and intelligence. A critical survey. *Psychological Bulletin*, 1938, 35, 727-737.

Nurcombe, B., and Parker, N. The idiot savant. *American Journal of Orthopsychiatry*, 1963, 33, 737-740.

O'Connor, N. Neuroticism and emotional instability in high-grade male defectives. *Journal of Neurology and Neurosurgical Psychiatry*, 1951, 14, 226-230.

Papageorgis, D. Pseudo-feeblemindedness and the concept of mental retardation. *American Journal of Mental Deficiency*, 1963, 68, 340-344.

Pearce, J.D.W. The limits of present knowledge on juvenile delinquency. In *Why delinquency?* Report of a conference on the scientific study of juvenile delinquency, London, 1949.

Philips, I. Children, mental retardation, and emotional disorder. In I. Philips (Ed.). *Prevention and treatment of mental retardation*. New York: Basic Books, 1966.

Plesset, M.R. Psychosis in adult mental defectives. *Psychiatric Quarterly*, 1941, 15, 574-588.

Pollock, H.M. Mental disease among mental defectives. *American Journal of Mental Deficiency*, 1945, 49, 477-480.

Redl, F., and Wineman, D. *Children who hate*. New York: Free Press, 1951.

Rogers, H.H., and Austin, O.L. Intelligence quotients of juvenile delinquents. *Journal of Juvenile Research*, 1934, 18, 103-106.

Rohan, J.C. Mental disorder in the adult defective. *Journal of Mental Science*, 1946, 92, 551-563.

Rollin, H.R. Personalities in mongolism with special reference to the incidence of catatonic psychosis. *American Journal of Mental Deficiency*, 1946, 51, 219-237.

Rouke, F.L. Recent contributions of psychology to the study of criminogenesis. In *Proceedings of the 2nd international congress on criminology*. Paris, 1950.

Schachter, F.F.; Meyer, L.R.; and Loomis, E.A., Jr. Childhood schizophrenia and mental retardation: Differential diagnosis before and after one year of psychotherapy. *American Journal of Orthopsychiatry*, 1962, 32, 584-595.

Shulman, H.M. *A study of problem boys and their brothers.* Albany: New York State Crime Commission, 1929.

Sloan, W. Mental deficiency as a symptom of personality disturbance. *American Journal of Mental Deficiency*, 1947, 52, 31-36.

Snyder, M.Λ. Λ comparison of mental traits and attitudes of delinquent boys and girls. *Journal of Juvenile Research*, 1931, 15, 181-191.

Sternlicht, M. A theoretical model for the psychological treatment of mental retardation. *American Journal of Mental Deficiency*, 1964, 68, 618-622.

_____. Fantasy aggression in delinquent and non-delinquent retardates. *American Journal of Mental Deficiency*, 1966, 70, 819-821.

Sternlicht, M.; Pustel, G.; and Deutsch, M.R. Suicidal tendencies among institutionalized retardates. *The Journal of Mental Subnormality*, 1970, 16, Part 2, No. 31, 1-10.

Sternlicht, M., and Silverg, E.F. The relationship between fantasy aggression and overt hostility in mental retardates. *American Journal of Mental Deficiency*, 1965, 70, 486-488.

Sutherland, E.H. Mental deficiency and crime. In K. Young (Ed.). *Social attitudes*. New York: Holt, 1931.

Tredgold, R.F., and Soddy, K. *Textbook of mental deficiency*. Baltimore: Williams and Wilkins, 1963.

Wallin, J.E.W. *Education of mentally handicapped children*. New York: Harper, 1955.

_____. *Mental deficiency, in relation to problems of genesis, social and occupational consequences, utilization, control, and prevention*. Brandon, Vt.: Journal of Clinical Psychology, 1956.

Wiener, G.; Crawford, E.E.; and Snyder, R.T. Some correlates of overt anxiety in mildly retarded patients. *American Journal of Mental Deficiency*, 1960, 64, 735-739.

Williams, F.R., and Belinson, L. Neurosis in a mental defective. *American Journal of Mental Deficiency*, 1953, 57, 601-612.

Woodward, M. Early experience and behavior disorders in severely subnormal children. *British Journal of Social and Clinical Psychology*, 1963, 2, 174-184.

_____. The role of low intelligence in delinquency. *British Journal of Delinquency*, 1955, 5, 281-303.

Wortis, J. Schizophrenic symptomatology in mentally retarded children. *American Journal of Psychiatry*, 1958, 115, 429-431.

Wyers, R.E., and Tarjan, G. Administrative practices to provide better psychiatric care of mental defectives. *American Journal of Mental Deficiency*, 1949, 54, 31-37.

6 Social Behavior and Social Problems

It is the purpose of the present chapter to explore the social realm of the world of the mental retardate, with special attention given to those problems of social adjustment with which the retardate must inevitably come to grapple in the course of his socialization in an intellectually normal world. Such problems, experienced almost universally by the retardate, are derived from behavior that is to be considered not pathogenic but rather maladaptive or maladjustive in character. Since he is required to perform his social functions in an environment which is generally overdemanding of his limited abilities and somewhat alien to his own life interests and goals, the retardate is bound to find himself facing problems and reacting with behavioral patterns which to some degree are specific and peculiar to him. (This is true even when the retardate is placed in a protective and relatively nondemanding environment, such as an institution, where the disciplinary controls effected might be expected to influence the expression of his social behavior and competence.) Often this situation is compounded by the fact that in many cases the retardate in question is a former institutional patient who must learn to acclimate himself to a world and way of life entirely new and different from what he had come to know during years of institutionalization. In such cases the retardate has not only to learn but to unlearn and to relearn as well. In addition, other persons' perceptions of the retardate's social behavior may be variable. As an example, Myers (1961) ascertained that special education teachers made numerous incorrect judgments concerning the social status of their students. Also popular attitudes and stereotypes may influence the way in which the retardate is evaluated by others.

The present discussion will first provide a general theoretical treatment of the nature of retardate adjustment, then discuss social reinforcement influences, next make an examination of various follow-up studies of retardate adjustment in the community, and finally focus upon certain actual experiments in social living which have been instituted as adjustment training experiences for retardates.

The Nature of Retardate Adjustment

Group acceptance is nearly always a problem for retardates, especially when viewed within the framework of a disparity between intellectual capabilities and social interests and needs. The question of the retardate's adjustment in society

101

is one that looms large both in terms of the percentage of retardates who reside in the community and in terms of the scope and pervasiveness of "adjustment" as a problem area in the life of each retardate. In fact, Clarke, Clarke, and Reiman (1958) have shown that IQ increments can be correlated with changes in the social behavior and adjustment of the retarded, while Capobianco and Cole (1960) have demonstrated that IQ seems to influence social participation. In this regard, Sternlicht and Siegel (1968) have shown that retardates' friendship patterns are very unstable.

It is generally estimated that at least 90 percent of all of the mental retardates in this country live in the community. Most of these individuals are mildly retarded, and Mitchell (1955) has shown that the mildly retarded generally are more competent socially than intellectually; familial retardates often are borderline or dull normal in their degree of social competency. Delp and Lorenz (1953) found that most retardates in the community exercised some degree of self-care and assisted in the handling of routine domestic tasks. Since many of these mild and borderline retardates marry and raise families, they must be realistically prepared for adult life. The day-to-day activities of the society, as Jordan (1961) has pointed out, will be as much their experiences as they are the experiences of the intellectually normal person:

For the homemaker there are decisions about child care and buying food. The children must be looked after, and the food must be chosen for the meals by multiple criteria of cost, nutrition, and availability. There is the selection of household chores and the planning of time in which to do them. For the working man there is the need to get to work in time, to use judgment and discretion in his assigned tasks, and in his relations with co-workers. At times independence of judgment may be necessary to fulfill the demands of one's position. The school age child is expected to find his way to school, avoiding the more enticing invitations to play that he meets on the way. He must get there on time and in much the same state of cleanliness that marked his departure from home. Once in school, he must be alert to the subtle ways in which the teacher indicates her demands. . . . He must subdue impulses and work in the presence of many distracting stimuli on material that is usually of an abstract order. (p. 8).

These illustrative samplings of the varieties and complexities of experiences which a member of society must regularly undergo in "second-nature" fashion point up the difficulties which the retardate inevitably confronts in his day-to-day adjustment in the community. From a social point of view, the retardate often lacks dependability, consideration for the feelings of others, and a sense of personal responsibility for his actions or a feeling of obligation to the community. However, if his environment is properly circumscribed and his daily functions appropriately delimited, the retardate can adapt smoothly and adequately to the world in which he finds himself.

Thus, one of the keys to a mental retardate's successful and happy adjustment to his social world is the adequacy of his social environment. While this in fact holds true for every human being, it creates special considerations in the case of the retardate because of the retardate's severe intellectual limitations. His poor self-concept, his feelings of rejection, his high rate of frustration, and his lack of adequate and sufficient social contacts all militate against the achievement of satisfactory social adjustment. For a retardate to function optimally in the community, his everyday world must, at least to some extent, be structured and planned for him in order to provide the necessary degree of protection and shelter from the fortuities and vicissitudes of life which are a part of normal existence; allowances also must be provided for the retardate's fluidity of interests and attitudes toward others. At the same time, however, care must be taken not to create a program or pattern which would be overly protective of the retardate's personality. Such a pattern could, according to the processes described in chapter 4, act to inhibit the retardate's strivings for autonomy by setting off a vicious cycle of protection-dependence-further protection. As Jordan and de Charms (1959) have pointed out, the retardate often is led away from, rather than toward, the development of those traits which are requisite for social competence. A "golden mean" formula for retardate adjustment must therefore be sought which eliminates the excesses of both social overexposure and social overprotection. On the one hand, the retardate should not be introduced to social situations which have such psychological stress or trauma value that they would tend to throw him into a severely anxious or catastrophic state. On the other hand, he should not regularly be sheltered from social experiences to the point where his self-concept becomes shrunken and his drive for independence crippled. It is interesting to note that both environmental extremes—overexposure leading to trauma and overprotection leading to overdependence—produce the same net result: namely, a personal ineffectiveness and a social maladjustment. To the extent, then, that the ecological formula for social adjustment is not properly weighted and balanced, adjustment problems can be expected to develop in the life of the retardate living in the community.

Before delving further into this area, however, it might be advisable to attempt to understand the influences of social reinforcement factors upon the behavior of retardates.

Social Reinforcement Variables and Behavior

Studies treating the role of social reinforcement in the behavior of retardates have yielded a variety of findings. The paradigm for such investigations generally has involved the application of traditional instrumental reinforcement techniques in controlled experimental situations utilizing rewards of a social, human, verbal, or (in the language of the area) high order secondary reinforcement nature.

In one such study, for example, Stevenson and Cruse (1961) investigated the effectiveness of social reinforcement upon the behavior of normal and institutionalized retarded children engaged in a simple, repetitive-task. The children were required to insert marbles of one color in one hole of a box and marbles of another color in a second hole. This was performed under three varying conditions of support: E made supportive comments about S's performance; E simply watched S perform and made no comments; or E left the room as S began performing. Performance differences were obtained among both the normal and the retarded children in accordance with the degree of support given. A study by Zigler, Hodgden, and Stevenson (1958), however, found that retarded children, unlike nonretarded children, tended to spend a greater length of time in a game situation under conditions of adult support than they did under conditions of nonsupport.

Utilizing a game situation too, Stevenson and Fahel (1961) examined the comparative effects of social reinforcement upon the performance of institutionalized and noninstitutionalized normal and retarded children. The children played a game involving one of several possible alternative responses under either a neutral condition (in which E was attentive but unresponsive) or a reward condition (in which E delivered supportive comments). Significant differences in increment of response over the base rate were achieved as a function of institutionalization, but not as a function of reward. Pursuing this variable of institutionalization further, Butterfield and Zigler (1965) studied groups of retarded children from two different kinds of institutions, one which had a permissive "homelike" atmosphere and the other a very restrictive atmosphere. While engaged in a marble-sorting game, one group from each institution received verbal social reinforcement while the other group received no reinforcement. The results of the study indicated that the introduction of social reinforcement produced a greater increase in performance among the children from the restrictive environment than among those from the permissive surroundings. The authors interpreted this as support for the general hypothesis that the more social deprivation a child experiences, the greater his motivation for social interaction and support.

Treating a different parameter of institutionalization, Stevenson and Knights (1962a) studied the effectiveness of social reinforcement after brief and extended periods of institutionalization. The results showed a higher level of response on a marble-in-the-hole game as a consequence of social reinforcement among retarded girls who were studied immediately upon their return to the institution than among those studied twelve weeks after their return.

Exploring still other possible variables in the situation, Stevenson and Knights (1962b) examined social reinforcement effects with normal and retarded children (performing a simple task) as a function of pretraining, sex of E, and sex of S. The results demonstrated the following: a pretrained group performed significantly differently from an untrained group; the sex of E influenced the performance of Ss of the opposite sex; and normal children performed significantly differently from retarded children. Terrell and Stevenson (1965) investigated another facet of subject and experimenter relationships by examining the effectiveness of normal and retarded peers as reinforcing agents. They discovered that the performance of normal Ss improved on a simple task when the reinforcing agent was a normal child, whereas the performance of retardates remained unaffected by the type of the reinforcing agent.

In an investigation employing a nonverbal mode of reinforcement (because of the Ss involved), Hollis (1965) studied the responses of profoundly retarded children and adolescents to various forms of social stimulation provided by an adult partner. He found that these various forms of social stimulation had definite and differential reinforcing effects. The order of preference for the social activities was as follows: signaling (E gestured and called to S by name and talked to him); petting (E stroked S); playing; passiveness (E engaged in no activity); and withdrawal (E crouched in a corner when S approached).

On the other hand, failure too can have significant motivating valence for retardates as well, as has already been pointed out in chapter 2. (For an amplified experimental treatment of the role of failure as a motivator in retardate performance, see Bialer and Cromwell, 1965; Lingren, 1967; and Sternlicht, Bialer, and Deutsch, 1970.)

It would thus appear, from the foregoing studies, that while certain limited systematic effects of social reinforcement upon the behavior of retardates have been demonstrated, these effects are not always consistent or widely generalizable. Obviously, a good deal of further research seems to be needed to explore the problem in a more thoroughgoing and exhaustive manner.

We are reasonably certain, however, that institutionalized retardates expect, and settle for, less success than do nonretarded children, that the effectiveness of reinforcing variables seems to be determined mainly by environmental situations that occur within the institutional setting, and that the behavior of the retardate is very strongly influenced by his immediate environmental surroundings.

Follow-up Studies of Retardate Adjustment

A more definitive picture of the social adjustment of the retardate, with its attendant problems, is provided by a variety of systematic research efforts reported in the literature in the form of longitudinal or follow-up studies of the community adjustment of individuals who had been diagnosed as mentally retarded. These studies have generally fallen into one of two classes. The first class of follow-up investigation includes those studies which have involved an examination of the subsequent adjustment of patients discharged, released, or paroled to the community from institutions for the mentally retarded (e.g., Bishop (1957); Brandon (1960); Craft (1958); Fernald (1919); Foley (1929); Johnson (1946); Kinder, Chase, and Buck (1941); Little and Johnson (1932);

Marchand (1956); Meyer (1951); Potter and McCollister (1926); Rudolf (1950); Stanley and Gunsburg (1956); Storrs (1924); Tarjan and Benson (1953); Windle, Stewart, and Brown (1961); and Wolfson (1956)). The second class of follow-up investigation includes those studies which have been concerned with an examination of the social adjustment of mentally retarded individuals who received treatment or training in their communities rather than in residential institutional facilities (e.g., Baller (1936); Bobroff (1956); Delp and Lorenz (1953); Kinder and Rutherford (1927); Kolstoe (1961); Lee, Hegge, and Voelker (1959); Lurie, Schlam, and Frieberg (1923); McKeon (1946); Phelps (1956); Peterson and Smith (1960); Shimberg and Reichenberg (1933); and Thomas (1943)). These studies all have undertaken to describe the successful or unsuccessful community adjustment of mental retardates and to delineate those personal and social factors which might play a significant role in that adjustment. The present treatment of the question will offer a sampling of studies which pinpoint and highlight the nature of retardate adjustment problems as these were discussed in a preliminary way in the previous section.

In a pioneer undertaking of the "institutional" class first described, Fernald (1919) conducted an investigation in the early part of this century of the careers of all the patients who had been discharged from the Waverly State School during a twenty-five year period ending in 1914. Fernald's study, which served as a methodological model for subsequent research undertakings in this area, secured its data by means of a letter inquiry sent to friends and relatives of the dischargees and a follow-up visit by a social worker who interviewed others in the community, such as agency personnel, police, and ministers. In this way, information was gathered from various agencies and services which reflected the frequency with which the former patients depended upon or offended the community. What Fernald found was that the general adjustment success of the retardates proved to be considerably better than would have been expected by institutional administrators and authorities in the field of retardation. Fernald himself admitted, as reported by Davies (1930), that "he had hesitated for two years to publish the results of this study because they seemed so much at variance with the then accepted theories dealing with mental deficiency (p. 196)." In particular, Fernald found that the males fared better than the females, with proportionately less antisocial behavior and greater community adjustment. In both the male and the female cases, the role played by friends and relatives in guiding and supervising the former patients appeared to have been the deciding factor in their social adjustment or maladjustment. The cases who were successful in their adjustment were those who had been counseled and aided by friends and relatives who provided proper supervision and direction for the dischargees. In contrast, the cases who were unsuccessful in their adjustment were those who had not received such guidance and supervision.

Thus, there are two features of Fernald's results which bear noting: first, the surprisingly good social adjustment of the retarded former patients; and second-

ly, the importance of guidance, supervision, and direction by friends and relatives in helping to effect a successful adjustment for the patient. These two
features point to the kinds of positive results in retardate adjustment which can
obtain if, as mentioned earlier in the chapter, the retardate's world is properly
structured and planned for him. This fact of retardate life throws up a real ob-
stacle to any attempt which is made to predict in an a priori fashion the future
social adjustment of an institutionalized retarded young man or woman. As important as the given personal potential of any retardate is in determining his
eventual adjustment, it is not always enough. One may think of it as perhaps a
necessary but not a sufficient condition for proper socialization. Not only must
the retardate by his personality be equipped to adjust, but society must by its
circumstances be equally fostering of such adjustment. There has to exist a
synergy or joint action between the retardate and the society in order for the
retardate's personality to breathe openly and to come to experience the full extent of its own capabilities.

In another follow-up research study which bears out this point, Matthews
(1922) examined the community adjustment of a sample of 100 boys paroled
from the Waverly State School, the same institution involved in Fernald's study.
In Matthews' investigation, which was performed several years after Fernald's
study, all of the subjects had participated in an organized institutionalized training program, all but two were placed in the community, and all were supervised
in the community by a social worker. Matthews' findings were very positive,
with all but three boys making a satisfactory adjustment to life in the community. It was Matthews' conclusion that the success of the boys she studied
was largely a function of the training which they had received while institutionalized at the Waverly State School. It thus appears that such prior training, combined with subsequent community placement and supervision, provided the
proper synergistic formula for successful social adjustment. Not only were the
retardates prepared for the community by appropriate training, but their subsequent experience in the community was thoughtfully arranged and individually
supervised.

In a contrasting follow-up study of the "noninstitutional" variety, Lee,
Hegge, and Voelker (1959) undertook an examination of social adequacy and
social failure among mentally retarded youth in Wayne County in Michigan. A
comparison was made between retarded students and normal students on such
items as school histories, family background, vocational attainment, types of
jobs held, police and social competence records, and service records in the armed
forces. The results of the study indicated that a great many of the retarded
group were not identified sufficiently early in their school training, a large percentage being ten years of age or older when first considered at all for special
class placement. With respect to general social adjustment, the findings showed
that the retarded students were less stable vocationally than the nonretarded
students, had poorer military records with greater incidence of discharges for
inept or unacceptable behavior, and had experienced longer periods of unem-

ployment, more frequent changes in jobs, and lower salaries. Violations of the law among the retarded subjects were equally high, with many serious offenses committed which led ultimately to prison or correctional school confinement. Similarly, out of wedlock pregnancy was significantly more frequent among the retarded girls than among the "normal" girls. It was the authors' conclusion that what had been provided educationally for the retardate was, in effect, too little and too late. While the educational provision offered by special class placement was a correct approach to the problem, it was an inadequate one as it existed. Earlier referral, diagnosis, and placement with appropriate ancillary services to the retarded student and his family, the authors suggest, might have produced a more positive result.

Thus, Lee, Hegge, and Voelker's study furnishes a concrete example of what can be expected in the way of retardate adjustment in the absence of a sufficiently lengthy and comprehensive training program for the retardate. As such, the study attests to the importance of a full and rounded approach which, as the present discussion has earlier emphasized, not only must prepare the retardate adequately but must plan his environment appropriately. This holds particularly true today, owing to the greater degree of variety, fluidity, and complexity in the contemporary world in contrast with the relatively circumscribed and localized character of the world which existed during the early part of the century at the time some of the investigations of retardate adjustment were first reported. As Goldstein (1964) has observed:

The years during and some years following Fernald's researches might be characterized as the comfortable years for the retardate, since this was the era of hand work and limited mobility. In contrast, the past decade or two have been stressful for the retardate because of the trend toward mobility and mechanization.

Where once the retardates could live well-circumscribed lives, they must now be as mobile as their peers in going from home to work to recreation and the like. Further, the know-how necessary to mobility have become more numerous and complex: bus schedules, fares, traffic rules, and courtesies are but a few of the everyday hurdles that the present-day retardate must take in his stride. . . .

In all probability, the data on the social adjustment of the retarded would take a different shape if it were not for the practice of educating and counseling the mentally retarded over the past three decades. More likely than not, the proportion adjusting adequately would be considerably less than in the past (pp. 237-238).

With this in mind, let us examine the kinds of community experiences which would tend to create difficulties for the retardate as he attempts to make his way in the everyday world. Just such a close-up examination of the circumstantial factors involved in the community failure of retardates released from institutions has been made in an investigation of the problem by Windle, Stewart, and Brown (1961), who studied the relationship between the mode of institutional release, types of patients, and subsequent community adjustment. Their investigation followed up the community adjustment of three groups of retarded patients released from Pacific State Hospital, each group having been placed on a different kind of community status: one group, mostly mildly retarded, was placed on vocational leave; the second group, also mostly mildly retarded, was placed on home leave; and the third group, mostly moderately retarded, was placed on family care. Each patient was followed for a four-year period, during which a social worker evaluated information on the patient gathered from the patient's family and from such social agencies as the police, the department of public welfare, and the armed forces. Failure in community adjustment was defined generally as reinstitutionalization for other than brief medical care. The results of the study indicated that the reasons for failure in adjustment varied considerably among the three groups. Failures on vocational leave most frequently involved inadequate work performance (e.g., inability to take orders, anxiety, and poor self-evaluation), inadequate interpersonal relations (e.g., jealousy, disrespect, quarrelsomeness, and dominating behavior), and voluntary departure from the leave situation. Failures on home leave most frequently consisted in antisocial behavior (e.g., crimes, sexual misbehavior, pregnancy, and minor antisocial actions). Failures on family care most often resulted from environmental lack of support (e.g., parental disinterest, closed home, parental interferences, and community objection), poor health (e.g., medical problems, seizures, and excessive need for care), and intolerable behavior (e.g., lack of proper hygiene habits, untidiness, temper, hyperactivity, destructiveness, and sleeping problems). These differences in the reasons for failure, the authors point out, offer evidence that different processes operate in the different leave programs to produce failure. The frequent failures of the family care patients for health and intolerable personal behavior indicate the unique problems of the moderately retarded patient. With health, there may be the additional factor of the emphasis placed by family caretakers on this aspect of the patient's adjustment. The high incidence of antisocial behavior among home leave patients, in contrast with vocational leave patients, possibly reflects the selection process which occurs within the institution prior to referral for placement (e.g., patients with a marked history of antisocial behavior would be carefully screened for vocational placement). The emotional ties between family and patient may be an additional factor in the high proportion of returns for antisocial behavior, i.e., there may be a relatively great reluctance to return one's own child voluntarily to the institution until a major difficulty necessitates police intervention. Moreover, it is likely that those factors in the home environment which originally led to the antisocial behavior and ultimately to commitment remain in effect to influence the patient while he is on home leave. Such an explanation was supported by the high percentage of failures arising from lack of support in the home leave situation. In the family care group, the percentage of failures resulting from lack of environmental support was much higher than in the home leave group, a fact which indicates the relative difficulty of maintaining foster homes for the moderately retarded. At the same time, there appears to be little risk of antisocial behavior among family care patients. Inadequate work performance, as might be expected, plays a large role in the failure of vocational leave patients by the very requirements of this type of placement. Existing anxieties and emotional difficulties express themselves in the work performance of the patient, which may result in complaints by the patient's supervisor or in the patient's own voluntary resignation from his vocational placement. According to the results of the study, there is a surprisingly great likelihood that interpersonal difficulties will occur in the quasi-vocational setting of vocational placements. This could be merely another manifestation of a patient's vocational maladjustment or it could be a reflection of a primary difficulty in interpersonal relations which manifests itself in all areas. The same interpersonal difficulties may exist in the home leave situation, but perhaps may go unnoticed because of the less intensive and comprehensive responsibility of the social worker in the home leave area.

The aforementioned findings of Windle, Stewart, and Brown (1961) appear to be generally reflective of the kinds of results which other investigators of the problem have reported. In studies of retardates in family care situations, Meyer (1951) and Bishop (1957) both reported data which agreed with those of Windle, Stewart, and Brown, with respect to the roles played by lack of environmental support and intolerable behavior in the retardate's maladjustment. In a related study on this point, Crump and Harry (1964) have found residence in foster homes to be a strong aid in the vocational rehabilitation of retardates. These foster homes assisted the retardates in learning and practicing good personal and social habits, and in learning to use leisure time wisely. In investigations of patients in vocational placement, Brown (1952), O'Connor (1957), and Collman and Newlyn (1956) reported results which were in general accord with Windle, Stewart, and Brown's findings on the factors involved in vocational maladjustment. Most of these studies, however, have indicated that many of these patients do succeed in their vocational adjustments. As an example, Collman and Newlyn (1956), in evaluating the post-school employment of a group of 223 mild retardates, showed that 61 percent were self-supporting and an additional 11 percent partially self-supporting.

In researches which studied combined home and vocational leave populations, Craft (1958), Potter and McCollister (1926), Rudolf (1950), Stanley and Gunzburg (1956), and Tarjan and Benson (1953) all disclosed data which, in affirmation of Windle, Stewart, and Brown's findings, indicated that bad conduct or character defects accounted for the majority of adjustment failures.

The various kinds of community maladjustment problems toward which the retardate himself, as we have just seen, contributes heavily in many cases point to the importance of before-the-fact identification of those traits and tendencies which would be most likely to lead to adjustment and those which would be most likely to lead to maladjustment. The question is thus raised: To what degree and in what possible way can one prognose or predict the kind of adjustment a given retardate is likely to effect when released to the community from an institution? This question has generated some degree of theoretical and research interest in the problem of retardate prognosis, particularly among psychologists, one of whose principal functions is to evaluate the retarded individual in terms of his intellectual and emotional functioning and his social and vocational potential (e.g., Fry (1956); Gunzburg (1959); Shafter (1957); and Sloan (1948)). While psychological studies on patient prognosis have yielded results that are not always consistent, certain conclusions can be drawn in a suggestive and tentative way, as Windle (1962) has done in his comprehensive review of the question. According to Windle's (1962) integration of the material, it appears that the older a patient is, up to an as yet unspecified age, at the time of release from an institution, the more likely he is to succeed on vocational or home placement. Both children and elderly people tend to adjust better than young adults in family care placements. On the other hand, those originally institutionalized at either a very young or a very mature age are less likely to be released to the community at all than those originally institutionalized between the ages of ten years and twenty years. The patient's sex seems to be prognostically unimportant for retardate adjustment. Patients with cultural-familial or undifferentiated diagnoses are more likely to be released from institutions than are patients with specific clinical disorders. Intelligence has been found to be highly related to likelihood of institutional release, though it has not been found to be an adequate predictor of subsequent community adjustment. The fact that it is extremely difficult, if not entirely impossible, to predict retardate adjustment purely from an intelligence measure points to the need for considering the total psychodiagnostic and clinical picture, and not merely an IQ score per se. The importance of this consideration cannot be overemphasized. All too often, a psychodiagnostic assessment and evaluation of a retardate is equated with an IQ score to the exclusion of other amplifying and modifying factors in the patient's intellectual and emotional functioning. It is the whole configuration of the retardate's personality which must be evaluated. The IQ level, while important to be sure, is only one of the many factors which must be considered in the psychological evaluation of the retardate. That such is the case can be illustrated by a comparative capsule analysis of three patients with comparable IQs in the mildly retarded-borderline category whom the authors have had the opportunity to study intensively at the Willowbrook State School in Staten Island, New York. In these three cases, despite the near identity of IQ scores, totally different predictions of adjustment would have had to be made on the basis of a configuration of all the psychological factors.

Baldwin is a basically cooperative adult male with an IQ of 69, who presents himself in a fairly spontaneous, self-assertive, and at times temperamental manner. Though he is well oriented to his circumscribed world within the institution, where he worked as a messenger, Baldwin would probably be in a quandary were he to find himself in a new and strange geographical location in the community. His memory for details is excellent, and while he might be able to recall with accuracy a set of travel directions, Baldwin could not at all be expected to translate the verbal knowledge into action in order to carry out the directions and thereby to navigate his way in the community. As a result, vocational placement in the community would not be feasible. Because of his somewhat idiosyncratic and temperamental qualities, Baldwin's adjustment in a family care situation is problematical. In view of Baldwin's social limitations, his continuous institutionalization since early childhood, and his satisfactory and content adjustment within the institution, a continuance of his present status would appear to be the most reasonable course for the patient.

Rachel is a pleasant late-adolescent female with an IQ of 68, who relates to others in a somewhat child-like and impulsive way. Part of Rachel's child-like behavior is her continual excessive curiosity. She has a tendency to tease others, though always in a playful, good-natured, and nonharmful way. At times, her manner is disarming. Rachel is well oriented to her environment and would probably be able to learn to negotiate her way to a limited extent in the community. She is able to perform domestic tasks well, and she is particularly skillful in sewing. In her case, placement in a family-care situation, in which she could employ her domestic skills, would seem to be a reasonable possibility. Her child-like behavior could easily be handled without difficulty and would create no real household management problem. Rachel should be able to make her way in the neighborhood were there an errand to perform, and to handle money to the extent required in making a small purchase. On the other hand, Rachel could not be expected to fend for herself in the community in the absence of a well-structured, supervised, and somewhat sheltered and delimited environment.

Stephen is a basically agreeable young adult male with an IQ of 71, who has a tendency to become defensive, hostile, and aggressive at times if he feels threatened, particularly by physical harm. His behavior is usually cooperative, and his motivation positive. If he has the feeling that he is being treated in a fair and honest way, he will behave and perform well in whatever situation he finds himself. Stephen has assorted job skills, particularly in the manual and mechanical realm, and his work habits are good. He is reasonably well oriented to the world at large, and he would have minimal difficulty in making his way from place to place in the community. For Stephen, vocational placement would be an appropriate community experience, with consideration of eventual discharge to the community in his own custody. In the right job setting with an understanding and democratic employer, Stephen could make a successful and productive community adjustment.

It is evident from the foregoing descriptions that the prognoses for these three retarded patients differ from one another to a significant degree, despite the fact that all three patients function intellectually within three IQ points of one another. Baldwin would need the full protective custody of an institutional environment. Rachel could adjust to the quasi-sheltered setting of a family-care placement. Stephen would be able to function in a vocational situation, make his way in the community at large, and eventually live the autonomous life of a full-fledged citizen. Thus, IQ score per se is insufficient as a basis for making a prognosis of social adjustment. One must consider the total psychological structuring of the patient's life, with all of its individual variations.

Experiments in Social Living Among Retardates

Directly related to the question of predicting a retardate's adjustment in the community is the problem of preparing and readying the retardate for such an experience. The existing training programs which have been instituted for this purpose have generally taken the form of experiments in social living of one kind or another among groups of retardates. A number of such social experiments, which usually consist in the establishment of some kind of community in miniature, have been reported in the literature. One of the forms which these experiments typically have taken is the development of student government programs in institutions for the mentally retarded, variously known as Merit Wards, Honor Wards, Self-Determination Wards, and Achievement Wards. Briefly, the Merit Ward refers to a segregated unit within an institution for the mentally retarded where, in return for certain privileges, patients are expected to accept greater responsibility in conducting their personal, social, and vocational lives. This concept of student government subscribes to the philosophy that providing youth with the opportunity and experience in self-determination within an institutional community enhances the individual's potential for adequate citizenship in the larger society to which he will eventually return. In 1938, Kephart found that the mere segregation of one group (cottage) from the other groups in a training school will result in greater group unity, and there will be a greater chance for self-determination among the patients. This philosophy is spelled out further by Shafter and Chandler (1960) in their offering of the following representative statements which have been made by institutional administrators about the Merit Ward system:

The underlying philosophy is to give the rehabilitable patients an opportunity to adjust to outside living and still have the protection of the institution. The Merit Wards serve as a means of determining discharge and give the institution an opportunity to observe adaptability, social adjustment, and ability to perform before he or she leaves the institution for living in our present day society.

The philosophy of this procedure is to instill in the patients an attitude that they can be trusted. It instills in them a feeling of self-confidence and the knowledge that they are potential candidates for wage placement or conditional discharge.

The cardinal purpose of the Merit Ward program is threefold: (1) To help vocational placement candidates gain social skills and values necessary to extra-mural living, (2) to provide an award for good institutional adjustment, and (3) to provide the professional staff with an opportunity for better evaluation of potentially rehabilitable patients (p. 1033).

A typical experiment in self-determination has been described by Kirk and Johnson (1951), who provide an account of a program concerned with the social rehabilitation of the educably retarded at the Wayne County Training School. In this experiment, retarded students were organized into unified subgroups which were homogeneous with respect to age and intellectual level. Through this homogeneity and unification, the experiment in student government gradually developed the principle of group acceptance as a potent disciplinary force. The selection of new members by the unified subgroups developed strong ties within the group, with the consequent social approval acting as the motivation for acceptable student behavior. The institution's desire to develop socially acceptable adjustment among the students was thus achieved without the imposition of institutional demands for conformity.

Klauminzer and Kille (1950) described a "conference method" technique which was utilized to bring together retarded boys to discuss some of the problems of their state school. Such discussion groups, the authors found, created a sense of responsibility in the retardates in relation to their school, and helped the boys to learn to cooperate in and as a group, and to analyze problems and proposals in a meaningful, governing fashion.

In a discussion of self-government in a children's institution, Putsch (1945) has similarly attested to the positive value of this kind of experiment. Group living, he states, provides youth with a worthwhile and constructive social experience. Self-government, he reports, can provide a consistently unified system of discipline by offering the children an opportunity to have a voice in its operation. As such, it can assist in inculcating in the children a feeling of responsibility for self-government. Davis, Kirkland, and Rostafinski (1963) have demonstrated the same point working with adult retarded women, as have Smith and Hartford (1959), with retarded adolescent boys.

Brown (1967) reports that, as a result of a study of the social systems of retardates, an institutional social group program was implemented with adolescents. A special cottage was set aside, and presided over by a social worker and a student. The emphasis in this program was on inter-system relationships composed of the unitary grouping of individual, family, and society. Bringing these various aspects into the life of the retardate broadened his abilities for social adaptation, and, incidentally, also helped the parents to handle better their attitudes toward having a retarded offspring.

Moorman (1967) has described the workings of a social education center (established within an institution for the retarded), which was designed to simulate, as nearly as possible, the milieu of a normal home. The ultimate goal of the program was to enable the participants to engage in normal community living, utilizing such activities as home maintenance training, budgeting, and self-improvement training. Eight boys and four girls (CAs 9-16; IQs 42-70) participated in the program, and they demonstrated increased social skills and favorable behavioral changes. They also ended up engaging in a wider variety of social situations.

Edgerton and Dingman (1964), working with institutionalized retardates, demonstrated that nonsupervised "dating" activities facilitated the learning of essential aspects of social living. As a consequence of such activities, the retardates learned to utilize subtle communications and to control their sexual impulses better, and, perhaps most important of all, grew to understand and to internalize the rules for acceptable social behavior.

What the principles of the Merit Ward all reduce to is the elementary concept, so important for the retardate, that with privileges comes responsibility. The particular privileges granted and the special responsibilities expected are varied, as indicated by Shafter and Chandler's survey (1960) of existing Merit Ward programs. The privileges usually include ground privileges, better quarters, more off-ground privileges, extra parties and entertainment, more professional staff attention, community day work, the free use of television, later bedtimes, self-government, more time off, more liberal vacation policy, and the use of special equipment. The responsibilities usually include maintenance of one's own discipline, care of room and/or ward, care of clothes, personal cleanliness, rendering of help to staff in special jobs and events, partial planning of one's own recreation, and traveling to and from work alone. The primary values and benefits of such experiments, as actually observed by administrators of a number of existing programs (Shafter and Chandler, 1960), include the following: the program serves as a preplacement trial at self-living; it acts as an incentive to other patients; it instills a feeling of confidence and trust in the participant; it eliminates or reduces the need for an attendant; it assists in the evaluation of, and steps up, a number of vocational placement candidates; and it increases employee morale. Such advantages are viewed by administrators to outweigh significantly the few disadvantages which the programs created, such as the engendering of jealousy among the nonparticipating patients in the institution. The positive net results of the Merit Ward program, some of them direct benefits to the participating patient and others general advantages to the institution, thus provide a suggestively hopeful picture of the usefulness of such social experiments in the preparation of retardates for community living.

Another approach to the social training of retardates, more traditionally and formally didactic in character than the Merit Ward experiment, involves the actual teaching of community adjustment in social orientation classes. As conceived by Pero (1955), the social orientation class is conducted "for the purpose of teaching and training students to make satisfactory social adjustments within the institution, and in the community should the students be released on a placement basis. . . . It is a teaching medium through which students are taught to become set in correct relation to institution standards, and proper community customs and standards (p. 390)." Pero reports the results of such an orientation class which was held for a group of twenty adolescent and adult mildly mentally retarded students at the State Home and Training School in Wheatridge, Colorado. All of these students had personality and behavior problems and a lack of social knowledge, and they were selected for the orientation class because of the possibility that they might eventually be released on community placement. The topics treated in the class, all enlarged upon by thorough explanation with accompanying question and answer periods, covered a wide variety of areas, including: "Attaining success through achievement and good deeds"; "Understanding limitations and adjusting to them"; "Profitable use of leisure time"; "What to do when faced by unfamiliar situations"; and "Finding a place as an individual, and as a member of a group." The classes continued over a three-year period, with many positive results. Among other things, the students acquired adequate training in solving many of their personal problems without the aid of an employee. They formed a code of ethical values which was helpful in their everyday living. There also was a notable improvement in their conduct and behavior within the institution. There were no escapes among the orientation students. There was an increase in the cultural training and development by those students who were functionally retarded. Students became familiar with the traditions and morals of society in general, as well as those within the institution. A sense of belonging was built up among the students. The students developed self-control, respect for the property of others, recognition of a need to assume their share of responsibility, personal contentment and happiness, increased work interests and more efficient work performance, a desire to succeed, self-confidence and self-reliance, emotional stability, and better human relationships. As was the case with the Merit Ward program, many of the nonparticipating students gained much from their contacts with the orientation students. The reported success of both these kinds of programs suggests the desirability of establishing such programs on a wide scale throughout institutions for the mentally retarded.

As an example of a community-based social group, Gershenson and Schreiber (1963) have described the operations of a coed social club of adolescent retardates in New York City. The group, consisting of as many as nineteen members (CAs 12-15, IQs 40s to 70s), engaged in a varied host of social and recreational activities. Some of the retardates were joiners, others isolates, and the total program was designed to provide the members with opportunities for encountering successful experiences. The authors did note, however, that the group activities must be carefully selected to suit the functioning level of the group *en toto*.

Thus, for those retardates who may be too handicapped for any type of employment situation, activity programs may be an answer. As described by Cortazzo (1964), these retardates are offered an opportunity to participate with others who are similarly retarded in training and in adjustment to activities of daily living. Such programs act as a buffer against any increase in social isolation and devaluation, and they also serve to develop positive peer and familial relationships.

References

Baller, W.R. A study of the present social status of a group of adults who, when they were in elementary schools, were classified as mentally deficient. *Genetic Psychology Monographs*, 1936, 18, 165-244.

Bialer, I., and Cromwell, R.L. Failure as motivation with mentally retarded children. *American Journal of Mental Deficiency*, 1965, 69, 680.

Bishop, E.B. Family care: The patients. *American Journal of Mental Deficiency*, 1957, 61, 583-591.

Bobroff, A. Economic adjustment of 121 adults formerly students in classes for mental retardates. *American Journal of Mental Deficiency*, 1956, 60, 525-535.

Brandon, M.W.G. A survey of 200 women discharged from a mental deficiency hospital. *Journal of Mental Science*, 1960, 106, 355-370.

Brown, D.L. The working convalescent care program for female patients at Rome State School. *American Journal of Mental Deficiency*, 1952, 56, 643-654.

Brown, L.N. Social work with retardates in their social systems. *Mental Retardation*, 1967, 5 (3), 17-20.

Butterfield, E.C., and Zigler, E. The influence of differing institutional social climates on the effectiveness of social reinforcement in the mentally retarded. *American Journal of Mental Deficiency*, 1965, 70, 48-56.

Capobianco, R., and Cole, D. Social behavior of mentally retarded children. *American Journal of Mental Deficiency*, 1960, 64, 638-651.

Clarke, A.D.B.; Clarke, A.M.; and Reiman, S. Cognitive and social changes in the feebleminded—three further studies. *British Journal of Psychology*, 1958, 49, 144-157.

Collman, R.D., and Newlyn, D. Employment success of educationally subnormal ex-pupils in England. *American Journal of Mental Deficiency*, 1956, 60, 733-744.

Cortazzo, A.D. Increasing sociability for the retarded through activity programs. *Journal of Rehabilitation*, 1964, 30 (2), 13-14.

Craft, M. Withdrawals from license in mental deficiency. *American Journal of Mental Deficiency*, 1958, 63, 47-49.

Crump, W.A., and Harry, W.M. Foster homes help mentally retarded. *Rehabilitation Record*, 1964, 5, 23-25.

Davies, S.P. *Social control of the mentally deficient*. New York: Crowell, 1930.

Davis, H.; Kirkland, M.; and Rostafinski, M. Self-government for retarded patients. *Mental Hospitals*, 1963, 14, 392-394.

Delp, H.A., and Lorenz, M. Follow-up of 84 public school special class pupils with IQs below 50. *American Journal of Mental Deficiency*, 1953, 58, 175-182.

Edgerton, R.B., and Dingman, H.F. Good reasons for bad supervision: "Dating" in a hospital for the mentally retarded. *Psychiatric Quarterly Supplement*, 1964, 38, 221-233.

Fernald, W.E. After-care study of the patients discharged from Waverly for a period of twenty-five years. *Ungraded*, 1919, 5, 25-31.

Foley, R.W. A study of patients discharged from the Rome State School for the twenty year period ending Dec. 31, 1924. *Journal of Psycho-Asthenia*, 1929, 34, 180-207.

Fry, L.M. A predictive measure of work success of high grade mental defectives *American Journal of Mental Deficiency*, 1956, 61, 402-408.

Gershenson, S., and Schreiber, M. Mentally retarded teenagers in a social group. *Children*, 1963, 10, 104-108.

Goldstein, H. Social and occupational adjustment. In H.A. Stevens, and R. Heber (Eds.) *Mental Retardation*. Chicago: University of Chicago, 1964. Pp. 214-258.

Gunzburg, H.C. Earl's moron-battery and social adjustment. *American Journal of Mental Deficiency*, 1959, 64, 92-103.

Hollis, J.H. The effects of social and nonsocial stimuli on the behavior of profoundly retarded children: Part I. Part II. *American Journal of Mental Deficiency*, 1965, 69, 755-771; 772-789.

Johnson, B.S. A study of cases discharged from Laconia State School from July 1, 1924 to July 1, 1934. *American Journal of Mental Deficiency*, 1946, 50, 437-445.

Jordan, T.E. *The mentally retarded*. Columbus: Charles E. Morrill, 1961; revised edition, 1965.

Jordan, T.E., and de Charms, R. The achievement motive in normal and mentally retarded children. *American Journal of Mental Deficiency*, 1959, 64, 457-466.

Kephart, N.C. A method of heightening social adjustment in an institutional group. *American Journal of Orthopsychiatry*, 1938, 8, 710-717.

Kinder, E.F.; Chase, A.; and Buck, E.W. Data secured during a follow-up study of girls discharged from supervised parole from Letchworth Village. *American Journal of Mental Deficiency*, 1941, 45, 572-578.

Kinder, E.F., and Rutherford, E. Social adjustment of retarded children. *Mental Hygiene*, 1927, 11, 811-833.

Kirk, S.A., and Johnson, G.O. *Educating the retarded child*. Boston: Houghton-Mifflin, 1951. Pp. 341-357.

Klauminzer, F.Z., and Kille, E.C. The conference method with older, mentally defective children. *American Journal of Mental Deficiency*, 1950, 55, 198-207.

Kolstoe, O.P. An examination of some characteristics which discriminate between employed and non-employed mentally retarded males. *American Journal of Mental Deficiency*, 1961, 66, 472-482.

Lee, J.L.; Hegge, T.G.; and Voelker, P.H. *A study of social adequacy and of social failure of mentally retarded youth in Wayne County, Michigan*. Michigan: Wayne State University, 1959.

Lingren, R.H. Anxiety, praise and reproof: Their effects upon learning and recall of MR boys. *American Journal of Mental Deficiency*, 1967, 72, 468.

Little, A.N., and Johnson, B.S. A study of the social and economic adjustment of 133 discharged parolees from Laconia State School. *Proceedings of the Association for the Study of the Feebleminded*, 1932, 56, 233-251.

Lurie, L.A.; Schlam, L.; and Frieberg, M. Critical analysis of the progress of fifty-five feebleminded children over a period of eight years. *American Journal of Orthopsychiatry*, 1932, 2, 58-59.

Marchand, J.G., Jr. Changes of psychometric test results in mental defective employment care patients. *American Journal of Mental Deficiency*, 1956, 60, 852-859.

Matthews, M. One hundred institutionally trained male defectives in the community under supervision. *Mental Hygiene*, 1922, 6, 332-342.

McKeon, R.M. Mentally retarded boys in wartime. *Mental Hygiene*, 1946, 30, 47-55.

Meyer, G.A. Twelve years of family care at Belchertown State School. *American Journal of Mental Deficiency*, 1951, 55, 414-417.

Mitchell, A. A study of the social competence of a group of institutionalized retarded children. *American Journal of Mental Deficiency*, 1955, 60, 354-361.

Moorman, C. The training centre: VI. A social education centre. *Journal of Mental Subnormality*, 1967, 13, 88-92.

Myers, R. Teacher's judgments of social success and sociometric scores. *American Journal of Mental Deficiency*, 1961, 65, 462-466.

O'Connor, N. The successful employment of the mentally handicapped. In L.T. Hilliard and B.H. Kirman (Eds.) *Mental Deficiency*. London: Churchill, 1957. Pp. 448-480.

Pero, J.F. Social orientation method of social training in an institution. *American Journal of Mental Deficiency*, 1955, 60, 390-396.

Peterson, L., and Smith L. A comparison of post-school adjustment of educable mentally retarded adults with that of adults of normal intelligence. *Exceptional Children*, 1960, 26, 404-408.

Phelps, H.R. Post-school adjustment of mentally retarded children in selected Ohio cities. *Exceptional Children*, 1956, 23, 58-62, 91.

Potter, H.W., and McCollister, C.L. A resume of parole work at Letchworth Village. *Proceedings of the American Association for the Study of the Feebleminded*, 1926, 31, 165-188.

Putsch, L. *Self-government in a children's institution*. New York: Child Welfare League of America, 1945.

Rudolf, G. De M. Improvement in mental defectives in colonies. *Journal of Mental Science*, 1950, 96, 272-275

Shafter, A.J. Criteria for selecting institutionalized mental defectives for vocational placement. *American Journal of Mental Deficiency*, 1957, 61, 599-616.

Shafter, A.J., and Chandler, C.S. Merit Wards—settings for social and vocational training. *American Journal of Mental Deficiency*, 1960, 64, 1029-1033.

Shimberg, M., and Reichenberg, W. The success and failure of subnormal problem children in the community. *Mental Hygiene*, 1933, 17, 451-465.

Sloan, W.P. Prediction of extra-mural adjustment of mental defectives by use of the Rorschach Test. *Journal of Consulting Psychology*, 1948, 12, 303-309.

Smith, R.V., and Hartford, R.J. A social group work program in an institution for the mentally retarded. *American Journal of Mental Deficiency*, 1959, 63, 897-902.

Stanley, R.J., and Gunzburg, H.C. A survey of residential licenses from a mental deficiency hospital. *International Journal of Social Psychiatry*, 1956, 2, 207-213.

Sternlicht, M., Bialer, I., and Deutsch, M.R. Influence of external incentives on motor performance of institutionalized retardates. *Journal of Mental Deficiency Research*, 1970, 14, 149-154.

Sternlicht, M., and Siegel, L. Time orientation and friendship patterns of institutionalized retardates. *Journal of Clinical Psychology*, 1968, 24, 26-27.

Stevenson, H., and Cruse, D. The effectiveness of social reinforcement with normal and feebleminded children. *Journal of Personality*, 1961, 29, 124-135.

Stevenson, H.W., and Fahel, L.S. The effect of social reinforcement on the performance of institutionalized and noninstitutionalized normal and feebleminded children. *Journal of Personality*, 1961, 29, 136-147.

Stevenson, H.W., and Knights, R.M. The effectiveness of social reinforcement after brief and extended institutionalization. *American Journal of Mental Deficiency* 1962a, 66, 589-594.

———. Social reinforcement with normal and retarded children as a function of pretraining, sex of E, and sex of S. *American Journal of Mental Deficiency*, 1962b, 66, 866-871.

Storrs, H.C. A report on an investigation made of cases discharged from Letchworth Village. *Journal of Psycho-Asthenia*, 1924, 34, 220-232.

Tarjan, G., and Benson, T. Report on the pilot study at Pacific Colony. *American Journal of Mental Deficiency*, 1953, 57, 453-462.

Terrell, C., and Stevenson, H.W. The effectiveness of normal and retarded peers as reinforcing agents. *American Journal of Mental Deficiency*, 1965, 70, 373-381.

Thomas, B.E. A study of factors used to make a prognoisis of social adjustment. *American Journal of Mental Deficiency*, 1943, 47, 334-336.

Windle, C.D. Prognosis of mental subnormals. *American Journal of Mental Deficiency, Monograph Supplement*, 1962, 66, 1-180.

Windle, C.D.; Stewart, E.; and Brown, S.J. Reasons for community failure of released patients. *American Journal of Mental Deficiency*, 1961, 66, 213-217.

Wolfson, N. Follow-up study of 92 male and 121 female patients who were discharged from Newark State School in 1946. *American Journal of Mental Deficiency*, 1956, 61, 224-238.

Zigler, E.H.; Hodgden, L.; and Stevenson, H.W. The effect of support on the performance of normal and feebleminded children. *Journal of Personality*, 1958, 26, 106-122.

7

Behavioral Adjustments in the Classroom

The problem of behavioral adjustments in the classroom is a matter of signal importance in the personal life of the retardate for a double reason: first, the classroom provides the retarded child with his first formal exposure to a large social situation in which he has to learn to adjust to others in a group setting; and secondly, the classroom learning experience represents exactly that entity which, by very definition, the retardate lacks and needs. The classroom is the place where the retardate is taught to grow both intellectually and socially, where he is offered the most concentrated and powerful antidote to those deficiencies of intelligence and personality which are the sine qua non of his being. It is here that one witnesses the most highly structured, planned, and formalized attempt to teach and to guide the retardate in the various realms of thinking and behaving. Nor should the curriculum for the retardate be conceived as a mostly academic affair with overriding emphasis upon the three R's. (If any three R's are taught, they should be repetition, routine, and relaxation.) Rather it must be an education in the broadest and most comprehensive sense of the word—an instruction in the matters of being, of living, and of relating to other human beings in the world. The philosophy of special education has been to shield the retardate from failure and to give him only artificial total success experiences. (The major aims in the education of mentally retarded children are an achievement of adequate social adjustment and the establishment and maintenance of good personal relationships with other people.) However, under certain conditions, retarded children can tolerate failure and be positively motivated by failure. As Bialer (1964) has suggested, this tends to indicate that providing the retarded school child with artificial total success and denying him the experience of recognizing and coping with failure may work to his disadvantage, at least insofar as preparation for the realities of post-school existence is concerned. However, the kinds of initial achievements that are gained by retardates may be extremely crucial determiners of subsequent performance and behavior.

All too often, however, and this is a basic problem which confronts the retardate in the classroom learning situation, the academic curriculum falls short of providing the kind of leveled-off and low-keyed experience which is so important to a person who enters the situation in the first place with a limited intellectual capacity. Some curriculum changes are occurring, however, and there has been a lessened emphasis on scholastic performance and a greater stress upon practical life experiences. In addition, special educators are trying to delineate small rather than aggregate units of the retardate's functioning, thereby permitting a more precise micro-identification of his assets and liabilities (and creating an individualized program around these). In addition, because schooling should be a preparation for adult living, and because social acceptability is an important aspect of the adult retardate's life, a concentrated effort to teach the retarded child the value of cooperative and coordinated experiences in socializing activities with his peers is warranted. In this connection, there remains a growing need for an interdisciplinary approach to the problems of the educable mentally retarded. A recent study by Sternlicht, Deutsch, and Alperin (1970) has highlighted this need by examining the relationship between psychological assessment and academic performance among institutionalized retardates. What the authors found was that considerable disagreement existed between the psychologist and the teacher over the question of academic potential among the students. They concluded that there remains a need for further examination of the relationship between measured psychological potential and actual classroom performance.

At the same time, however, one cannot exclude entirely the teaching of the three R's to the retarded child, for, to a certain extent, these serve as basic raw materials which the retardate uses in his general life adjustment. What is necessary in this regard is to work out a specialized approach in the teaching of the basic subjects which takes into account both the generally limited intellectual capacity of the retardate and the individual variability among retardates in their approach to a learning situation. As Abel and Kinder (1942) have stated:

Children are expected to succeed in school—particularly, they are expected to succeed in the three R's. Without the ability to read and write and compute any child actually is, and also as she grows older feels herself to be, handicapped not merely in her school situation but also at home and in her own community. The subnormal girl wants to read books, newspapers, signboards, as do other girls. She wants to receive and to write letters. She does not want to be considered a 'dummy' by her peers. Usually she is strongly motivated to acquire some skill in the fundamental school subjects if she has not experienced failure and discouragement all along the line in the elementary school classroom. Furthermore, the subnormal girl who acquires at least some ability to read, spell, write, and solve simple problems in arithmetic is in a better position to make educational and social adjustments than is the less literate girl (pp. 58-59).

Thus, whereas, the three R's must be geared carefully to the level of the retardate's capacity to absorb, they cannot be and should not be eliminated from the teaching program altogether. What is important to bear in mind is that the retardate's learning ability is not different in *kind* from that of the intellectually normal person, but merely different in *degree*. The retardate does not utilize a different order of thought process in the learning situation from that which the normal person uses; rather he is limited in the rate at which he can absorb the learning material and in the level which he can ultimately reach. That such is the case is attested to by a host of experimental studies which have explored the durability of learning in the retardate. Investigations by Baumeister (1963),

Hetherington and Banta (1962), and Johnson and Blake (1960), for example, all have suggested that once he has acquired verbal associations, though his rate of acquisition may be relatively slow, the retardate will remember these associations almost as well as the intellectually normal person. Two other studies of verbal learning among retardates and among normals—Deutsch and Sternlicht (1967), and Sternlicht and Deutsch (1966)—bear out this point more graphically. These two studies investigated certain theoretical aspects of the so-called von-Restorff effect, i.e., the phenomenon of superior recall of items that are isolated in a series of otherwise homogeneous items, and found that while the normal subjects demonstrated a higher level of recall of the isolated item in the series than did the retarded subjects, the normals and retardates both recalled the isolated item according to the same perceptual pattern. As Sternlicht and Deutsch (1966) observed:

It should be noted that the isolation effect . . . is of somewhat smaller magnitude in the mentally retarded Ss tested in the present experiment than in the intellectually superior Ss tested in the authors' previous experiment. This difference in degree can be attributed partly perhaps to the limited learning and memory capacity of the retardate under optimal conditions, such that less than half of the retardates (15 out of 40) were able to recall the isolated item correctly, whereas almost all of the college students (57 out of 60) were able to recall the isolated item correctly. At the same time, however, the fact that the isolation effect obtains at all with the mentally retarded S suggests a similarity in the learning and memory patterns of normals and retardates (pp.67-68).

Thus, the learning patterns and cognitive styles of retardates are essentially the same as those of normals, with only the degree and level of learning varying between the two groups. There is a quantitative difference, but not necessarily a qualitative one. As Baumeister (1967) has said in a discussion of learning deficiencies in the retardate:

This is not to say that we should expect to see a set of behavioral laws that apply to retardates and not to normals and vice versa. In writing a formula for behavioral output, one might expect to see essentially the same set of terms for both populations but with the values of certain constants differing (p. 182).

It thus appears that the problems of the retardate in the classroom center not so much around his performance abilities per se, but rather around the total behavioral context in which his performance is embedded. This behavioral context includes the whole personality of the retardate, and more particularly those personality traits which were discussed in chapter 4, most notably his rigidity, his distractibility, his low frustration tolerance, his impulsivity, and his aggressiveness. It is this complex of personal factors which forms the behavioral nucleus that creates special classroom difficulties for the retardate, and which calls for appropriate techniques and procedures to deal with them. In fact, as Snyder,

Jefferson, and Strauss (1965) have shown, greater emphasis should be placed upon personality variables, particularly the self-concept, than on IQs in considering a special education program. In addition, the mere entrance into a school situation may present problems for the retardate, who may have already experienced prior difficulties, thus placing him in an especially vulnerable position. As an example, the retardate may be made to feel "different" from his schoolmates, since he generally starts his schooling at a later age, and he may be teased and ridiculed by his peers. Accordingly, the present discussion will consider some of these difficulties, with particular emphasis upon two principal situational dimensions of the problem: first, the relationship between class composition and behavioral adjustment; and secondly, the effect of teacher attitudes and approaches upon the retardate's classroom behavior.

The Relationship Between Class
Composition and Behavioral Adjustment

While there is more than one dimension in terms of which one may consider the question of the composition of a group of classroom students, the most important in its effect upon the behavioral adjustment of the retardate is that of intellectual homogeneity and heterogeneity of the student population. This problem, which has been treated widely in the literature, reduces itself to the question of special-class vs. regular-class placement for the retarded student (e.g., Baldwin (1958); Blatt (1958); Fine (1967); Johnson (1950); Johnson (1961); Johnson and Kirk (1950); Jordan and de Charms (1959); Kaplan (1961); Kern and Pfaeffle (1963); Mayer (1966); Mullen and Itkin (1961); Ross (1965); Sparks and Blackman (1965); and Thurstone (1959)). The question is posed: Which is more conducive to healthy behavioral, personal, and social adjustment in the mental retardate: placement in a special class composed entirely of other retarded students or placement in a regular class composed primarily of intellectually normal students? There has been no simple and straightforward answer to this question, but rather a set of cogent and meaningful arguments on both sides of the issue. On the one hand, those investigators who have found special-class placement to be more advantageous to the retardate have emphasized the fact that the retardate will adjust better among a group of his peers because of his feeling of familiarity and acceptance. On the other hand, those investigators who have found regular-class placement to be more beneficial have pointed to the fact that the retardate will be better stimulated and motivated (especially, but not exclusively, in the academic sphere) in the company of a group of intellectually normal students and will thus be better able to achieve full actualization of his potentialities.

Support for the latter position is provided by various studies which have demonstrated that retarded children enrolled in regular classes tend to be superior in educational achievement to those placed in special classes. In an early investigation of this type, Bennett (1932) compared two IQ-matched groups of 50 retarded children each, one in regular classes and the other in special classes, and found that the regular-class students were superior to the special-class students in educational achievement and in such areas as speech and motor coordination. Similarly, Pertsch (1936), in a study which match-paired 278 retarded children in regular special classes in terms of chronological age, mental age, IQ, sex, and racial extraction, found that those who remained in the regular grades were superior in both educational achievement and personal adjustment. It has been pointed out, however, that in both these studies an experimental error in the form of a selection bias exists, such that it is precisely those mentally retarded children who are inferior educationally and more troublesome behaviorally who are most likely to be the ones selected for special-class placement. Bennett and Pertsch both recognized this problem themselves and took note of it in their reports. In relation to this selection factor, Bennett (1932) states: ". . . In general, the findings that are given below could not be explained without further research. They may be due either to segregation in special classes or they may be due to selection—to the factor involved in the identification of special class children by the teachers who nominate them and by the authorities who select them (p. 76)." And Pertsch (1936) said in this connection: "The uniformly superior attainment of the graded groups cannot be interpreted as entirely due to the policy of non-segregation since the factor of selection may be an actual determiner (p. 82)." (In this regard, McCoy (1963) discovered that the academic achievement of the mentally retarded was significantly influenced by such ego factors as the realistic degree of their self-confidence, the amount of realism in their levels of aspiration, and the way in which they view themselves as being accepted by their peers.) Carrying the effect of this kind of selection error one step further, Cowen (1938) made a statistical reanalysis of Pertsch's data and discovered that in actuality the percentage of mean gain in educational achievement was for the most part greater for the special-class group than for the regular-class group, a reversal of what Pertsch had found.

In an effort to control for the aforementioned selection error, Blatt (1958) undertook an investigation comparing the physical, academic, and personality status of seventy-five retarded children and young adolescents attending special classes and that of fifty retarded children and young adolescents attending regular classes in communities in which there are no special classes. The two groups were equated on the variables of chronological age, mental age, intelligence, and sex. The results of the study indicate generally that no significant differences exist between special-class and regular-class retarded students in the three areas investigated. In the physical area, the power of the retarded children, as measured by the vertical jump, their grip strength as measured by the hand dynamometer, and their motor ability, as measured by the Brace Scale of Motor Ability, was not significantly different in the two groups. In the academic realm, the reading, arithmetic, and language achievement of the retarded students as measured by the California Achievement Tests was not significantly different in the two groups. In the personal sphere, the personal and social adjustment of the retarded subjects, as measured by the California Test of Personality, was not significantly different in the two groups. It should be noted here that while the procedure used by Blatt minimized the effect of selection error, it did not eliminate it altogether. As Kirk (1964) has observed in this connection: "Although Blatt partially controlled the selection factor, he did not succeed in eliminating this very important factor, since his two groups are still not comparable. One group contained the obvious cases who were referred to special classes, and the other group contained both the obvious cases who would have been referred had there been special classes in that community and also the less obvious cases who normally would have remained in the regular classes (p. 58)." At the same time, however, despite this remaining selection bias favoring regular-class placement, Blatt reported a suggestive exception to his general finding in favor of the special-class group. As rated by teachers using as-yet unvalidated scales of social maturity and emotional stability, the special-class students were found to be more socially mature and emotionally stable than the regular-class students. This result is worthy of further consideration because it is a finding that has been reflected in other studies which have explored more fully the problem of social adjustment and class placement.

In one such study on a total of 1,273 retarded children in regular and special classes, Thurstone (1959) found that sociometric and teacher ratings of the social acceptance and adjustment of the two groups showed a superiority of the special-class students. "If their ratings are sound," Thurstone asserted, "mentally handicapped children in special classes are emotionally better adjusted, have a higher regard for their own mental ability, participate more widely in learning and social activities, and possess more traits desired by their peers than do their counterparts in regular grades (p. 59)."

The kinds of results obtained by Thurstone, as well as by other investigators (e.g., Ellenbogen (1957); Jordan (1959); Miller (1956); and Mullen and Itkin (1961)), favoring special-class placement for the retardate in the area of social adjustment can perhaps be understood in the light of the findings of an earlier study by Johnson (1950), which explored the social position of mentally retarded children in regular elementary school classes. In particular, Johnson wanted to know the answers to the following questions: (1) Are the mentally retarded children in regular classes accepted, isolated, or rejected?; (2) To what extent are the mentally retarded children in regular classes accepted, isolated, or rejected?; and (3) Is there any difference in the social position of groups of children classified according to different degrees of intellectual ability, i.e., is there any difference in the social position of a lower mentally retarded group (IQ below 60), an upper mentally retarded group (IQ from 60 through 69), a borderline group (IQ from 70 through 88), and an intellectually normal group? The study was conducted in two communities in which there were no special classes for the mentally retarded, thereby insuring that all the educable mentally retarded in the communities' public schools were included in the investigation. During a personal interview, a sociometric questionnaire was administered individually to each of 688 children who were asked the following questions designed to determine their best friends: "Who are the children in your class that you like the best?"; "If you were to have your seat changed, who would you like to have sit in the seat next to you?"; and "Who are the children in your class that you like to play with the best?" In addition, each child was asked the following questions designed to determine which classmates he did not like and rejected as companions: "If you were to have your seats changed, who wouldn't you like to have sit in the seat next to you?"; "Who are the children in your class that you do not like to play with?"; and "Who are the children in your class that you do not like?" Every child was further asked his reasons for accepting or rejecting other children. The results of the study indicated that the mentally retarded children were significantly more rejected than were the intellectually normal children. In addition, the borderline children were more rejected than the intellectually normal children, the retarded children were more rejected than the borderline children, and the lower mentally retarded children were the most rejected of all. Thus, the higher the intelligence of the children, the less rejected they were by their classmates. Concerning the reasons for rejection, the retarded children were usually rejected because of their behavior in the classroom, at the playground, and away from the school. The majority of the reasons involved certain behaviors, compensatory in character, on the part of the retardate, such as bullying, fighting, misbehaving, showing off, swearing, lying, and cheating. It was pointed out by Johnson that such behaviorisms may well have been the consequence of the retardate's inability to compete in intellectually demanding situations. On the other hand, the retarded children were seldom rejected because of poor academic achievement. On the basis of his findings, Johnson drew the conclusion that the regular classes were not meeting the needs of the mentally retarded children. "In addition to being significantly different from their classmates intellectually and academically," Johnson (1950) asserted, "the mentally-handicapped children were also segregated socially in spite of their physical presence within the grade group. This implies that in public school education, segregation does not necessarily mean removing a child from his group and placing him in a special class. It means that a child may be socially segregated although physically a part of the group (p. 86)." The behaviors on the part of the retardate which subject him to this kind of segregation by his classmates have their roots in the nature of the regular-classroom experience. As Johnson (1950) has further pointed out:

A probable explanation of these compensatory behaviors in the mentally-handicapped children may be made on the basis of what we know of the psychology of adjustment. It has been stated that a behavior problem is a result of the discrepancy between the child's capacity to behave and the requirements of the environment. The mentally-handicapped child is expected to be one of the group whether or not the individual subject matter areas have been scaled down to meet his limited capacities and abilities. He is expected to maintain discriminative standards (standards of right and wrong, standards of participation in group activities and games, standards of behavior, standards of cooperation, standards of social etiquette, etc.) that are beyond his abilities. With the imposition of too much discriminative strain, his integration is broken down resulting in the various forms of bizzare and disintegrated activities and behaviorisms observed, such as swearing, stealing, lying, bullying, teasing, etc. (p. 87).

The discrepancy between the child's capacity to behave and the requirements of the environment, of which Johnson (1950) speaks, is a problem which was discussed in chapter 4 as a general consideration in the functioning of the retardate's personality. This discrepancy was seen to be an essential frame of reference for understanding many of the retardate's personality traits. When applied to the retardate's behavioral adjustment in the classroom, the discrepancy between individual capacity and environmental requirements serves to highlight the essential nature of the retardate's personality in a concrete, everyday situation. When the retarded child is confronted by circumstances which are beyond his grasp and with which he therefore cannot satisfactorily cope, he responds with a host of negative behaviors, all embedded in the basic experience of anxiety. To the extent that the regular school class creates such a discrepancy by setting out-of-reach standards of learning for the retardate, an anxious or catastrophic reaction can be expected to occur. It is this reaction which accounts for the various negative and disruptive behaviors which were observed in Johnson's study of mental retardates in regular classes. To the extent that the special school class eliminates or decreases this anxious reaction by reducing the discrepancy which causes it, the retardate can be expected to make an easier and smoother adjustment in the classroom. As Johnson (1950) has put it:

The purpose of the special class curricula is to meet the needs of mentally-handicapped children. Emphasis is placed upon cooperation, social and community adjustment, and the development of good habits and personal cleanliness. The areas in which mentally-handicapped children suffer failure in the regular grades are not emphasized. Instead, emphasis is placed upon their growth and development so that they will become well-adjusted, socially acceptable, contributing members of the community (p. 87).

This argument in favor of special-class placement over regular-class placement for the retardate received added support from a study by Johnson and Kirk (1950), which examined further the question of segregation of retardates in regular classes. Concerned with possible limitations of the aforementioned study by Johnson (1950); the authors asked the question: Were the regular classes in which the study was made so academic and so traditional that they failed to emphasize social adjustments sufficiently to produce an acceptance of the mentally retarded children in these classes? They undertook to answer the question by conducting the same kind of investigation in the setting of a progressive school, which stressed social adjustment rather than academic achievement in the teaching curriculum. The results of the study were very similar to those of Johnson's investigation in the traditional schools, the percentages of isolates and rejectees among the mentally retarded students in the progressive school classes being almost identical with the percentages in the traditional school classes. The reasons for rejection also were similar. Very few of the intellectually normal children rejected the mentally retarded children because they did not learn so fast as the other children, because they did not read, or because they could not achieve in the academic areas. Rather, they rejected the retarded children because of their behaviorisms. These behaviorisms were of a type that can be interpreted as compensations for frustration resulting from failure in school situations in which the retardates cannot compete. Typical answers given as reasons for rejection of the retarded child in both the traditional and the progressive schools were "he teases me," "he cheats in games," "he pulls my hair," "he hits me over the head with his lunch bucket," "he says bad things," "he takes my jumping rope," "he steals my bicycles," and "he stinks." The upshot of these two studies is that although mentally retarded children are physically present and nominally integrated with normal children in a regular class, whether of the traditional or of the progressive type, they are actually segregated in these classes by the intellectually normal children themselves.

In a related sociometric study of 155 mildly and moderately retarded children in public school special classes, Jacobs and Pierce (1968) found a relationship between rejection and the presence of characteristics typically associated with neurological deficit. Those retardates were most rejected who exhibited a short attention span, hyperactivity, emotional lability, and impulsivity.

In an even more demanding test of the social position of the mentally retarded child in regular school classes, Baldwin (1958) studied the problem in the regular classes of a public school system that provided special classes for the mentally retarded as well. Baldwin felt that it was highly probable that the mentally retarded children who were the most objectionable to their classmates had been among the first to be placed in the special classes. In view of this earlier discussed selective factor, it was assumed by Baldwin that a higher degree of social acceptance by their classmates would be found among the regular-class retarded children whom she was studying than among the regular-class retarded children whom Johnson had studied. The results of the investigation, obtained from sociometric tests and personal interviews on 31 mentally retarded children, did not, however, bear out Baldwin's expectation. The degree of social acceptance of the mentally retarded children in regular classes was much lower than that of the intellectually normal children in the same classes. This finding thus reflects the same trend that was observed in Johnson's study. As in Johnson's study, too, it was the antisocial and disruptive behavior of the retarded children that was resented by the other students, and in this case, by the teachers as well. The reasons most frequently given for not accepting the mentally retarded child were: "he bothers us," "he talks back to the teacher," "she's lazy," "she fights too much," "she can't do anything," "he talks too much," "he never studies," "he disturbs our class," and "he can't play." Baldwin's interpretation of the retardate's antisocial behavior agrees with that of Johnson: a form of compensation for a lack of mental ability to cope with a situation in which the mentally retarded child feels inadequate.

In an expanded study of the problem which offers further support of the position taken by Johnson (1950) and Baldwin (1958), Kern and Pfaeffle (1963) made a comparison of the social adjustment of a total of 93 mentally retarded children in three different educational settings: regular classes, special classes for retarded children in a regular school, and classes for retarded children in a special school for the retarded. The results of the study, based upon measures of social adjustment as assessed by the Elementary Form of the California Test of Personality, revealed that the special-school children showed the best overall social adjustment, the regular-class retardates demonstrated the poorest overall adjustment, and the special-class children assumed an intermediate position with regard to social adjustment. These findings thus lend support to the belief that specially-placed retarded children will make a more satisfactory classroom adjustment, although, as Barksdale (1961) has pointed out, placement in a special class per se does not necessarily insure acceptance. In addition, they provide data concerning the relative efficacy of the particular type of special placement: the special school vs. the special class. This subquestion of special placement for the retardate has itself been the subject of considerable dispute among noted authorities in the area. For example, Kirk and Johnson (1951), on the one hand, have been critical of the special-school approach, feeling that the special class is better able to provide for the social needs of retarded students. Wallin (1955), on the other hand, has appeared to favor the special school over the special class, believing that the disadvantages of special schools are greatly exaggerated. The results of Kern and Pfaeffle's study favoring special-school placement shed some light on this largely experimentally virgin area.

The question of class placement for the retardate, however, remains an unsolved problem, largely because there are two ways to look at the question of retardate adjustment. The first is to conceive of adjustment in immediate terms, i.e., the retardate's psychological and social comfort, security, ease of mind, and lack of anxiety and tension in the classroom learning situation itself. This is the general frame of reference for those who advocate special-class placement. The second is to conceive of adjustment in longer-range terms, i.e., the retardate's eventual and ultimate adjustment to his community and world at large, beyond what tensions or discomforts he might have to experience momentarily in the classroom. This is the general frame of reference for those who advocate regular-class placement. A study by Jordan and de Charms (1959) of achievement motivation in regular-class and special-class retarded students pin-points this double aspect of the problem. Their findings indicated that while less academic achievement results from special-class placement, less fear of failure is engendered at the same time. (Based upon a review of the literature, Sparks and Blackman (1965) also arrived at essentially similar conclusions.) The authors suggested that the resolution of this dilemma is to be made in terms of an a priori value decision concerning the purpose for organizing special curricula for the retarded. In teaching the retardate, should the emphasis be placed upon achievement and assimilation into a normal social group as a necessary basis for successful social adjustment in an intellectually normal world, or should the emphasis be placed upon immediate classroom security and acceptance as a requisite condition for emotional and social stability for the retarded? In a follow-up study of educable mentally retarded children trained in both special and regular classes, Porter and Milazzo (1958) found that those who had been in the special classes adjusted better to social standards, formed more permanent community ties (i.e., they drifted less from place to place), and were economically more self-sufficient.

The aforementioned question can be reformulated in terms of social exposure and protection as these were discussed in chapter 6: To what extent should the retardate's classroom learning experience be specially structured, delimited, and circumscribed for him in order to provide the necessary degree of protection and shelter from the demands of the normal classroom environment, without at the same time shrinking his self-concept and crippling his drive for independence? As was the case with social adjustment in general, the answer is to be found in a "golden mean" formula for classroom adjustment which eliminates the excesses of both social overexposure and social overprotection. In terms of actual classroom structure and function, this might mean the development of some kind of intermediate class-room situation containing elements and features of both regular-class and special-class learning.

The Effect of Teacher Attitudes and Approaches Upon the Retardate's Classroom Behavior

A factor equally as important as class composition in the behavioral adjustment of the retardate in the classroom is the attitude and the approach of the teacher. Since the classroom serves as the setting for the retarded child's first formal and sustained exposure to a large social situation, the teacher of the retardate must function not only as a transmitter of information, conveyor of knowledge, and stimulator of ideas, but as a guide, counselor, leader, disciplinarian, and even temporary surrogate parent. As such, her role is a complex and vital one, demanding much from the teacher in the way of training, of experience, and of intuitive know-how. Not only should the educational program be worked out to meet the needs and abilities of the retarded child, but the teachers of this program should be specially trained. The teacher plays an immensely important role in the life of the child, and a good teacher (that is, good for the particular child) can do a great deal to help in his adjustment, while a teacher unsympathetic to the child can injure him in various ways. A well-trained teacher, however, should also be similar to a "good" parent. That is, she should not be detached and objective, but she should be intimately involved with her students and ready to assist them in any area where assistance is needed (e.g., toileting).

Of all of the questions a teacher must consider in connection with the behavioral adjustment of her retarded students, perhaps the most immediate and self-presenting one is the matter of discipline. Given the retarded child's typical personality traits and characteristics, including rigidity, distractibility, low frustration tolerance, impulsivity, and aggressiveness, one can expect a host of behavioral shortcomings, weaknesses, and excesses on the part of the retardate which would constitute a major disciplinary and administrative problem in the classroom. One difficult-to-manage child with a hyperactive, impulsive, noisy behavioral pattern could easily disrupt the orderly group learning experience of an entire class. Similarly, an aggressive, assaultive, abusive youngster would work havoc with a planned class lesson. To a lesser extent, an extremely withdrawn or frightened or reticent or recalcitrant boy or girl would become a special problem if only for the reason that he or she would come to require a very individual teaching approach, perhaps even in the form of tutoring or psychotherapy.

The fact that children of all of these types might be in attendance in the very same class compounds the problem many times over. In light of the manifold nature of the situation, no simple and straightforward prescription for a type of teaching discipline appears to be appropriate or meaningful. One general maxim, however, is that praise should be employed lavishly and punishment rarely, if at all. Each situation must be treated on an individual basis, and the type of discipline geared to the special requirements of the particular class in question. In some situations, a firm and controlling hand is required, whereas in other situations a more permissive and democratic orientation is needed. For all practical purposes, the question becomes: To what extent can a permissive and democratic classroom approach in fact be introduced to the retardate in a reasonable and beneficial way? In a study which helps to answer precisely this question, Harris (1953) undertook to explore the reactions of a group of sixteen institutionalized educably retarded adolescent girls to a permissive atmosphere in an academic classroom. It was the purpose of this study to learn whether or not these girls could adequately control one another and themselves in such a democratic classroom atomosphere, and, if so, whether such a situation was beneficial or detrimental to the development of social maturity and emotional stability. By "permissive atmosphere," the teacher of these girls had in mind the following:

It is one in which the girl, regardless of her behavior, can sense that she is accepted and is free to do and say what she wishes without the fear of being constantly reprimanded for doing so. How the teacher feels is very important in creating this atmosphere, because the pupils will be very apt to sense the deceit if what she does is not an outgrowth of what she really feels. She must accept the girl wholeheartedly, looking upon her not as someone to be disliked and punished because of her unacceptable behavior but as a victim of circumstances, displaying the type of behavior which seems best suited as a means of supplying her present needs (p. 434).

While the girls who composed the class were not selected on the basis of the presence or absence of emotional disturbance, many of them were in fact rather unstable. For example, one of the girls, Sally, would say of herself: "I have been with bad people all my life. My mother has said that I would always be bad. I've decided she is right, and I might as well be bad." Similarly, each of the girls presented an emotional or behavioral classroom problem of one kind or another. Martha, for example, once asked why she hated everybody but God and herself and sometimes even hated herself. Lena did nothing but sit for a long time. She neither worked nor played, and when urged to do so, would say that there was no use, that she was a jailbird, and, as her family had said, would never amount to anything. Bertha was an accomplished procrastinator. She seldom worked or played, but talked a great deal about what she intended to do in the future. For example, she did not intend to study in school because she was going to night school when she returned home and would study there. She would not work in the work areas because she was going to have a big house all to herself when she got older and would then not need to work. Myra would do only the things she wanted to do, when she wanted to do them. She realized that she should not be that way but felt that she could not change herself. Marilyn would say repeatedly: "the harder you try, the less you get." Imogene wept at any slight frustration. May would only sit and stare into space or hang onto the teacher's arm. Anna would pick something up and slam it down, crumple or tear paper, or direct a violent, seemingly unprovoked tirade at another person. Betty did very little work in class. She talked constantly to girls around her, wrote letters to boys, and when not doing either, would stare vacantly into space. Often, at the sound of a boy's voice outside, she would rush to the window. Once, after going to the window, she bolted out of the room and down two flights of stairs toward the outside and the boys' side of the grounds before the teacher could stop her.

The permissive tone that was set for this class of girls is captured in the following description of the opening class session:

The teacher asked the girls what they wanted her to do when they did not behave as they should. She got the following replies: 'Smack them one.' 'Sit them in the corner.' 'Stand them in the corner.' 'Send them to the office.' 'Take their work away from them.' To these suggestions she objected saying that she did not like to do such things to them, because she would not like to be punished that way for her own misbehavior. They said that it would be different for her because she was the teacher; but she insisted on their making some other plan, saying that punishment would not make them really want to do better in the future. Some felt they might say that they were sorry for doing what was wrong. Sally said that this would never do. The girls, she said, would just say they were sorry and continue to misbehave. She sounded the warning that the teacher 'could never stand it' if she did not punish. The majority of the girls agreed with her. The teacher still insisted, however, that she did not want to punish. Someone suggested that expressing sorrow might work if the girls 'were right in their hearts.' Others made comments of that kind, and by questioning the teacher brought out their meaning: that this would work if the expression of sorrow really meant an intention not to do wrong again. It was then decided that the girls would 'take care of themselves,' that if one girl could not refrain from disturbing the group she would go away by herself. Sally raised her hand in a gesture and said, 'You will not have any trouble with me' (p. 438).

The results of the study were essentially positive: the number of times that the teacher had to assume control of a situation, the number of major disturbances involving all or a great majority of the class, and the number of minor disturbances involving less than half of the class were all greater during the first third of the year than during the last third. A descriptive report of a particular class session depicts the operation of the permissive approach and portrays its self-regulatory effect upon the behavior of the group of girls:

Martha constantly wandered around among the girls and bothered them by talking. Elaine asked her not to bother her. Martha said she would do as she pleased. Myra said she wished the girls who were keeping her from working would stay in the living department. Conversation of this kind continued for some time, with Martha using some profane language in response to criticism from the girls. Sally then said that they should not blame Martha for what she was doing as she did it because she was 'dumb,' that everyone here was 'dumb': This brought angry looks and retorts from Bertha, Elaine, Myra, Anna and Lillian. Bertha said she would 'lick' Sally for that statement. Sally immediately walked toward Bertha with clenched fists. The teacher started to intervene, but they all chorused that she should stay out of it, that they could take care of it. And they did. They took Sally to her seat and stood beside her until she showed a willingness to stay there. The teacher suggested to Martha that she might ask the Director if she (Martha) could come to school for a short time in the morning instead of in the afternoon. Martha said that she herself would see him and bolted out of the room (pp. 439-440).

The quality of functional autonomy and self-responsibility which expressed itself among the group of girls in this situation reflects an important behavioral principle which is especially operative in the classroom learning situation. It is the principle that one learns best by doing, and, one may add, rather than by being told what to do. The more the retarded child can participate actively in his own learning experience, the more real this experience will be for him and the more healthful for his growing personality. As Abel and Kinder (1942) have stressed:

As is well known, subnormal adolescents, like younger children, can be taught most effectively through activity programs. A great deal has been written on this subject. Girls who can decorate a schoolroom, go to a store and buy chintz and thread for making curtains, actually sell novelties they make in school, design posters advertising a dance exhibit or a Christmas sale of their own, and dramatize a story based on a motion picture they have seen, draw pictures or make clay models of objects seen on a trip to a zoo, river front, mill or dairy—these girls seem to participate more fully both emotionally and intellectually in whatever they are learning by these methods than they would if they listened passively to a teacher's description or sat quietly at their desks looking at pictures. A group of subnormal girls once listened to the playing of Mozart's 'Eine Kleine Nachtmusik' by a visiting amateur quartet. As the music proceeded, music that was doubtless too complicated for an untutored audience, to say nothing of subnormals, the girls began to keep time with their feet. At the end they clapped vigorously and said the music was 'fun.' They were severly reprimanded by a teacher for being rude to the visitors and were given a lecture on manners. In reality these girls had responded to the rhythm of the music and enjoyed the experience in a way that would not have been possible if their listening role had been more passive. One girl said 'I could dance to that music. Is he going to write more?'

In a further study of this problem, Harris and Sievers (1959), working with eighteen adolescent retarded girls in a permissive classroom situation, noted that over a one to two year period, the girls exhibited an increase in positive behavior (with a corresponding decrease in negative behavior) in the classroom. It would thus appear that, other things being equal, the more permissive the classroom atmosphere, the more likely it will be that retarded students will participate in classroom activities in an active, involved, and total way. At the same time, however, it must be recognized that there are circumstances and situations which necessitate the application of other teaching approaches and modes of discipline. In this connection, Harris (1955) has identified three basic teacher attitudes toward the retarded student: the first is the already-discussed permissive attitude which the teacher effectively expresses understanding of the student's problems, excusing or ignoring negative behavior; the second is the suggestive rational attitude, in which the teacher tries to objectify the student's behavior, asking the student to find reasons for his overt behavior pattern and attempting to change this behavior; and the third is the disciplinary attitude, by which the teacher uses various means to control and to manage a student's problem behavior, including group pressure, exclusion from activities, and confinement of the student to his seat. Harris (1956) says:

In an ideal situation for treatment and rehabilitation the teacher would be permissive until the pupil had no feeling of rejection toward her. At this time, she would try to suggest and reason with the pupil concerning her negative behavior. When the pupil understood the difference between positive and negative attitudes and seemingly wanted to or felt that she should conform, the teacher would be disciplinary if necessary in order to bring about the adjustment to the change from the environment in the treatment situation to that of social living in the community, especially the working world (pp. 542-543).

As might be expected, however, it is not always possible to carry out this ideal procedure. In reacting to a given student in a class, the teacher must always consider what is best for the others in the group as well.

The necessity for combining various disciplinary approaches while teaching the retardate must be recognized as an important principle in effecting satisfactory behavioral adjustments in the classroom. Permissiveness for the retardate in the classroom learning situation, as Harris and Sievers (1959) have pointed out, must be differentiated from complete laissez faire. While the retardate needs personal freedom in order to grow fully, he requires structuring as well in order to direct and to channel this growth. Permissiveness for its own sake without proper structuring would lead to chaos and anxiety for the retardate. In an experimental program for training retarded children with emotional problems in a religious school, Birner (1955) has exercised this proper disciplinary balance with positive results. On the one hand, no child was ever punished in any way, nor was any child ever made to feel inadequate. (This required that the frustration tolerance of the staff be inexhaustible.) On the other hand, limits were set in terms of the group's behavior. No fighting was permitted, and if a child came into the setting and demonstrated aggressive or antisocial behavior, the psychologist could at any time remove the child from the group for a short talk. Among the beneficial effects of this program were the following: one child who had been a complete social isolate made a friend for the first time in his life; the aggressive trends manifested in the early sessions tended to reduce themselves once the children felt more secure; and definite gains in the children's relation to their environment were reflected in a study of figure drawings over an eight-month period.

A recent development in the teaching of the retardate, representing a radical departure from normal classroom procedure, is the use of automated instructional devices or teaching machines in place of the traditional teacher (e.g., Sprague and Binder (1962); and Stolurow (1963)). In a study by Blackman and Capobianco (1965), retardates taught by such automated teaching devices demonstrated greater improvement in personal and social deportment than retardates taught by traditional special-class techniques. The authors viewed this improvement in behavior as the result of a settling effect of automated instruction upon the retarded student, and they pointed to three possible factors responsible for this effect: first, the teaching machines are "self-placed" without overt pressures exerted by the teacher, thereby reducing the retardate's frustration; secondly, immediate feedback in the form of red and green lights indicating the correctness or incorrectness of responses permits consistent reinforcement for the retarded student; and thirdly, the novelty of the teaching machine itself may have motivated the retardate, increasing his attention and interest.

Others, such as Birnbrauer, et al. (1965) and Smith and Quackenbush (1960), also have obtained behavioral improvements in retardates with the employment of programed instructional methods, but Birnbrauer, et al. have ascribed the improvement as being a function of the utilization of a token reinforcement system rather than as a consequence of the instructional technique per se. At Willowbrook, we also have observed behavioral and scholastic improvements with the employment of a "Talking Typewriter" (Edison Responsive Environment Learning System), especially in terms of heightened motivation. A teacher's report of a ten-year-old, mildly retarded girl bears this out well.

Initially the subject's behavior was guarded, nervous, and generally withdrawn. Her agitation upon entering the booth was visibly intense. Consequently, the booth assistant accompanied her during her machine sessions, for a period of two weeks. At this point, Marilyn expressed a desire to complete her machine work unaccompanied.

If one were to observe Marilyn's behavior at this time (one year later), one would find a highly motivated child, a child who approaches most tasks with a high degree of self-assurance.

In considering many of the foregoing observations and interpretations, however, one must not lose sight of the forest for the trees. Whereas the retardate's frustration might be momentarily reduced and his attention maximized in the automated learning situation, there are other matters of much greater moment and more lasting significance for the retardate in this situation, the most notable of which is the absence of human contact and social interaction in such an automated learning experience. The retardate's need for human contact and emotional richness, particularly in the formative years, has been amply demonstrated, as pointed out in chapter 3 in the discussion of the severely deleterious effect of psychological and social deprivation upon the retarded child. In these terms, no matter how ostensibly effective a teaching machine may be in the momentary situation, there can be no adequate mechanical substitute for the warmth, love, and understanding which only a human teacher can provide. Without these emotional entities, there could be no behavioral adjustment for the retardate at all.

References

Abel, T.M., and Kinder, E.F. *The subnormal adolescent girl*. New York: Columbia University, 1942.

Baldwin, W.K. The social position of the educable mentally retarded child in the regular grades in the public schools. *Exceptional Children*, 1958, 25, 106-108, 112.

Barksdale, M. Social problems of mentally retarded children. *Mental Hygiene*, 1961, 45, 509-512.

Baumeister, A.A. A comparison of normals and retardates with respect to incidental and intentional learning. *American Journal of Mental Deficiency*, 1963, 68, 404-408.

———. Learning abilities of the mentally retarded. In A.A. Baumeister (Ed.) *Mental Retardation*. Chicago: Aldine, 1967.

Bennett, A. *A comparative study of subnormal children in the elementary grades*. Teacher's College contributions to education, No. 510. New York: Teacher's College, Columbia University, 1932.

Bialer, I. Enhancing prospects for personal and social mobility in the mentally retarded. Paper presented at the Eastern Regional Conference of the Council for Exceptional Children, Washington, D.C., Dec. 1964.

Birnbrauer, J.S.; Bijou, S.W.; Wolf, M.M.; and Kidder, J.D. Programed instruction in the classroom. In L.P. Ullmann and L. Krasner (Eds.) *Case studies in behavior modification*. New York: Holt, 1965. Pp. 358-363.

Birner, L. An experimental program for retarded children in a part-time congregational religious school. *American Journal of Mental Deficiency*, 1955, 60, 95-97.

Blackman, L.S., and Capobianco, R.J. An evaluation of programmed instruction with the mentally retarded utilizing teaching machines. *American Journal of Mental Deficiency*, 1965, 70, 262-269.

Blatt, B. The physical, personality, and academic status of children who are mentally retarded attending special classes as compared with children who are mentally retarded attending regular classes. *American Journal of Mental Deficiency*, 1958, 62, 810-818.

Cowen, P.A. Special class vs. grade groups for subnormal pupils. *School and Society*, 1938, 48, 27-28.

Deutsch, M.R., and Sternlicht, M. The role of "surprise" in the von Restorff effect. *Journal of General Psychology*, 1967, 76, 151-159.

Ellenhogen, M.L. A comparative study of some aspects of academic and special adjustment of two groups of mentally retarded children in special classes and in regular grades. Unpublished doctoral dissertation, Northwestern University, 1957.

Fine, M.J. Attitudes of regular and special class teachers toward the educable mentally retarded child. *Exceptional Children*, 1967, 34, 429-430.

Harris, L.M. Reactions of adolescent, mentally deficient girls to a permissive atmosphere in an academic schoolroom. *American Journal of Mental Deficiency*, 1953, 57, 434-446.

———. A method for studying and treating behavior problems in the schoolroom. *American Journal of Mental Deficiency*, 1955, 59, 595-600.

_____ . Exploring the relationship between the teacher's attitudes and the overt behavior of the pupil. *American Journal of Mental Deficiency*, 1956, 60, 536-544.

Harris, L.M., and Sievers, D.J. A study to measure changes in behavior of aggressive mentally retarded adolescent girls in a permissive classroom. *American Journal of Mental Deficiency*, 1959, 63, 975-980.

Hetherington, E.M., and Banta, T.J. Incidental and intentional learning in normal and mentally retarded children. *Journal of Comparative and Physiological Psychology*, 1962, 55, 402-404.

Jacobs, J.F., and Pierce, M.L. The social position of retardates with brain damage associated characteristics. *Exceptional Children*, 1968, 34, 677-681.

Johnson, G.O. A study of the social position of mentally handicapped children in the regular grades. *American Journal of Mental Deficiency*, 1950, 55, 60-89.

_____ . *A comparative study of the personal and social adjustment of mentally handicapped children placed in special classes with mentally handicapped children who remain in regular classes.* Syracuse: Syracuse University, 1961.

Johnson, G.O., and Blake, K.A. *Learning performance of retarded and normal children.* Syracuse: Syracuse University, 1960.

Johnson, G.O., and Kirk, S.A. Are mentally handicapped children segregated in the regular grades? *Journal of Exceptional Children*, 1950, 17, 65-68, 87-88.

Jordan, A.M. Personal-social traits of mentally handicapped children. In T.G. Thurstone (Ed.) *An evaluation of educating mentally handicapped children in special classes and in regular classes.* Chapel Hill: University of North Carolina, 1959.

Jordan, T.C., and de Charms, R. The achievement motive in normal and mentally retarded children. *American Journal of Mental Deficiency*, 1959, 64, 457-466.

Kaplan, M.S. An investigation of the anxiety levels of mentally handicapped children with special consideration of the effects of special education classes. Unpublished doctoral dissertation, Michigan State University, 1961.

Kern, W.H., and Pfaeffle, H. A comparison of social adjustment of mentally retarded children in various educational settings. *American Journal of Mental Deficiency*, 1963, 67, 407-413.

Kirk, S.A. Research in education. In H.A. Stevens and R. Heber (Eds.) *Mental Retardation.* Chicago: University of Chicago, 1964.

Kirk, S.A., and Johnson, G.O. *Educating the retarded child.* Cambridge: Houghton Mifflin, 1951.

Mayer, C.L. The relationship of early special class placement and the self-concepts of mentally handicapped children. *Exceptional Children*, 1966, 33, 77-81.

Miller, R. Social status and socioempathetic differences among mentally superior, mentally typical and mentally retarded children. *Exceptional Children*, 1956, 23, 114-119.

Mullen, F.A., and Itkin, W. *Achievement and adjustment of educable mentally handicapped children in special classes and in regular grades*. Chicago: Chicago Board of Education, 1961.

McCoy, G. Some ego factors associated with academic success and failure of educable mentally retarded pupils. *Exceptional Children*, 1963, 30, 80-84.

Pertsch, C.F. A comparative study of the progress of subnormal pupils in the grades and in special classes. Unpublished doctoral dissertation. Teacher's College, Columbia University, 1936.

Porter, R.B., and Milazzo, T.C. A comparison of mentally retarded adults who attended a special class with those who attended regular classes. *Exceptional Children*, 1958, 24, 410-412.

Ross, E.M. Reactions to frustration of retardates in special and in regular classes. *Dissertation Abstracts*, 1965, 26, 2316.

Smith, E.A., and Quackenbush, J. Devereux teaching aids employed in presenting elementary mathematics in a special education setting. *Psychological Reports*, 1960, 7, 333-336.

Snyder, R.; Jefferson, W.; and Strauss, R. Personality variables as determiners of academic achievement of the mildly retarded. *Mental Retardation*, 1965, 3, 15-18.

Sparks, H.L., and Blackman, L.S. What is special about special education revisited: The mentally retarded. *Exceptional Children*, 1965, 31, 242-247.

Sprague, R.L., and Binder, A. Automated arithmetic instruction for the retarded. Progress report, P.H.S. Grant M-5647 (A), 1962.

Sternlicht, M., and Deutsch, M.R. Cognition in the mentally retarded: the von Restorff effect. *Journal of Mental Deficiency Research*, 1966, 10, 63-68.

Sternlicht, M., Deutsch, M., and Alperin, N. Psychological evaluations and teacher assessments of institutionalized retardates. *Psychology in the Schools*, 1970, 7, 164-167.

Stolurow, L.M. Programmed instruction for the mentally retarded. *Review of Educational Research*, 1963, 33, 126-136.

Thurstone, T.G. *An evaluation of educating mentally handicapped children in special classes and in regular grades*. Chapel Hill: University of North Carolina, 1959.

Wallin, J.E.W. *The education of handicapped children*. New York: Harper, 1955.

8

The Adult Retardate

In order to live a full and happy life with a reasonable degree of personal independence and self-sufficiency, the retardate ultimately must find himself gainfully employed in a job which both offers a creative outlet for his talents and skills and provides a living wage to accommodate his daily economic needs. As such, the retardate's employment situation becomes the focal point of his existence as he enters adulthood, giving both form and substance to his entire personal and social world and representing the end-product of the process of "education for living," which should commence as soon as the mental retardation is recognized. It becomes equally the most difficult and trying experience of his life, because for the first time he is of necessity torn from the sheltered and protective world of childhood and adolescence, and called upon to perform and to produce in the intellectually normal and highly competitive world about him. In a word, as our society understands it, he is expected to become an adult. It is this state of adulthood, with all of its personal and social overtones and implications, that is perhaps the single most difficult act for the retardate to achieve. In this connection, Seidenfeld (1962) has declared that the rehabilitation goal for the mentally retarded is "to provide conditions and circumstances that permit the retarded to perform the activities of daily life and to learn how to behave socially and vocationally in such a manner that they may compete successfully within that segment of their milieu that is within normal limits (p. 17)."

The problems which the retardate experiences in pursuit of his adult goals, together with the benefits he reaps, will be the subject of the present chapter. In order to provide a rounded and complementary picture of the retardate's life in the adult work-a-day world, two basic realms or phases of this world will be explored: first, his vocational and occupational adjustment; and secondly, his leisure time pursuits.

The Vocational and Occupational Adjustment of the Retardate

In his transition from the classroom to the job, the retardate enters a world and way of life which is not only new and alien to him, but which is in many ways incompatible with his entire personality. He finds himself in a situation which by its very nature removes those protective wraps with which he remained covered in the school learning situation and exposes him to the competitive and often harsh realities of the work-a-day world. The expectations which others hold of the retardate in an employment situation are centered not primarily around the retardate's own self-fulfillment, but around the fulfillment of a task for its own sake. Mistakes or errors which are committed in the performance of the job task cannot be treated with the same degree of understanding and tolerance as they would be if they occurred in the learning of an academic class lesson. The classroom is a learning situation; the job is a performance situation. Thus, whereas the retardate might typically have his shortcomings, deficiencies, and idiosyncracies catered to and indulged while he is in school, he encounters a significantly less catering and indulgent attitude when on the job. His feelings and sensitivities take second place to the job performance itself and, in the process, his personality often becomes ruffled. Then, too, most retardates have no specific vocational plans upon leaving school—they do not know what kind of job, if any, they can get.

As a result, the retardate is called upon to assume a significantly greater share of the burden of adjustment than he had ever known before. He must now meet his environment more than halfway because of the economic realities of a work situation which requires that a job be done. All those traits of the retardate's personality discussed in chapter 4—his rigidity, his distractibility, his low frustration tolerance, his impulsivity, and his aggressiveness—are put supremely to the test in a typical employment situation. He must be able to meet a daily schedule in a punctual way, to accept orders from authority figures, to relate to others, often as part of a working team, and, most essential of all, to perform a task or series of tasks according to certain externally imposed and generally accepted standards of competence. These manifold job requirements place great tension and stress upon the retardate, and they tend, over a period of time, to bring his personal tolerances closer and closer to the breaking point. Under such conditions, a single error in performance or a criticism from a supervisor or a misunderstanding with a fellow employee is enough to trigger an emotional outburst which might appear to be inappropriate and unjustified when viewed by others, but which is entirely reasonable and understandable when viewed from the standpoint of the retardate himself, who sees the event as a culmination of a series of mishappenings—the proverbial "straw that broke the camel's back."

It thus can easily be seen that the retardate's on-the-job adjustment is a complex and involved affair which calls not only for an appreciation of work demands and job conditions in and of themselves, but also for an understanding of the retardate's personality and its functioning in stressful adult situations. We now recognize that the vocational capacities of the mentally retarded are fluid and that they depend upon increased personal, social, and vocational adaptability. Personality and attitudes may be more important than specific job skills. The complexity of the problem is reflected in the fact that the literature in this area has been multifaceted in character, forthcoming from a variety of disciplinary sources, including psychology, sociology, social work, education, occupational therapy, and vocational rehabilitation (e.g., Badham (1955); Cohen (1960); Collmann and Newlyn (1956); Cowan and Goldman (1959); Gambaro and Schell (1966); Guerrero (1967); Horne and Allen (1942); Kliebhan (1967); Madison (1964); Tizard, Litt, and O'Connor (1950); and Younie and Colombatto (1964)).

In view of the unavoidably difficult and strained situation which exists for the retardate in an employment setting, the greatest care should be taken not only to place the retardate in a job which is appropriate to his ability and temperament, but also to provide the retardate with the proper training and preparation for the actual work experience. As Kolstoe (1961) and Gorelick (1966) have indicated, training and personality, rather than intelligence per se, seem to be the most important determinants of employment success among the mildly mentally retarded. Similarly, Windle, Stewart, and Brown (1961) found that vocational leave patients who failed to make an adequate community adjustment did so mainly on account of inadequate work performance and interpersonal relationships. Shawn (1964) confirmed this latter point. Meyer (1960) and others view a program of group therapy as a basic aspect of any training atmosphere.

At Willowbrook State School, the most frequent complaints from supervisors in job areas concerning their patient-employees focus on "inability to get along with others," "poor self-control," and "inability to accept constructive criticism." As an example, Sarah is a twenty-year-old young lady, who had been admitted to Willowbrook State School at the age of eleven. She attended the educational program there, and, at the age of eighteen, was referred to the (New York State) Division of Vocational Rehabilitation (D.V.R.) for job training. At that time, she had a WAIS IQ of 61, and had achieved the following academic levels: reading 3.5, arithmetic 4.3, and spelling 5.7. Sarah completed D.V.R. training and was placed in a full-time job (food service) and in a foster home. She kept her job only a few months, losing it because she was too easily distracted by the younger male employees. In addition, she refused to come and go from her foster home at regular hours, and she failed to notify her foster mother of her whereabouts. Consequently, it became necessary to return Sarah to Willowbrook, where she currently is receiving group therapy and additional social training.

In an effort to provide the kind of job preparation which the retardate requires, specialized on-the-job training programs, known as "sheltered workshops," or community day work programs, have been instituted widely in what might be considered dress rehearsal experiences for the retardate's ultimate job placement. As it has evolved, the sheltered workshop has come to be viewed actually as a dual concept. As DiMichael (1954) has stated, the sheltered workshop should be considered at once a training resource for those retardates who can be placed in outside employment and a place of long-term employment itself for those retardates who cannot make the grade in competitive employment. As has been pointed out elsewhere (U.S. Dept. of Health, Education and Welfare, 1965), a period of preparation in a sheltered workshop can be an important culmination of the series of experiences leading to vocational adjustment, either where the retardate is not quite ready for competitive placement upon completion of training or where the retardate must mature socially before competitive placement is possible. The sheltered workshop has a distinct advantage in enabling control and manipulation of the work program, whereby trainees can be moved from one job to another at a rate commensurate with needs and abilities, and also where work can be halted as needs for specific instruction emerge, and where appropriate models for imitation can be provided. The workshop can be particularly useful in stressing attributes which may be generalized to any job situation, such as the importance of punctuality, good grooming, and appropriate socialization with fellow workers. This is especially important since, with the acquisition of greater social and personal adaptability, the retarded are able to make a much more successful vocational adjustment. As Blanton (1966) has demonstrated, adequate and effective socialization must precede vocational training and job placement. At the same time, the sheltered workshop experience must not become so sheltered that it fails to provide the retardate with realistic work situations or to make work demands upon the retardate relevant to those he will encounter upon placement in the community. Bitter (1967), however, is convinced that most problems in a workshop setting can be offset by competent professional handling, including those relating to social immaturity.

What the sheltered workshop appears to do for the retardate is to apply to the vocational sphere the "golden mean" formula for retardate adjustment which was discussed in chapter 6. According to this formula, the retardate's world must be structured and planned for him in a way that eliminates the excesses of both social overexposure and social overprotection. On the one hand, the retardate should not be introduced to situations which have such psychological stress or trauma value that they would tend to throw him into a severely anxious or catastrophic state. On the other hand, he should not be regularly sheltered from social experiences to the point where his self-concept becomes atrophied and his drive for independence crippled. When applied to the vocational sphere, this "golden mean" formula requires that the retardate's work world be structured and planned to eliminate the extremes of both excessive work demands and overly protective work conditions. On the one hand, the retardate should not be introduced to work situations which have such stress or disturbance value that they would tend to throw him into a severely anxious or catastrophic state. On the other hand, he should not be regularly sheltered from on-the-job experiences to the point where his ability to function in an employment setting becomes impaired. It is just such a balance between the extremes of job overexposure and job overprotection which the sheltered workshop strives to achieve. In order to understand more concretely how this "golden mean" formula operates in a sheltered workshop, let us examine a typical ongoing workshop program and its effect upon the performance of the retardate.

A typical sheltered workshop undertaking, operative within the framework of a state institution for the mentally retarded, has been described by Cohen (1961). As originally planned, individuals were to be assigned to the workshop for industrial experience for any of three reasons: the expectation that they will return to an industrial community; the severity or multiplicity of handicaps which limit both participation in the regular vocational training program and opportunity for eventual free release to the community; or as a phase of their regular vocational training program. Considering the training problems presented by the retardates, it was determined that approximately ten individuals should be assigned for each half day. A number of different work projects would be handled simultaneously and, although production was considered important, a strong instructional flavor would be desired. The complexity of tasks with which a retardate is given experiences is dependent upon his ability to perform. Initially, individuals assigned to the workshop would be given relatively simple manual tasks such as sorting, envelope stuffing or hand sanding. As the retardate demonstrates mastery of the simple tasks and, in addition, potential to perform more complicated tasks, the use of hand tools and ultimately machinery would be introduced. Those retardates who have the capability may be afforded experiences with the entire array of equipment. In addition to the technical training itself, every effort must be made to provide as realistic an employment situation as possible in terms of job responsibility, punctuality, cleanliness, neatness, and value of product or service. As an example, a standard time clock and time cards for each retardate assigned to the workshop could be installed. Punching in and out would be required, just as it is on regular employment, to instill a structured sense of punctuality. An incidental benefit provided by this particular experience may be a marked progress on the part of individuals who previously had little concept of time. The focus of the workshop program is on an evaluation of the retardate's performance and on the development of desirable habits and attitudes as well as a realistic concern for supplies and equipment consumed. Each retardate should receive a regular monthly evaluation which would indicate his development and growth within the program. These evaluations are extremely helpful in determining future programing for the retardate. Initially, quantitative production standards should not be heavily emphasized. Rather, the retardate should be taught and encouraged to be concerned with the quality of items produced. Care should be taken to insure that any work projects which are considered can be handled by mental retardates. As an example, an assembly operation of the fabric for institutional bed springs was selected as the initial work project in the workshop described by Cohen. Since such work is considered to be very tedious, time consuming, and thus uneconomical in the institution which originally had the assignment, it was given as a subcontract to the workshop on an experimental basis. The assembly operations of this project could all be broken down into steps easily mastered by the workshop trainees. The technique of analyzing complexity and sequence to adapt even relatively difficult operations to the ability level of the retardate can be employed successfully in all work projects. In the assembly of cardboard shoe boxes, for example, the various steps of the operations included the use of jigs and fixtures for the cutting of gummed paper for the edges, the shaping and assembly of the shoe carton, and the preparation of completed boxes for shipment. Every workshop trainee should be able to take part in at least one step of such an operation. Similar techniques, reports Cohen, have been employed in the assembly of a teaching device, the manufacturing of scratch pads, and the collating, binding, and mailing of thousands of copies of a catalog.

In a demonstration of work potential among retardates, Tate and Baroff (1967) have described in detail the training of retardates in one of the aforementioned operations, namely the assembly of electrical relay panels used in teaching machines. The trainees were a group of moderately and mildly retarded institutionalized males (IQs 40-60) in the late adolescent-young adult age range (CAs 18-36), some with very limited communication. The first problem in the organization of the work project for the trainees was to analyze a complete relay panel into separate tasks which the retardate could be trained to perform. This analysis yielded about twenty operations which were placed in what appeared to be a reasonable sequence. The result was a detailed plan for an assembly line operation. Next, tentative training techniques were decided upon for each of the tasks and a reinforcement or 'reward system formulated. In general, the effort of the workshop was directed toward insuring the success of each worker from the beginning of training, step by step, until he was competently performing a task on his own. Each trainee was introduced to the workshop in as nonthreatening a manner as possible, and each was given time to adapt to and to feel comfortable in the workshop environment. The jobs were broken down into discrete parts, a simple first task selected, and the worker trained in each step. Teaching the worker to make wire connections and to solder them served as an example of this discrete, step-by-step training technique. A practice board consisting of solder lugs nailed to a one-foot wood square was used. The lugs were spaced about one inch apart at the top of the board and gradually brought closer together at the bottom. The worker started at the top where there was plenty of working room and proceeded down the board working within less and less space. The supervisor first demonstrated how to attach the wire to the lug, then showed how to solder the connection. After two or three demonstrations, the worker was talked through the steps several times with praise given for every correct response. When he completed the practice board satisfactorily, the worker was instructed in similar fashion to solder wires to the relays. The worker's first attempts on the relays typically were successful, but his performance would deteriorate after several days. It then was necessary for the supervisor again to give instructions and to supervise closely for several more days, thereby obtaining a resultant improvement in soldering performance. Satisfactory soldering work was maintained by periodic supervision. Periodic reinforcement also was used exclusively, and this consisted largely of verbal praise, attention from the trainer, assured success, and an hourly pay rate of ten cents. When trainees experienced difficulty in learning a task, either the training technique or the steps in the task were modified. In teaching the retardates to cut wire the proper length for the relays, for example, a board with two marks on it was used, the worker being required to stretch a length of wire across the board and to cut it off at the mark. Because it was difficult to keep the wire straight, however, wires of various lengths resulted. The problem was solved by the use of wood blocks with holes bored to wire length which enabled the worker to cut all wires to proper length by inserting the wires in the holes and cutting them off even with the end of the blocks.

Examination of the aforementioned procedures and techniques in operation within the sheltered workshop discloses three general principles which appear to be essential to the implementation of the golden mean formula in the vocational training of the retardate. The first principle involves the creation of a work atmosphere which is maximally nonthreatening to the retardate and optimally conducive to a feeling of ease, comfort, and general acceptance. The second principle consists in the simplification and discrete breakdown of job tasks to the point where each task can be understood and mastered with relative ease by the retardate. The third principle calls for a modification of training procedures and techniques to accommodate the retardate's limited learning abilities when he finds himself unable to grasp the several steps in a particular job task. These three principles—nonthreateningness of environment, simplification of tasks, and modification of techniques—serve to bring about the proper degree of protection, shelter, and structured organization of the work environment necessary to the smooth and satisfactory adjustment of the retardate in what he might otherwise find to be an inordinately competitive, demanding, and traumatic experience. By focusing upon the individual capacity of each retardate to absorb a given work task, the sheltered workshop minimizes the competitive and demanding aspects of the normal work situation. It permits the retardate to learn at his own rate, and to master each task with a feeling of confidence and a sense of accomplishment. When the retardate is able to learn in this way, his learning will have a more solid foundation and a more durable character.

That the three principles of the sheltered workshop do in fact work to bring about successful learning is attested to by the ultimate job performance of the participating workers. One such worker is described by Tate and Baroff (1967):

The most understanding worker was a 31-year-old multiply handicapped resident with an IQ score of 53 who had been institutionalized for 19 years. He walked with a shuffling gait, had a drooping jaw, and his speech was barely intelligible. Within six months he had mastered all phases of relay panel assembly and could carry out the final electrical test. He was one of several residents who completely assembled a panel from start to finish and then checked it out electrically (p. 406).

An outstanding example of a comprehensive community-based sheltered workshop type of operation is the Federation of the Handicapped's "Special

Work Adjustment Program," or SWAP (Federation of the Handicapped, 1966). This program was designed primarily to demonstrate the value of a multidimensional placement-oriented special work adjustment program in promoting the employability and satisfactory community adjustment of mentally retarded school dropouts. A unique feature of SWAP is that the retardate starts earning pay from the moment he enters the program and continues to do so throughout its duration. The program calls for a twenty-six-week experience, divided into three phases: (1) an initial three-week Diagnostic Vocational Evaluation (part of which involves rotating the retardate through a series of vocational experiences designed to evaluate his vocational interests and capacities and part of which consists of remunerative bench work); (2) a 15-week service program of Personal Adjustment Training (during which the client undergoes a more intensive vocational experience in selected training areas); and (3) a final eight-week Supportive Work Experience (during which an intensive, individualized placement program is begun on the trainee's behalf, if he has not already been placed). The trainee is counseled throughout, and additional aspects of the program include remedial arithmetic and reading work, where needed, recreational and social sessions, post-placement counseling, if called for, and parent-counseling sessions. The program's success has been demonstrated via a 73 percent success rate.

The sheltered workshop performance of retardates has been the subject of more systematic scrutiny in a variety of studies which have been particularly concerned with the prediction of competitive employment following workshop training (e.g., Appell, Williams, and Fishell (1962), (1965); Kolstoe (1960, 1961); and Warren (1961)) or with occupational adjustment to the workshop itself (e.g., Higbee (1966); Newhaus (1967); and Wagner and Hawver (1965)). On the matter of workshop adjustment, Wagner and Hawver (1965) reported rather high positive correlations between various psychological tests and workshop performance as determined by the chief workshop supervisor, who placed the workers in rank order by means of a rating scale. In a study designed to formulate a method of enlisting supervisory personnel in the assessment of workshop performance of retardates, Higbee (1966) determined the relationship between workshop performance and performance on the verbal and nonverbal subtests of the Wechsler Adult Intelligence Scale (WAIS). The method of assessment required six workshop supervisors to select employees whom they knew well and then to rank them into what are called stanine distributions, i.e., rating scales with a nine-point distribution of scores, which were then combined to form a master stanine rating of workshop performance. Correlations of workshop performance with the WAIS verbal and nonverbal IQs were both positive and significant, though the verbal IQ correlated at a much lower level of significance than did the nonverbal IQ. This finding suggests that the verbal ability of these retarded workers bears only slight relationship to their workshop performance, a result which is not unexpected. In Higbee's study, the raters were instructed to rate the workers against four criteria assumed to be related to performance in the workshop: namely, production, efficiency, ability to follow directions, and ability to work independently. Further application of the method, suggests Higbee, might concentrate on these criteria singly or be made specific to actual tasks performed by sheltered workers, such as speed in envelope stuffing or efficiency with the stuffing machine. Employing the method to rate workers in nonperformance areas in the workshop, such as personal appeal or relationships with other workers, would seem to have application as well.

While the sheltered workshop appears to provide the ideal training experience for the retardate, such sheltered workshop programs constitute in fact a relatively small proportion of the existing retardate training facilities. To what extent, then, do these other training sources serve the vocational needs of the adult retardate? In a representative study of this question, Cowan and Goldman (1959) undertook to examine whether these other places of training can adequately prepare the mental retardate for eventual job placement. The authors advanced three hypotheses: (1) the mental retardate, as a result of vocational training, will be able to secure and to hold a job more successfully than a matched nontrained group; (2) the retardate's ability to secure and to hold a job will vary directly with the IQ level; and (3) vocational success can be predicted from the efforts made in attempting to locate a job, formal education, and past work experience. A group of twenty mental retardates, with no accompanying physical disability, who received vocational training from the Department of Vocational Rehabilitation of the State of Kansas was matched with a group of twenty nontrained mental retardates on such factors as age, sex, race, IQ, education, past work experience, and elapsed time since their IQ testing. All of the subjects were interviewed to discover what had transpired since the time of training for the experimental (trained) group and since the time of testing for the control (nontrained) group. Information was secured concerning which individuals had secured employment and how long they had remained employed, whether those employed of the trained group had found jobs in the area of their training, and whether they had been successful in making a vocational adjustment. An adequate vocational adjustment was said to exist if the individual had held a paying position for at least twelve months. A remunerative position consisted of employment where the individual was receiving at least the existing minimum state wage ($1.00 per hour) and was working enough hours during the week to result in a salary that was satisfactory to him. The results of the study indicated that the trained group of retardates had a significantly larger number of vocationally successful individuals than the nontrained group. This success, however, was found to be unrelated to the retardate's IQ level, formal education, or past work experience. In their discussion of the demonstrated importance of training for the retardate's ultimate job adjustment, Cowan and Goldman point out that training means more to the mentally retarded than just an opportunity to learn new skills. It means that someone is interested in them, that someone is there to encourage their efforts and to help them handle the disappointments and frustrations that arise in the course of their work experience.

Recognizing the critical role which vocational training plays in the occupational adjustment of the retardate, we might examine precisely what some of these training techniques comprise. As has been pointed out elsewhere (U.S. Dept. of Health, Education and Welfare, 1965), such techniques can be divided into several types according to the vocational goals toward which they are directed: those techniques which are concerned with the improvement of productive capacity; those techniques which are directed toward the enhancement of personal or social effectiveness; and those techniques which are devoted to the overcoming of specific lags in vocational development.

The techniques for improving productive capacity include a variety of particular procedures. One such procedure consists of what might be called occupational preparation and involves providing information dealing with the world of work and with work-related activities, such as where and how to apply for a job, completing an application form, following instructions, cashing a check, and knowing about social security. Another procedure is that of generalized work training, by means of which a work personality may be developed through controlled work experiences. Still another procedure involves job tryouts, whereby a retardate is exposed to brief periods of work experience in various types of occupational activities. A very important and basic procedure is occupational training itself, which acquaints the retardate with a specific type of work, such as cafeteria work and maintenance work in the school, and provides practice in task performance. A related procedure is skill training in which the retardate is trained in specialized skilled vocations, such as body and fender worker, and mechanic's helper. A somewhat differently oriented procedure is that of employer preparation, i.e., acquainting a prospective employer or workshop supervisor with the assets and liabilities of a retardate who is to be referred for on-the-job training, work experience, or sheltered employment. Identification with work models constitutes yet another procedure which involves the retardate's working in tandem with capable peers or adult trainers with whom the retardate can identify. Field trips in which the retardate makes visits to industrial or business firms in the community in which the retardate may work comprise another valuable training procedure.

The techniques for enhancing personal or social effectiveness similarly embrace a number of special procedures. One is group interaction, involving discussion and drama activities which provide experiences in social situations, and possibly planned trips to use community social and leisure facilities and to engage in shared experiences. Another procedure, which is actually a specialized variety of group interaction, is role playing, i.e., the creation of life situations in which the retardate plays the part of specific personalities, in this case in simulated employment situations, e.g., the retardate may play the part of an interviewee or interviewer, either asking for help or answering questions posed by another member of the group. Still another procedure involves planned experience in new situations, recognition of hazardous or dangerous situations, and training in asking for help, including knowledge of the types of people from whom assistance can be requested.

The training techniques for overcoming specific lags in vocational development likewise assume various forms. Acclimitization to work constitutes one such procedural form, and it involves accustoming the retardate to work under conditions other than those typical of school and training settings, and preparing him for the achievement demands and social requirements of a work setting. This acclimitization would include work under conditions of motivation on a remunerative basis in a facility which simulates a true work setting, and would emphasize development of an appropriate work role pattern by the retardate. Training in sensorimotor skills relevent to job performance is another training procedure, the objectives being to prepare the retardate for the perceptual, manual, and motor demands of the work sector in which he will function. Such sensorimotor training includes assessment of the retardate's developmental sensorimotor status in a work situation similar to that in which he will engage. This may be accomplished through job tryouts and work experiences in settings which permit an analysis of performance. Breakdown of the job into component tasks helps to facilitate assessment of assets and deficits in sensorimotor skills affecting performance. Training in socially maturing activities forms another procedure, with the aim of increasing the retardate's ability to handle himself effectively in work-related social situations, such as traveling to and from work, participating in leisure activities within the work group, and engaging in interpersonal relations at work. Several techniques are employed for this purpose: the retardate's community awareness is increased through mobility training and knowledge of transportation resources, with the utilization of such training techniques as messenger work, reinforcement for recognition of salient neighborhood characteristics, and guided mobility practice, as is done with blind persons; his communication skills are cultivated through various group activities, and include recognition of signs, reading as required, verbal expression, ability to follow instructions, and responsiveness to social cues; and his recognition of hazardous or difficult situations is developed by having the retardate request assistance in familiar and unfamiliar experimentally-arranged experiences. The expansion of the retardate's horizons in the vocational sphere and the concomitant enhancement of his self-concept as a worker are two further procedures essential to a rounded training experience. The goals of these procedures are twofold: first, to increase the retardate's potential for independent action by involving him continuously in organized activities which enhance his perception and reaction to all types of stimulation; and secondly, to nurture the retardate's perception of himself as a competent individual who can function in 'an achievement-demanding work setting.

In order to implement the various training techniques, as well as to guide the retardate at each step in the course of his vocational career, an adequate counseling procedure is necessary, whereby the retardate is provided with a constant individual source of information, advice, direction, supervision, and psychological support during his daily trials and tribulations. The retardate enters the world of employment as a virtual "babe in the woods" who needs to be watched over by someone in whom he can confide and who in turn can steer him over the proper course. As Rosenberg (1956) has pointed out:

The young severely handicapped trainee who has had little or no contact with the competitive working world comes to a training program with serious misconceptions concerning the field of work. He knows little of what is required in a productive environment. A factory he pictures as a 'sweat shop' arrangement where one works constantly with a foreman looking over his back. He enters a trade-training program with extreme feelings of insecurity and inferiority. Since birth he had led a sheltered existence, never venturing more than a few blocks away from his own home, always depending on his parents for any decisions that needed to be made. Prevented by his parents from reaching out into the social world, he has developed no ability to cope with life's problems and sorely needs to be guided along the lines of emotional and vocational growth (p. 4).

For such an individual, repeated exercises are necessary in those elementary behaviors and practices which normal individuals regularly take for granted and pursue in second-nature fashion. With the retardate, such behaviors cannot be taken for granted. For a normal individual, being properly dressed and groomed for a job interview is an obvious and self-evident requirement. For a retardate, it is a piece of behavior which is somewhat remote from his immediate considerations and which must be imprinted and impressed on the prospective interviewee. As Rosenberg (1956) has pointed out in his discussion of group counseling with prospective job interviewees, it is necessary to proceed slowly and cautiously through each phase of the job interview, emphasizing such elementary items as following travel directions and arriving on time for the interview, making an appropriate introduction to the employer, and, as was mentioned earlier, being properly dressed and groomed. Such a simple matter as entering a room, extending a hand for a handshake greeting, and stating simply why one has come may, in a job-seeking situation, be a quite formidable task for the retardate. Through the use of role playing in such matters, Rosenberg has found that the prospective interviewees became well acquainted with typical questions presented by employers. They developed a prepared response useful in discussing their training, their productive speed, and related matters. In playing the part of the employer or of the job applicant, each group member having a chance at both roles, the participants found release of tension and escape from anxiety concerning their own real-life situations. In the ensuing discussions, they gained strength from one another, talking freely about their experiences and inadequacies.

In addition to role playing, a "key situation" technique was employed by which the counselor presented hypothetical job situations for group decision.

Through this technique, which is a useful device for engaging the retardates' interest and response, and for sharpening their judgmental abilities, the counselor draws out the trainees' concepts and feelings by confronting them with the necessity for immediate decisions. Rosenberg found that the trainees experienced great difficulties along this line, having only a limited conception of the consequences of a given alternative. One such hypothetical situation was the following: "Your working hours are from 9:00 a.m. to 5:00 p.m. Employer asks you to drop off a package at the post office on your way home. This has occurred on several occasions after 5:00 p.m. and taken you somewhat out of your way. What would you do?" Some trainees felt that the employer was exploiting them and would "have it out" with him. There were others who refused to do the task for the employer because it involved giving service beyond 5:00 p.m. In general, the group felt that they would perform the given task to the best of their ability. Group members argued with those who refused to do this task for the employer. There was a great deal of interchange of feeling. Those who had never worked were the ones who refused. As their improper action was interpreted to them by group members, they realized their mistakes and seemed to accept the general feeling. Another hypothetical situation was posed in this way: "What would you do if your employer asked you to come in and work on Saturdays?" The same people who refused to work after 5:00 expressed serious doubts that they would work on Saturdays. The majority of the group responded positively, indicating they would be willing to work on Saturday. As the session progressed, there was a positive response from all members. Other situations presented included the following: "You were taught in your trade training program a specific method for performing a job task. The employer prefers that you do it his way. What is your decision?" "An employee asked for a raise after working ten days. Was this a proper action?" "You were promised a wage increase after working six months. If your employer failed to give it to you what would you do?" To these typical situations, the group reacted actively and verbally. There were always a few who presented rationalizations for their negative actions. The unfavorable responses came from those whose work experience was limited. They did not know how to react to these various situations. Such ambivalent reactions to key situations were the result of their basic insecurity, lack of job experiences, inability to make their own immediate decisions, and difficulty in accepting responsibility. Members often did not realize that their improper action might lead to dismissal. As their negative actions were carefully interpreted to them, they gained greatly in insight and forethought from the group's reaction to their improper decisions. The group as a whole also seemed to benefit from exposure to these various hypothetical situations. Individual counselors noted changes in those of their counselees who were part of the group counseling program. They appeared more verbal in their individual sessions and, among the younger counselees, there were signs of vocational maturity and adjustment. These individuals seemed more secure, more confident of their abilities and eventual independence in the working world, and more strongly motivated toward immediate employment. In the trade training sessions, improvement was noted in the trainees' interest, motivation, and productive speed. Individuals appeared to be more sincere in their desire to be considered for immediate job placement. There was definite growth in their interpersonal relationships as well.

A similar type of program has been outlined by Wanderer and Sternlicht (1964), termed "Alternative Guidance." With this approach, the leader offers a group of patients a problem situation, and then posits a series of alternative solutions. By allowing the retardate to choose a solution, the leader is able to facilitate the development of realistic attitudes, and consequent adaptive behavior, on the part of a patient who may lack the resources to do it himself.

It thus becomes evident that vocational counseling can serve as a demonstrable aid in the general vocational adjustment of the retardate. As Goldstein (1964) has written:

... studies indicate that counseling and guidance play critical roles in the preparation and placement of retarded workers. In many ways, these services may be contributing to the consistency in the employment picture that the training program played in the social adjustment of former inmates of institutions. Without the benefits of counseling and guidance, the proportion of workers getting and holding jobs might have showed a continuous reduction over the years (p. 250).

At the same time, one cannot minimize the vocational adjustment problems of the retardate. The real test of such adjustment comes when the retardate actually finds himself on the job and confronted by a variety of novel and difficult situations which create tension and stress for him and which can work havoc with his already anxious and fragile personality.

The problems of the retardate on the job fall basically into one of three categories: the retardate's job performance itself, his relationship to his supervisor or employer, and his relationship to his fellow employees. All three areas are sensitive to the retardate's typical personal characteristics, readily engaging and evoking such traits and tendencies as his rigidity, his distractibility, his low frustration tolerance, his impulsivity, and his aggressiveness.

Perhaps the most salient and self-evident difficulty which the retardate confronts on the job is the very fact of the limited ability or skills that he possesses, relative to those of the intellectually normal individual. This limitation reflects itself in quality of performance, in quantity of production, and in speed of operation. It may also involve certain behaviors which call for insight, judgment, and independent decision-making ability, which are qualities that the retardate is sorely lacking. The problems of quality, quantity, and speed of performance need not, however, be major sources of difficulty in and of themselves. If an employer or supervisor recognizes the performance limitations of a retarded worker and gears his expectation to these limitations, the lower level of performance should not act to produce any special adjustment problems for the retardate. It is only when an employer or supervisor has an unrealistic expectation of the retardate and acts with an attitude of hypercriticalness or hostile authority that a catalyst for possible friction is created. The retardate is extremely sensitive to his limitations and becomes easily disturbed if they are held up to ridicule or thrust in his face. His reaction may become catastrophic, with a resulting disorganization of behavior. Whatever he might have been able to do before becomes lost to him as he finds himself in the throes of an attack of anxiety which pervades his entire existence.

His ensuing behavior might take one of several forms. He might become outwardly aggressive, extrapunitive as it were, directing hostility and blame for the situations against the employer or supervisor or even against the work task itself. Such a reaction could be accompanied by a physical outburst, e.g., the retardate might typically spew forth verbal vulgarities or slam down a piece of work equipment or material onto the table or floor. His physical aggressiveness, however, would remain diffuse and random in character, directed against an abstract or inanimate object rather than against the employer or supervisor himself. On the other hand, many retardates in such a situation would turn their aggression inward, acting intropunitively as it were, and would blame themselves for the frustration. This reaction would be marked behaviorally by a verbal tightening up with no oral response forthcoming whatsoever. In addition, the retardate might begin to pout or to cry. (For a complete description of the extrapunitive and intropunitive types of reaction to frustration which a retardate might display, see Angelino and Shedd (1956), Portnoy and Stacey (1954), and Rosenzweig (1945), as well as a later portion of the present chapter.) A reaction with more serious consequences, and one which an employer may be less able to understand or to accept, is the retardate's impulsive walking off the job. Such a reaction should not be interpreted by the employer as a voluntary and rational decision by the retardate in which he chooses to resign, but rather must be understood simply as an expression of a state of anxiety and disorganization in which "leaving the field," as it were, remains the only possible course of behavior open to the retardate. Escape from the situation becomes the easiest way for the retardate to cope with such anxiety. After a "cooling-off" period, accompanied by proper counseling with a vocational worker and by direct talking-out with the employer himself, the retardate could return to the job in an even better state of adjustment than prior to the difficulty.

Such a working out of an on-the-job problem requires, of course, great patience, forbearance, understanding, and even compassion on the part of the employer. The average employer, however, is not prepared to accommodate an employee in such a magnanimous way under the circumstances, and is more likely to accept the worker's walking off on its face and to dismiss him forthwith. The impulsivity and defiance expressed in such employee behavior is considered undesirable and even intolerable from both a personal and an economic stand-point. It is for this reason that the proper understanding and empathy between an employer and a retarded worker are of paramount importance in the retardate's successful job adjustment. This understanding and empathy must be established from the very beginning of the retardate's tenure on the job, so that the employer has full knowledge of the kind of person who will be in his employ and can therefore accept him for what he is. Toward this end, the retardate's credentials should be openly made known to the prospective employer by the vocational counselor and any questions which the employer might have should be freely discussed. In certain cases, the employer might decide, for the best interests of everyone concerned, that the retardate in question would not be suitable for the job. While such a decision is naturally disappointing and upsetting to the retardate, it is a more desirable state of affairs than would develop if the retardate were to be blindly accepted for the position, to adjust poorly, and perhaps eventually to be dismissed from his job because of inadequate performance. The likelihood of success on the job is significantly increased when the employer accepts the retardate with full knowledge of his deficiencies, limitations, and personal idiosyncracies. At the same time, the question of job success involves many other factors beyond the immediate influence or control of the employer himself.

These factors, which range widely, have been pinpointed and highlighted by Peckham (1951), in a study of a sample of eighty representative cases followed up in the Office of Vocational Rehabilitation of the State of Michigan. Of all of the problems which the retardate experiences immediately following initial job placement, perhaps the most universal is that of acceptance by his fellow workers. Such behaviors as ridicule, teasing, and practical joking constitute a severe and ever-recurring difficulty for the retardate on the job. In many ways, the question of acceptance by his fellow workers has a much more penetrating effect on the personality of the retardate than does the question of acceptance by his employer or supervisor. The employer or supervisor represents an authority figure to the retardate, and someone generally in a different social class and distant life station. The retardate's fellow workers, however, represent a community of peers who belong to the same social and economic world as does the retardate and who in effect form a mirror image of the retardate himself. Rejection by his peers thus constitutes a real and devastating injury to the retardate's own self-image. This is the same kind of problem of rejection which the retardate experiences in the regular class of a public elementary school, as was discussed in chapter 7, with one important difference. In the classroom situation, the teacher has a more influential and controlling role, since it is her very function to instruct children in every area of their lives, including interpersonal relationships. As such, the teacher can easily and properly intercede in cases of group rejection or ridicule of a retarded child in the classroom. In the job situation, on the other hand, the employer or supervisor cannot intercede so easily nor does he see it as his function to do so. The workers under his supervision are adults who are on the job not for the primary purpose of being taught or edified, but rather for the purpose of performing a task and performing it well. As a result, the retardate is left largely to his own resources to solve such personal and social problems. The task, needless to say, is not an easy one. When one reflects on the initial strangeness and discomfort which most intellectually normal people experience on a new job, he can easily appreciate the terrible pain and suffering which a retardate must undergo in the face of overt rejection by his fellow workers in a new job situation. It is at times such as this that the guiding hand of the vocational counselor is so important to the retardate, often making the difference between success and failure on the job.

A related problem, described by Peckham (1951), which is equally common to retardates on the job, is that of a general lack of social and vocational sophistication on the part of the retardate. In this connection, the retardate frequently displays a rather naive disregard for such basic items as punctuality on the job, dress, and general deportment. He sometimes finds it difficult to manage the problem of transportation, particularly in urban areas, and if the problem is complicated by some particular circumstance from time to time, he might not even try to get to work, nor would he phone his employer about it. Similarly, with such items as vacation or sick leave, the retardate often does not take management into his confidence, but simply absents himself until such time as he deems it advisable to return. There also is a lack of general know-how and wherewithal which the retardate displays when placed on his first job, including the handling of such matters as the cafeteria, the time clock, and even the rest room.

Another job problem which the retardate frequently experiences is that of salary dissatisfaction. This dissatisfaction arises largely from the fact that the retardate fails to recognize that the kind of job to which he is ordinarily assigned is not so important economically to the employer as are certain other types of jobs, with the result that the salary differentials are confusing to him. In a number of instances, the retardate comes to have the feeling that he is being victimized, and accordingly he may quit his job to look for something better.

A factor compounding this problem, which the authors have found in their own experience, is the fact that the retardate very often entertains unrealistic salary expectations during the time that he is in the process of seeking a job. The thought that he is about to become his own breadwinner, as it were, is a quite exciting, self-flattering, and ego-expanding one. As a result, he permits himself the luxury of letting his mind wander to consider all the wonderful and long-desired material things that a salary will be able to bring him. Not only, therefore, will he, in his phantasies, have spent his paychecks before he has even secured a job, but he will have established in his mind an unrealistic image of what his purchasing power actually will be. As a person about to become economically self-sufficient, he gears his thinking along the lines of spendthriftiness with little consideration of the limits which a given salary will necessarily impose.

When the retardate actually does secure a job and earn a salary, the problem of budgeting thus poses a number of genuine difficulties for him. Here the retardate demonstrates a lack of capacity to handle his pay check adequately. Money which should be allocated for such essential items as lodging, board, and laundry might be dissipated on trivialities and luxuries, such as motion pictures, sports, radio, or camera equipment, and magazines and phonograph records. This kind of irresponsible management of personal affairs, so typical of the retardate's lack of proper judgment and forethought, comes to present real job-connected problems during each period immediately prior to payday. The retardate might find himself obliged to borrow in order to meet his immediate needs, or, as an unavoidable alternative, perhaps having to postpone payment of his room rent, to do without adequate meals, or to come to work wearing unlaundered clothes.

Still another job problem, and one which is inextricably involved with the entire concept of job adjustment, is the retardate's general lack of initiative and job responsibility. Upon completing a task, for example, the retardate might typically sit and wait for his supervisor to discover that the work was done rather than make an inquiry on his own part about what to do next. In some cases, the retardate might be prone to continue performing an operation incorrectly rather than ask for help. This quality is so part-and-parcel of the retardate's passive and dependent personality, at the same time as it is so generalized and abstract in its character, that it presents a difficulty which is not entirely amenable to change. It is much easier, for example, to point out to the retardate the foolishness of spending money on phonograph records instead of rent than it is to explain the meaning of job initiative and responsibility. In the matters of initiative, judgment, and responsibility, it is perhaps necessary to be most lenient and accepting of the retardate, meeting him more than halfway, if optimal job adjustment is to be effected.

A related problem, described by Peckham (1951), is that of thoughtless quitting of the job, without regard for the immediate consequences of unemployment. Discounting the earlier discussed walking off the job because of momentary upset and anxiety, most job quitting by retardates is attributable to purely capricious behaviors involving such generalized factors as laziness and irresponsibility.

To a lesser extent, status anxiety on the part of the family can act as a disruptive influence on the retardate's job adjustment. The parents of a working retardate sometimes find it difficult to accept the fact that their child should attempt employment at a level beneath the family dignity. Often these feelings become communicated to the child himself, thereby creating a source of confusion and disturbance to the retardate, who is at the time trying to make his own independent way in the world as an adult. At the same time, some retardates, without the influence of their families, develop status anxiety on their own. They assume unrealistic self-attitudes about their abilities and talents, making it very difficult for them to accept employment opportunities of a modest nature.

A problem related to the aforementioned family status anxiety, though operative in a different way, is that of familial overprotection. In the interest of protecting and sheltering their child, the family of the retardate might insist on certain employment restrictions, such as requiring that the job be located close to home, that the individual be accompanied to and from work by a relative or family friend, and that the nature of the job and the retardate's job associates be of high character.

A special job adjustment problem, also described by Peckham (1951), which can arise in certain cases is the retardate's either limited ability or virtual inability to read. Such written matter as printed job instructions, bulletin board announcements, and work tags on materials can create awkward situations for the retardate, who would be likely to have difficulty in reading such printed matter with real comprehension and proper interpretation. In many instances, the retardate is inclined to bluff his way through the situation, either by guessing at the meaning of the printed matter or by ignorning it altogether. Such haphazard or evasive ways of handling the situation can create very real job problems, in terms of disruption and confusion of work procedures and possible economic loss to the employer.

In light of the problems typically experienced by the retardate on the job, we might examine those personal traits and characteristics which would be considered desirable for a retardate's vocational success. The findings of a study by Michal-Smith (1950) afford a capsule view of such characteristics, relating them to four broad industrial occupational areas: manual, repetitive, machine operation, and social (i.e., those jobs which involve contact with the public). Striking differences in the relative importance of personal characteristics found to be important in manual, repetitive, and machine work are considered to be of less than average importance in jobs which involve meeting the public. It appears that in the manual, repetitive, and machine operation areas, acting in a nonclumsy way and not becoming easily fatigued are both important personal characteristics desirable for the retardate's successful job adjustment. In addition, showing caution and avoiding danger are behavioral characteristics important in the manual and machine operation areas, while not being forgetful is singly important in the manual area, and performing responsible routine chores in the repetitive area. In the social area, however, such items as being emotionally even tempered, feeling loyal to the company, and appearing personally attractive are of prime importance in job adjustment for the retardate. By way of contrast, two of these very same items—company loyalty and personal attractiveness—are demonstrably unimportant characteristics for successful adjustment in the manual and machine operation areas, while personal attractiveness is singly unimportant in the repetitive area. The tendency to assume new duties willingly is unimportant as an adjustment trait in the manual and machine operation areas, while the ability to act flexibly and to change one's work habits is, as might be expected, unimportant in the repetitive area. A characteristic which appears to be universally unimportant for retardate adjustment in all four occupational areas is the ability to systematize one's own work. This is understandable in light of the fact that the work which is typically assigned to a retardate is of such a nature that the factor of systematization or organization of the material has been eliminated as a working problem.

In analyzing job success among retardates, however, it must be recognized that no single factor or even small cluster of factors can account comprehensively for a retardate's satisfactory or unsatisfactory job adjustment. Rather, it is necessary to take into consideration the whole employment configuration, with all its interactive and reciprocal effects. As Abel (1940) has observed concerning the employer-employee relationship in her study of the vocational adjustment of subnormal girls:

The ways in which the girl reacted to her new employer, the modifications in her behavior as a result of his attitudes toward her, the manner in which the employer, in turn, reacted to the girl, and the modifications in his attitudes, as a result of the girl's behavior, all formed reciprocal relationships that helped determine success and failure. Sometimes factors in the girl's personality influenced her successful adjustment, at other times, the employer's sympathetic or understanding attitude turned the tide in this direction (p. 70).

The Leisure-Time Pursuits of the Retardate

It is during the adult retardate's nonworking hours that he affords us a glimpse of himself which remains inaccessible in the various other situations in which we see him in the course of his life. Whether in an institution, at school, or on the job, the retardate would always find himself in a more-or-less constricting and constraining environment which would have the effect of creating some degree of external pressure and stress. During his nonworking hours as an adult in the community, however, the retardate suddenly comes to experience himself as a truly free agent in the world. His time is his own, his physical movement is largely unhampered, and his choice of personal expression is left entirely to himself. He becomes, at least manifestly, an autonomous being, unfettered by externally imposed rules and regulations, time schedules, and institutional codes of behavior. What the retardate does and does not do in his leisure time with his newly discovered freedom is the subject of our present discussion.

In examining his extracurricular life, as it were, it might be helpful to keep in mind the image of the retardate which is conjured up in the following characterization offered by Mickelson (1951): "The mentally deficient are just like other people; only more so (p. 313)." Perhaps one could elaborate by declaring that the retarded are just like other people who live near them in the same lower socio-economic neighborhood. In general, as Goldstein (1964) has suggested, most adult retardates living in the community make reasonably successful adjustments. As has been emphasized as a recurrent theme throughout the present work, the retardate can best be understood not as a strange, odd, or idiosyncratic creature, but rather as an individual with certain deficiencies and limitations which tend to highlight and to exaggerate his behaviors, such that, relative to the normal person, these behaviors might appear at times qualitatively different and idiomorphic in character. The fact is that the retardate has the same kinds of desires, wishes, and dreams and the same human need to work out his own destiny as does the intellectually normal individual. He is merely somewhat more circumscribed in the goals which he sets for himself, and correspondingly more limited in his ability to realize his aspirations. The retardate's life goals are more modest, and he goes about attaining them in a less hurried way. Accordingly, in his daily leisure-time activities, the retardate can be expected to pursue the same general kinds of recreational pleasures, amusements, entertainments, and diversions as an intellectually normal individual, but to go about them in his own way and at his own level. He may go to the motion pictures, though he is less likely to see a foreign film or an avant-garde comedy than a Western or an Abbott and Costello picture. The retardate may attend a musical event, though his interests here would run almost exclusively toward music in the popular or jazz vein. In the dating and courting sphere, he can be expected generally to operate in a less formalized and structured way than would an intellectually normal individual. His dates would tend to arise more or less spontaneously and would lack the thought out and planned quality that is so characteristic of the behavior of the intellectually normal young man who is trying to win the favor of a young lady. A typically retarded couple on a date "play it by ear" to a significantly greater extent than most other people in our society. There are fewer of the trappings that surround the normal evening out, with the possible result that the retardate comes to know and to experience his dating partner in a more direct and immediate way. The dates themselves are more simple and modest than those of the intellectually normal. For example, a special dining-out experience for the normal person in a large cosmopolitan city might consist in reservations at a deluxe establishment. For the retardate, on the other hand, a special dining-out experience would probably involve visiting a simple and unpretentious chain eatery or even a modern and glossy cafeteria. The mere presence of napery in an eating establishment might provide more than enough atmosphere to make the restaurant a special place for the retardate. His food preferences are, as might be expected, similarly simple and unsophisticated. He is by and large a "meat and potatoes" man, who is most comfortable and contented eating a pizza pie, fried chicken with French fried potatoes, spaghetti and meat balls, or, perhaps his favorite, a hamburger.

The informal and plain character of the retardate's leisure-time pursuits expresses itself, too, in the diffuse, random, and marginal quality of his daily off-the-job activities. Window shopping, for example, which is classically representative of this quality, is one of the retardate's most frequently pursued and cherished pleasures. The female retardate, particularly, can make a whole day's enjoyment out of such wandering about before store windows, and even relish it into the evening as well, talking about the beautiful things she has seen and would probably love to have. While there is a paucity of systematic study of such leisure-time pursuits among retardates, several notable works have been produced which touch upon this area (e.g., Kennedy (1948); Peck and Stephens (1945); Saenger (1957); and Edgerton (1967)). One of these investigations, a report by Saenger (1957), supports the present view concerning the retardate's general tendency toward random, marginal, and passive activities. Saenger's study, which is a quite comprehensive and detailed undertaking, investigated the community adjustment of a large sample of adult retardates living in New York City. Concerning their daily activities, Saenger reported that much of the time which the retardate spends outside the home is taken up with merely hanging around the street by himself. Approximately one-half of the retardates occupied themselves in this manner, lounging around public places such as neighborhood stores and, in rarer instances, visiting pool rooms. These activities, it is important to point out, did not usually lead to prolonged or intensive contacts. Most of the retardates only exchanged greetings with neighbors or played with the neighbors' children. The spectator quality of many of the retardate's activities was captured in the following description of one particular retardate offered by a respondent in Saenger's study:

When he goes out it is to go to a ball game, basketball game or any other sport. Yes, he loves to watch them, but has never tried to play anything not even with the boys in our neighborhood. He does not like to try it, he'd rather watch. He goes with us to watch these games because he does not know how to travel alone. He spends a lot of time around the grocery store in the corner of our block (p. 103).

Going to ball games also is an extremely popular pastime among retardates, as is seeing motion pictures, and together these two activities are engaged in generally by over 75 percent of the retardates in the community. Visiting relatives is an equally popular activity, and, to a slightly lesser extent, visiting friends. It is with these people, of course, that the retardate experiences the greatest comfort and acceptance, such that he would naturally gravitate toward such experiences in the course of his daily activities. Attending recreational centers and workshops are much less frequently pursued activities. This is not unexpected, since such activities represent more structured and formalized, as well as stranger and less familiar, experiences for the retardate.

When the retardate remains at home in the course of the day or evening, he devotes the overwhelming majority of his time to either watching television or listening to the radio. In his study, Saenger (1957) reports that 97 percent of the retardates' leisure time at home is spent in this manner. In these terms, as Saenger mentions, television and to a lesser extent radio appear to be a major blessing for the retardate. They provide him with the ideal passive spectator entertainment, for they are conveniently situated in his own home, they can be varied from channel to channel or station to station, and they can be turned on or off at will. Looking at books, papers and magazines comprises another popular diversion, as does conversation with others. (With the severely retarded, the greatest leisure time problem is sluggishness, underactivity.)

In addition to engaging in pleasurable activities per se, the retardate living with his family spends a good portion of his time at home helping around the house. Approximately one-half of the retardates studied by Saenger help in such chores as cleaning their own rooms, making their own beds, and picking up and putting away their own clothes and belongings. A little less than one-third of the retardates perform these chores on an occasional rather than a regular basis. Similarly, approximately one-half of the retardates living with their families regularly help with dusting, sweeping, cleaning, and dishwashing, with slightly fewer retardates executing these household tasks only occasionally. About two out of every five retardates can be expected to assist in the preparation of food. In general, the female retardate makes a particularly good housekeeper, being both quite capable and highly motivated in this area. Running errands and minding children are two additional help activities of which the retardate is particularly fond. The extent to which he may actually perform such tasks is dependent, however, upon his ability to negotiate his way in the neighborhood, and upon the trust which may be placed in him to take total charge of a small child in the absence of other adult supervision.

It must be borne in mind that, while certain general, composite statements about the leisure-time pursuits of the retardate may be ventured, there are wide individual differences among retardates even as there are among intellectually normal people. This is most readily evident in the extent and style of social life which various retardates pursue. Saenger's (1957) interviews, for example, reveal that social friendships among retardates range all the way from engaging in parallel play to spending time together without doing much to going together to the motion pictures or on dates. One of the qualities, mentioned earlier, that does seem to run through all of these relationships is the rather circumscribed, unembellished, and even sudden character of the retardate's social experiences. The following characterization of a female retardate offered in Saenger's (1957) study serves as an example: " 'She has a girl friend, H. is her name, who was in the same class. She often comes and visits R. They usually watch T.V. or they chat on the divan. But I don't know quite why, R. can't take too much of her. Suddenly she will rise up and say to H., "It's time for you to go home now." And poor H. has to leave. But that's the only friend she has.' (p.105)." The question of having friends, as Saenger (1957) and Edgerton (1967) have pointed out, must be viewed not only from the point of view of the adjustment of the retardate, but also in terms of a lessening of the burden he may be to his parents. Having friends means being wanted, a condition which holds especially true for the retardate, who experiences so much rejection and alienation in the course of his life. According to Saenger's findings, slightly more than half of the adult retardates in the community have friends. This proportion, however, decreases rapidly and significantly as the retardate grows older: between the ages of 21 and 25, 62 percent of the retardates have friends; between the ages of 26 and 30, this figure decreases to 50 percent; and from the age of 31, there is a drop to only 35 percent. Such a sharp decline in friendships with increasing age is partly attributable to the fact that normal children, who are counted among the friends of the retardate, are less likely to play with the older retardate than with the younger one.

The growing isolation which the retardate experiences in his more advanced years constitutes one of the more serious and sad of his leisure-time adjustments. The nostalgically lonely and lugubrious quality of this experience is poignantly captured in the following excerpt from Saenger's (1957) report, rendered by a retardate himself:

Well, I go to the movies in the neighborhood—sometimes downtown to the Paramount, places like that. Friday nights (nights off) I go downtown a lot—I go to dances a lot—by myself. You know, to dance halls where you pay to dance with the girls. And, sure, I go to the bar. I drink a little. I like to go there to talk to the guys. Nobody gyps me. . . . Well, I really don't have any personal friends now, I know a lot of people but no one I would really call a real friend. When I was younger, I had a lot of friends on the block—guys my own age. We used to play ball, swim, go to the movies together. But as they got older they got married and sort of drifted off. I don't see them. I guess I could if I called them up. I think they'd ask me over their house. But I never do (p. 108).

For the retardate who never marries, as well as for the one who has not yet fully reached that stage in his adult career, the question of his relationship with the opposite sex becomes an increasingly important and pressing one in his daily life. Not only does the retardate largely have the same problem of managing his basic physical drives, needs, and desires as the intellectually normal person; he has, in addition, the problem of maintaining them as a constituent and integral part of his total functioning personality. To the extent that he is subject to greater restrictions on his sexual expression through increased control and supervision of his social life, the retardate's needs in the sexual sphere will become exaggerated and consequently isolated from his total personality. The repeated admonitions he receives in this area from his parents or guardians, the limitations placed on his evening-time schedules, and the chaperonage to which he is often subjected, in the interest of his own protection and well being, all necessarily introduce complications into the retardate's pursuit of a normal and healthy heterosexual life.

Whereas Saenger (1957) reports that the majority of retardates whom he studied show no interest in the opposite sex, there is reason to believe that sexual interest and activity, at least among the very mildly retarded, flourish today to a much greater extent than Saenger's figures would suggest. (Most probably, heterosexual interests increase as intellectual functioning decreases, and sexual behavior would also appear to be closely related to the retardate's level of emotional development, rather than to his or her level of physical development. Thus, the severely retarded demonstrate limited sexual drives and interests, and their behavior in this sphere generally is exploratory and characteristic of that which one might expect in a young child.) It has been the authors' observation that even the mildly retarded who reside in an institutional setting have a quite considerable interest in, awareness of, and even degree of, sophistication concerning the opposite sex. Kissing, necking, and petting are activities not at all outside the retardate's normal behavioral repertoire, and he can be expected, circumstances and situations permitting, to indulge in sexual relations on a more than rarely occurring basis. There are, of course, many exceptions in both directions. Some retardates display a significant disinterest in, lack of awareness of, and naivete concerning the opposite sex and the entire sexual process. For such retardates, a sex education experience is desirable, in the style of one described by Thorne (1957), which was designed for females and which handled such matters as the origin of babies, prenatal care, fetal and infant development, sterilization, menstruation, and menopause, as well as the subject of good grooming and dating behavior. Certain other retardates, on the other hand, demonstrate a precociousness, hypersensitization, and overdemonstrativeness in the sexual realm. Many of the phantasies and dreams which retardates disclose in the course of psychotherapy are rather vivid and full in their sexual content, reflecting the retardate's deeper occupation with thoughts and feelings in the sexual sphere. In cases where he is prevented from releasing his physical urges in a heterosexual relationship, the retardate can be expected, as can the intellectually normal individual, to engage in masturbatory behavior. Such behavior may be equally common among retardates who show no interest in the opposite sex and have no overt heterosexual inclinations whatsoever.

In his examination of the sexual behavior of community-based retarded ex-patients, Edgerton (1967) discovered that none of the stereotypic views about them were correct. He illustrated that the experiences of retarded persons with sex and marriage were varied, but that, for the most part, they were on the conventional side.

The question of marriage is a reasonably widespread matter of concern to retardates, perhaps more so among the women than among the men. The interest is often, however, a merely fleeting, remote, and phantasized activity, rather than an actual pursuit after matrimony. According to Saenger (1957), interest in getting married is found in one out of five retardates, with actual marriage being consummated in only a few isolated cases. Among the very mildly retarded, however, as evidenced in a classical study by Kennedy (1948) of community adjustment among retardates, marriage becomes more than a rarity, and, depending upon the stability and compatibility of the partners, can turn out to be a successful, happy, and productive experience. Certainly, in many cases marriage would be desirable from the viewpoint of attaining a mutually satisfying and supportive relationship, comradeship, and a more reasonable social adjustment. It does appear to be the case, though, as Kennedy (1948) reports, that retardates exhibit a greater incidence of divorce and desertion than do intellectually normal individuals. This pattern is consistent with the retardate's tendencies toward impulsive and whimsical behavior. However, as Kratter (1958) and Shaw and Wright (1960) have concluded, many borderline retardates make quite satisfactory housekeepers and parents, provided that their circumstances are familiar and that they do not have too many children. Edgerton (1967), in agreement with Kennedy, found that the majority of the retarded ex-patients that he studied were married, and that some of this group were married to nonretarded individuals. In fact, he concluded that the group's sexual and marital lives were more "normal" and "better regulated" than he would have predicted on the basis of their manifest intellectual limitations.

In the midst of his pleasures, diversions, and delights, however, there are bound to be momentary situational disappointments and frustrations for the retardate, as there are for everybody. A baseball game that is rained out, a date that fails to materialize, a color television set that the retardate wants so much but cannot afford—such experiences and situations with their obstacles and disappointments set up frustrations in the retardate which are difficult for him to handle. The intellectually normal person can accept such minor frustrations and take them in stride. A retardate, however, cannot postpone gratification in the same way in matters which to him are of more central importance in his life. The ways in which a retardate responds to such leisure-time frustrations may be varied.

Some light has been shed on this matter by studies which have utilized a special psychological projective technique, the Rosenzweig Picture-Frustration Study, devised for the purpose of analyzing an individual's modes of responding in frustrating situations. In particular, the technique measures the direction in which an individual turns his aggression in the face of typical daily frustrations. It consists of a series of cartoon-like drawings, representing incidents of everyday life in which one character is shown saying something of frustrating significance to another, the subject who is administered the technique being asked to write in the reply that would be made by the second person. From the responses which the subject gives, a measurement can be made of the general direction which the individual's aggression takes in terms of placing blame for the frustrating situation: "extrapunitive," if the blame is directed against others; "intropunitive," if the blame is directed against himself; and "impunitive," if the blame is glossed over or minimized. An investigation by Portnoy and Stacey (1954), which utilized the Rosenzweig Picture-Frustration Study, has found that the retardate typically responds to frustration in an extrapunitive manner, directing aggression and blame against others in his environment rather than turning them inward upon himself. This is a reasonable expectation in light of the retardate's somewhat weak personality controls and his fragile self-concept. A later study by Angelino and Shed (1956) discovered that, with increasing age, however, the retardate's reaction becomes more intropunitive in character, with blame directed to a greater extent against the retardate himself. While such investigative research is still in the early experimental stage, it suggests that as the retardate grows older, the aggressive components of his personality become somewhat more restrained in character and less subject to the operation of explosive emotional forces. At the same time, the source and character of the frustration itself must be considered in any analysis of the retardate's frustration-induced behavior. Being ridiculed or teased by another member of the community, being personally rejected by a partner on a date, and being prevented from seeing a baseball game or going to the motion pictures all represent frustrating experiences, but each has a special and individual quality all its own.

Beyond his immediate and daily pleasures and diversions, however, one must consider some of the deeper and more durable leisure-time yearnings of the retardate: not merely his momentary delights and frustrations, but his projected and personal feelings about his life, his world, and his destiny. While it is true that the retardate is heavily anchored to his momentary and concrete situational world of the present, he nevertheless does entertain inner feelings about life in general, which may not be readily accessible unless expressly tapped by the appropriate psychological techniques.

One such technique, described in chapter 4, has been employed by Sternlicht (1967), and involves gleaning the values held by retardates from their responses on a projective psychological instrument—the Sentence-Completion Test. From these responses, Sternlicht has been able to construct a picture of the retardate's world of perceptions, attitudes, and values in several basic areas, including his relationship to significant people in his life, his emotions and his self-concept, his conduct, behavior, and morality, and his general life views and attitudes. What Sternlicht has found is that, in their relationship with other people who are emotionally significant in their lives, particularly loved ones, retardates of both sexes see their mother in a slightly more favorable light than they do their father, in terms of what they perceive their parents' inherent qualities to be, in terms of what their parents do for them, and in terms of how their parents love them. Concerning other people in general, retardates tend to respond to rejection by others with a similar rejection or negation of the other person and a general refusal to become very much involved in or affected by the other person's attitude. This attitude of noninvolvement, as felt and expressed by the retardate himself, has its behavioral counterpart, as we have seen, in the marginal and cursory quality of many of the retardate's leisure-time relationships. A basic theme in the motivational life of the retardate, as further revealed by Sternlicht, is the retardate's concern with the idea of being good, with an accompanying fear of his own hostility and aggression. In this connection, the retardate considers his own show or feeling of love for others to be less important than his good behavior and deportment as a condition for gaining another's affection. This attitude is consistent with the retardate's generally rather dependent and passive orientation to the world. On the subject of love itself, the retardate views the phenomenon usually in a generalized and wholesome way, with less emphasis on its more physical and romantic manifestations. The retardate's moral life is guided basically by two underlying principles: being good in and of itself, and avoiding one's own strong hostility and aggression. His views of life in general are predominantly positive views, and his thoughts about the future are happy thoughts.

The retardate's subjective phenomenological world thus appears to present a possibly more optimistic and hopeful picture of his life and his future than the retardate's daily ordeals and frustrations might otherwise tend to evoke. That the retardate can emerge with such a personally positive view of life bears witness to his ultimate strength of spirit. Given this wellspring of faith which resides in the retardate's personality, no effort should be spared to provide for the retardate the kind of life which does justice to such faith. Toward this end, every attempt should be made to assist the retardate, to nurture his talents, to cultivate his skills, to enable him to realize his own inner core of being so that he might ultimately establish for himself a comfortable niche in life and find his own special place in the sun.

References

Abel, T.M. A study of a group of subnormal girls successfully adjusted in industry and the community. *American Journal of Mental Deficiency*, 1940, 45, 66-72.

Angelino, H., and Shedd, C.L. A study of the reactions to "frustration" of a group of mentally retarded children as measured by the Rosenzweig Picture-Frustration Study. *Psychological Newsletter*, 1956, 8, 49-54.

Appell, M.J.; Williams, C.M.; and Fishell, K.N. Factors in the job holding ability of the mentally retarded. *Vocational Guidance Quarterly*, 1965, 13, 127-130.

——. Significant factors in placing mental retardates from a workshop situation. *Personnel and Guidance Journal*, 1962, 41, 260-265.

Badham, J.N. The outside employment of hospitalized mentally defective patients as a step towards resocialization. *American Journal of Mental Deficiency*, 1955, 59, 666-680.

Bitter, J.A. Using employer job-sites in evaluation of the mentally retarded for employability. *Mental Retardation*, 1967, 5 (3), 21-22.

Blanton, R.E. A study of the vocational adjustment of the educable mentally retarded. *Dissertation Abstract*, 1966, 27-A, 879.

171

Cohen, J.S. An analysis of vocational failures of mental retardates placed in the community after a period of institutionalization. *American Journal of Mental Deficiency*, 1960, 65, 371-375.

Cohen, J.S. A workshop operation within the framework of a state institution. *American Journal of Mental Deficiency*, 1961, 66, 51-56.

Collmann, R.D., and Newlyn, D. Employment success of educationally subnormal expupils in England. *American Journal of Mental Deficiency*, 1956, 60, 733-743.

Cowan, L., and Goldman, M. The selection of the mentally deficient for vocational training and the effect of this training on vocational success. *Journal of Consulting Psychology*, 1959, 23, 78-84.

DiMichael, S.G. *Sheltered workshops for the mentally retarded*. New York: National Association for Retarded Children, 1954.

Edgerton, R.B. *The cloak of competence (Stigma in the lives of the mentally retarded)*. Berkeley: University of California, 1967.

Federation of the Handicapped. The effectiveness of a placement-oriented special work adjustment program for mentally retarded adolescents and young adults with a history of school drop-out. Progress Report, 1966 (mimeo).

Gambaro, S., and Schell, R.E. Prediction of the employability of students in a special education work-training program using the Porteus Maze Test and a rating scale of personal effectiveness. *Educational and Psychological Measurement*, 1966, 26, 1021-1029.

Goldstein, H. Social and occupational adjustment. In H.A. Stevens and R. Heber (Eds.). *Mental Retardation*. Chicago: University of Chicago, 1964.

Gorelick, M.C. *An assessment of vocational realism of high school and post-high school educable mentally retarded adolescents*. Los Angeles: Exceptional Children's Foundation, 1966.

Guerrero, C. Work Therapy for the retarded. *Staff*, 1967, 4, 6.

Higbee, W.R. Supervisors as raters in the assessment of workshop performance of retarded sheltered employees. *American Journal of Mental Deficiency*, 1966, 71, 447-450.

Horne, B.M., and Allen, M.L. A study of the vocational orientation of institutionalized adolescent mentally defective girls. *American Journal of Mental Deficiency*, 1942, 46, 485-495.

Kennedy, R.J.R. *The social adjustment of morons in a Connecticut city*. Willport, Connecticut: Commission to Survey Resources in Connecticut, 1948.

Kliebhan, J.M. Effects of goal-setting and modeling on job performance of retarded adolescents. *American Journal of Mental Deficiency*, 1967, 72, 220-226.

Kolstoe, O.P. The employment, evaluation and training program. *American Journal of Mental Deficiency*, 1960, 65, 17-31.

_____. An examination of some characteristics which discriminate between employed and not-employed mentally retarded males. *American Journal of Mental Deficiency*, 1961, 66, 472-482.

Kratter, F.E. A modern approach to mental deficiency. *North Carolina Medical Journal*, 1958, 19, 268-271.

Madison, H.L. Work placement success for the mentally retarded. *American Journal of Mental Deficiency*, 1964, 69, 50-53.

Michal-Smith, H. Study of the personal characteristics desirable for the vocational success of the mentally deficient. *American Journal of Mental Deficiency*, 1950, 55, 139-143.

Mickelson, P. Minnesota's guardianship program as a basis for community supervision. *American Journal of Mental Deficiency*, 1951, 56, 313-325.

Neuhaus, E.C. Training the mentally retarded for competitive employment. *Exceptional Children*, 1967, 33, 625-628.

Peck, J.R., and Stephens, W.B. Marriage of young adult male retardates. *American Journal of Mental Deficiency*, 1945, 50, 818-827.

Peckham, R. Problems in job adjustment of the mentally retarded. *American Journal of Mental Deficiency*, 1951, 56, 448-453.

Portnoy, B., and Stacey, C.L. A comparative study of Negro and white subnormals on the children's form of the Rosenzweig Picture-Frustration Test. *American Journal of Mental Deficiency*, 1954, 59, 272-278.

Rosenberg, B. Group vocational counseling in a rehabilitation center. *Journal of Rehabilitation*, 1956, 22, 4-6; 20.

Rosenzweig, S. The Picture-Association Method and its application in a study of reactions to frustration. *Journal of Personality*, 1945, 14, 3-23.

Saenger, G. *The adjustment of severely retarded adults in the community*. A report to the N.Y. State Interdepartmental Health Resources Board. Albany, 1957.

Seidenfeld, M.A. *Mental retardation: A further assessment of the problem*. Washington, D.C.: U.S. Department of Health, Education and Welfare, Office of Vocational Rehabilitation, 1962.

Selkin, J., and Meyer, G. Group therapy enters the sheltered workshop. *Journal of Rehabilitation*, 1960, 26 (5), 8-9.

Shafter, A.J. Criteria for selecting institutionalized mental defectives for vocational placement. *American Journal of Mental Deficiency*, 1957, 61, 599-616.

Shaw, C.H., and Wright, C.H. The married mental defective: A follow-up study. *Lancet*, 1960, 30, 273-274.

Shawn, B. Review of a work-experience program. *Mental Retardation*, 1964, 2 (6), 360-364.

Sternlicht, M. Adolescent retardates' values, as gleaned from sentence-completion responses. Paper presented at annual meeting, Eastern Psychological Association, Boston, April, 1967.

Tate, B.G., and Baroff, G.S. Training the mentally retarded in the production of a complex product: A demonstration of work potential. *Exceptional Children*, 1967, 34, 405-408.

Thorne, G.D. Sex education of mentally retarded girls. *American Journal of Mental Deficiency*, 1957, 62, 460-463.

Tizard, J.; Litt, B.; and O'Connor, N. The employability of high-grade mental defectives. II. *American Journal of Mental Deficiency*, 1950, 55, 144-157.

U.S. Department of Health, Education and Welfare. *Vocational rehabilitation of the mentally retarded*, 1965.

Wagner, E.E., and Hawver, D.A. Correlations between psychological tests and sheltered workshop performance for severely retarded adults. *American Journal of Mental Deficiency*, 1965, 69, 685-691.

Wanderer, Z.W., and Sternlicht, M. Alternative guidance: A psychotherapeutic approach to mental deficiency. *International Mental Health Research Newsletter*, 1964, 7, 13-15.

Warren, F.G. Ratings of employed and unemployed mentally handicapped males on personality and work factors. *American Journal of Mental Deficiency*, 1961, 65, 629-633.

Windle, C.D.; Stewart, E.; and Brown, S.J. Reasons for community failure of released patients. *American Journal of Mental Deficiency*, 1961, 66, 213-217.

Younie, W.J., and Colombatto, J.J. A survey of some current practices in off-campus work-experience programs. *Mental Retardation*, 1964, 2, 136-142.

Index

Abstract concepts, 11
Academic achievement:
  institution and, 49
  personality integration, 5
Academic curriculum, 123
Acceptance, 101
  by fellow workers, 158
  need for, 4, 52
Achievement motivation, 133
Activity, shifts in, 64–65
Activity programs, 116
  teaching through, 137
Adjustments:
  behavioral, 123–142
  coping with, 50
  employment, 144
  failure in, 109
  follow-up studies, 105–113
  immediate, 132
  nature of, 101–103
  of parents, 40
  teacher's role in, 134
  theoretical treatment, 101
Adult goals, 143
Adult retardate, 143–173
Aggression, 157
  controlling, 58
  fear of, 72
Aggressiveness, 12, 15
Alternative guidance, 156
Amusements, 163
Animal-reared child, 42–45
Antisocial behavior, 132
Anxiety, 89
  effect of, 21
  over status, 160–161
Approach, to classroom behavior, 133
Assaultiveness, 15, 17
Attitude:
  constructing, 169
  parental, 37, 40

of teacher, 133–139
Authority, acceptance of, 144
Autism, behavior and, 3, 87
Automated instructional devices, 138
Autonomy:
  functional, 136
  strivings for, 103

Behavior, 75–100
  animal child, 43
  antisocial, 132
  classroom, 125
  compulsive, 93–94
  criminality and, 86–87
  factors in, 89–95
  among idiots, 15
  institutionalization and, 51
  permissive approach, 136
  reinforcement variables, 103–105
  retarded/normal, 25
  sexual, 167
  social, 101–122
  as variable, 25, 103–105
Behavioral adjustments, 123–142
  class composition, 126–133
Behavior disorders, incidence, 87
Belonging, need for, 116
Biological differences, 21
Borderline normals, 27
Brain damage, 10

Capabilities, distrust in, 60
Class placement, 132
Classroom:
  behavioral adjustments, 123–142
  teacher's attitude, 133–139
Clinically feebleminded, defined, 27
Cognitive development, 2
Communications, 18
  parent-child, 41
Community adjustment, 106, 108–110

175

Community day work, 145–148
Community placement, 116
Compensatory reactions, 60
Competition, need for, 11
Compulsion-obsession, 93, 94
Conference method technique, 114
Conscience, ineffective, 81
Courting, 163
Co-workers, relationship with, 157
Criminal behavior, 75–79
Criminality, 86–87
Criticism, accepting, 145
Crying, 17
Cultural deprivation, 10
Cultural-familial retardates, 9
Cultural variables, 10

Dating, 163
Defective delinquent, 77
Defense mechanisms, 58, 89, 92
Defensiveness, 60
Delinquent behavior, 75–79
Demands, impossible, 63
Demented schizophrenic, 88
Dependability, 102
Depressing effect, institution as, 48
Depression, 94
  withdrawal and, 92, 93
Deprivation, 33, 41–46
Desertion, incidence of, 167
Development:
  institutionalization and, 49
  slowness in, 3
  stages of, 2
Deviant behavior, 75–100
  personality structure and, 79–84
Diagnosis, ambiguity in, 84
Differentiation, 65–66
Direction, importance of, 107
Disappointment, responding to, 167
Disciplinary approaches, 138
Disciplinary attitude, 137
Discipline:
  classroom, 134

group acceptance, 115
Disorganization, 93
Distractibility, 68–69
Divorce, 69, 168
Drug addiction, 14

Eating habits, 14, 17
Education, basic, 123, 124
Educational achievement, 127
Educational provisions, 108
Ego, 79, 91, 92
Ego assessment, 81–82
Ego development, 25
Ego maturation, 5
Ego resources, 58
Ego skills, developing, 58
Ego structure, rigidity in, 64
Eidetic imagery, 11
Emotional adjustment, 88
Emotional disturbance:
  criminality and, 86–87
  factors in, 89–95
  mental retardation and, 84, 87
  symptoms of, 95–96
Emotional functioning, 57
Emotional maladjustment, 10
Emotional problems, needs and, 25
Emotional security, 4
Emotional ties, 71
Empathy, need for, 158
Employer, relationship with, 156, 157
Employment:
  competitive, 150
  success in, 145
Enrichment programs, 50
Entertainment, 163
Enuresis, 15
Environment:
  home, importance of, 36
  power of, 45, 48
  reactions to, 101
Environmental influences, 35–56
Errors, treating, 144
Escape mechanisms, 157

Ethical values, forming, 116
Extrapunitive blame, 167

Failure, motivating force, 105, 123
Family:
  emotional ties, 71
  importance of, 3
  retardate's role in, 41
  role of, 35, 36–41
Fantasy aggression, 82
Father, regard for, 72
Faulty perception, 80
Feelings, analysis of, 57
Friends, adjustment to, 165
Frustration, 83, 103
  compensating for, 131
  hostility and, 62
  reaction to, 21
  response to, 167
Frustration tolerance, 83

Goal direction, failure in, 59
God, concept of, 72
"Golden mean" formula, 133, 144
Good (quality), concern for, 72
Group acceptance, 101, 114
Group living, 114
Group rejection, 158
Guidance, importance of, 107
Guilt, burden of (legal), 84
Guilt feelings, 23
  dysfunction, 80
  of parents, 38

Heredity:
  background, 47
  retardation in, 37
Heterosexual relationships, 166–167
Home-familial milieu, 36
Home situation, effect of, 23
Homosexuality, 25, 83
Hostility, 12, 57, 62–63, 157
  controlling, 58

fear of, 72
Household chores, 165
Human experience, need for, 45, 47
Hyperactivity, 17

Id, 79
Ideal self, 61
Idiot, studies of, 16
Idiot savant, 18–20, 93
Illegitimacy, effect of, 43, 44
Impulsiveness, 82
Impunitive blame, 168
Inadequacy, feeling of, 92
Incentive, need for, 5
Indulgent attitude, 144
Industrial experience, obtaining, 147
Infantilism, 38
Inhibitions, controlling, 58
Initiative, lack of, 160
Insecurity, 93
Instinct, reality and, 79
Institutionalization, 3, 35, 46–53
  behavior functioning in, 22
  contemporary concept, 53
  depressing effect of, 48
  "punishing monster," 52
  social reinforcement, 104
  a variable, 24
Intellectual abilities, 18
Intellectual functioning, 24, 88
Intellectual homogeneity, 126
Intellectual performance, 78
Intellectual resources, 50
Intelligence, 5
  of delinquent, 76
  rejection and, 129
Interest contraction, 88
Interpersonal relationships, 26, 109
Inter-system relationships, 114
Intropunitive blame, 168
Isolation, 35, 41–46
  age and, 166

Jealousy, 83

Job:
  appropriateness of, 145
  motivational factor, 156
Job interview, preparation for, 154
Job performance, 149, 156
Job responsibility, 144
Job tasks, breakdown of, 149
Judgment, ineffective functioning, 82
Judgmental abilities, 155

Learning ability, degrees of, 124
Learning experience, 137
Learning level, degrees of, 125
Leave programs, failures in, 109
Leisure time, 162–170
Life goals, 163
Limitations, sensitivity to, 157
Love, need for, 4, 52
Love relationships, 58
Low intelligence, 10

Maladjustment, history of, 3
Maladjustment problems, 110–111
Marriage, 166, 167
Masturbation, 17
Material goods, desire for, 72
Memory feats, 20
Mental age, differentiation and, 66
Mental retardation syndrome, 10
Mental retardation:
  defined, 9
  deviant behavior and, 75–79
  emotional disturbance and, 84, 87
  meaning of, 9–34
  symptoms, 95–96
  theory of, 65
Mistakes, treating, 144
Money handling, 160
Mongolism, 12–13, 69, 91
Morons, crimes and, 21
Mother, regard for, 72
Mother-love, need for, 52
Motivation:
  achievement as, 133
  failure as, 105, 123

heightened, 139
institutionalization and, 46
job as, 156
Motivational variations, 66–67
Musical talent, 20

Need patterns, 11
Needs:
  classroom, 129
  emotional problems and, 25
Negative experiences, 60
Neurological deficit, 10
Neurosis, demarcation, 84
Nonviolence, attitude of, 169
Nonverbal reinforcement, 105

Observational techniques, 6
Occupational adjustment, 152
Occupational therapy, 17
Oligophrenic response, 10
On-the-job adjustment, 144
Orientation, difference/similarity, 3–6
Other-directedness, 67–68, 89
Overcompensation, 39
Overprotection, 38

Parent-child relationships, 3–4, 16, 36,
  38–40
Parents:
  demands of, on child, 40
  problems, 18
Perception, constructing, 169
Performance differences, 104
Permissive attitude, 134–136
  structuring of, 138
Personal adjustment, 127
Personal effectiveness, enhancing, 152
Personal relationships, 123
Personality:
  development of, 1–8
  environmental influences, 35–36
  institutionalization and, 49
  isolation type, 50
  theoretical concern, 27
  structure of, 57–59

Personality disorders, frequency, 28
Personality dynamics, 9–34
  brain damage and, 11
  generalized observations, 25
  patterns, 9
Personality integration, 5
Personality structure, 79–84
Personality studies, 1, 70–73
Personality traits, 57–74
  understanding of, 130
Praise, using, 134
Productive capacity, improving, 152
Programmed instructional methods, 139
Pseudofeeblemindedness, 10, 85
Psychopathology, basic patterns, 94
Psychosis, demarcation of, 84
Punishment, use of, 134

Radio, as amusement, 164
Rational attitude, 137
Rating scales, utilizing, 6
Reading ability, 161
Reading problem, 77
Reality:
  instinct and, 79
  testing, 58
Recreation, 163
Recreation therapy, 14
Rehabilitation, 113
Reinforcement variables, 103–105
Rejection, 37, 40–41, 103
  fear of, 11
  by peers, 129, 158
  reasons for, 131
  response to, 168
Repression, defense mechanism, 58
Retardation, theory of, 65
Responsibility, 102
  accepting, 155
  importance of, 115
  lack of, 160
Rigidity, 57, 64–70
  detrimental effect, 21

Sampling, studies of, 2

Schizophrenia, 22, 88, 90–91
Scholastic performance, 123
Security, need for, 58
Segregation, 130, 131
Self-attitudes, 36
  negative, 50
Self-concept, 57–74
  adjustment and, 103
  atrophying, 144
  constituents of, 79
  nature of, 59–61
  psychological contruct, 1
Self-confidence, 28
Self-control, 145
Self-determination, 113, 114
Self-government, 113–114
Self-image, enhancing, 58
Self-living, 115
Self-responsibility, 136
Sex differentiation, 23
Sex relationships, 166–167
Sex role development, 4
Sexual frustration, 83
Sexual identification, 23
Sheltered workshops, 24, 145–148
  principles of, 149
Shifting paradigm, 64–65
Situations. reacting to, 155
Skills, limitations on, 156
Social acceptance, 131
  rating, 128
Social adjustment, 105–113
  adequate, 123
  comparisons, 132
  noninstitutional, 107
  stressing, 131
Social deprivation, 69
Social effectiveness, enhancing, 152
Social living, 113–116
  learning aspects, 115
Social maturity, 4
Social orientation, 115
Social position, demands of, 131
Social problems, 101–122
Social reinforcement, 103–105

Sociopathic personalities, 76
Sophistication, social/vocational, 159
Special classes, 126–133
Special Work Adjustment Program,
    149–150
Speech:
  limitations on, 15, 17
  patterns, 15
Sports programs, 164
Stacey study, 71–72
Status, anxiety over, 160–161
Sternlicht study, 72–73
Stimulation, environmental, 24, 45, 47
Stimulus:
  abnormal reactions to, 69
  home life as, 47
  receptivity of, 21
Stress, withstanding, 82
Stubbornness, 14
Success, 158, 161
Suicide, 94–95
Superego, 58–79
Supervision, 24, 107
Supervisor, relationship with, 156, 157
Syphilis, 19

Teacher, attitude of, 133–139
Teaching approach, 134
Teaching machines, 138
Television, as amusement, 164
Temper tantrums, 15, 22
Tests, types and uses, 6
Thorazine, use of, 15, 17
Toilet training, 14, 17, 19, 43
Training, importance of, 107
Training experience, 151
Training problems, 147
Training techniques, modifying, 149
Training, techniques, 148–149
  implementing, 153

Truancy, 22
Trust, need for, 113
Two-group approach, 21

Understanding:
  lack of, 80
  need for, 158
Unemployment, 160

Values, constructing, 169
Variables, 103–105
  anxiety as, 89
  behavioral manifestation, 25
  behavioral/situational, 2
  institutionalization as, 24
  motivational, 66–67
Verbal associations, 125
Verbal behavior, 14
Verbal stimulation, 21
Vocational adjustment, 143–162
Vocational development, techniques,
    153
Vocational maladjustments, 110
Vocational needs, training and, 151
Vocational rehabilitation, 110
Vocational therapy, 20
von Restorff effect, 125

Wages:
  dissatisfaction with, 159
  as incentive, 150
Wild children, 42–45
Withdrawal, 94
  defense pattern, 89, 90, 91
Work atmosphere, 149
Work habits, complaints about, 145
Work performance, failure in, 109
Work potential, 148
Workshop program, 147

About the Authors

Manny Sternlicht, a clinical psychologist whose work combines an academic background with an active research orientation, is currently Assistant Director at Willowbrook State School (where he has been since 1960) and Professor of Psychology at Yeshiva University.

He earned a masters degree in school psychology and one in experimental psychology. He completed his doctoral studies at Yeshiva University, where he was awarded a Ph.D. in June of 1960. He interned in clinical psychology at Kings County Hospital, and has served as a clinical psychologist at the Institute for Juvenile Research and as Chairman of the Psychology Department at Rockford College.

Dr. Sternlicht has presented many professional papers on the subject of mental retardation at conventions, and has published more than 50 articles on the subject.

He is a member of most of the major national organizations in psychology, and is a Fellow of the American Association on Mental Deficiency, as well as Chairman of the Mental Retardation Committee of the New York Society of Clinical Psychologists.

He is married to the former Madeline Goldstein, and has three children, Elliot, Harold and Jeffrey.

Martin R. Deutsch is a psychological clinician, researcher, and theorist who has specialized in the diagnosis and treatment of the mentally retarded for nearly a decade, since his appointment as Senior Clinical Psychologist at the Willowbrook State School in Staten Island, New York. He has conducted studies in memory function, IQ measurement, and abnormal behavior in the retarded.

Mr. Deutsch was born in Brooklyn, New York in 1934. He received an A.B. degree cum laude with distinction in psychology from Brandeis University in 1955, and an M.A. degree in psychology from Bryn Mawr College in 1960. During his graduate tenure, he served as psychological research assistant at both Swarthmore College and Bryn Mawr College, where he engaged in experimental research within the theoretical domain of Gestalt psychology. He was next appointed as research associate of a visual perception laboratory at National Analysts, Inc. in Philadelphia. Mr. Deutch was greatly influenced and encouraged by his teacher and friend, the late Kurt Goldstein both at Brandeis University and in later years. Following a number of years of clinical work in criminology and geriatrics, Mr. Deutsch undertook the specialty of mental retardation. In his present capacity as psychodiagnostician, psychotherapist, and researcher at the Willowbrook State School for the mentally retarded, Mr. Deutsch utilizes the techniques of the clinic and the laboratory in equal measure.

The many published products of his efforts include his well-known investigations of the von Restorff memory phenomenon, as well as a study in IQ measurement which has led to a suggested revision of the Wechsler intelligence norms for the retarded. His most recent research contributions are in the form of an exploratory investigation and accompanying theory of suicide among retardates and an empirical demonstration of the value of temporary institutionalization in habilitating the mentally retarded.

Assisted in his research by his wife, Gragina, Mr. Deutsch has lately been directing his efforts toward the formulation of a new theory of human behavior which he calls "empirical humanism" and which he proposes as an explanatory alternative to traditional scientific psychology.